When Ideas Fail

This study offers an ideational explanation of Russia's relative failure to establish a functioning market economy and thus sets up a new and original perspective for discussion. In post-Soviet Russia, a clash between imported foreground ideas and deep domestic background ideas has led to an ideational division among the elite of the country. Within economic science, this led to the emergence of two thought collectives, (in the sense of Ludwik Fleck), with entirely different understandings of social reality.

This ideational division translated into incoherent policy measures, the emergence of institutional hybrids and thus, all in all, into institutional instability. Empirically, the book is based on a systematic, qualitative analysis of the writings of Soviet/Russian economists between 1987 and 2012. A central insight of the book is that when it comes to the diffusion of economic ideas beyond the core group of Western developed countries, the relationship between imported (foreground) economic ideas and culturally and historically deeply rooted patterns of thought (background ideas) constitutes a major problem.

This groundbreaking book thus makes an important contribution both to Central Eastern and Eastern European area studies and to the current debate on ideas and institutions in the social sciences.

Joachim Zweynert is Professor of International Political Economy at Witten/Herdecke University, Germany. He studied economics and political science at Hamburg University, Germany.

Routledge Studies in the European Economy

For a full list of titles in this series, please visit www.routledge.com/series/SE0431

36 **The New European Industrial Policy**
Global Competitiveness and the Manufacturing Renaissance
Franco Mosconi

37 **A Global Perspective on the European Economic Crisis**
Edited by Bruno Dallago, Gert Guri and John McGowan

38 **Migration in the Mediterranean**
Socio-economic Perspectives
Edited by Elena Ambrosetti, Donatella Strangio and Catherine Wihtol de Wenden

39 **Transformation and Crisis in Central and Eastern Europe**
Challenges and Prospects
Steven Rosefielde and Bruno Dallago

40 **Labour and Social Transformation in Central and Eastern Europe**
Europeanization and Beyond
Edited by Violaine Delteil and Vassil Kirov

41 **The Contemporary Crisis of the European Union**
Prospects for the Future
Ivan T. Berend

42 **Ageing, Lifestyles and Economic Crises**
The New People of the Mediterranean
Edited by Thierry Blöss
In Collaboration with Isabelle Blöss-Widmer, Elena Ambrosetti, Michèle Pagès and Sébastien Oliveau

43 **When Ideas Fail**
Economic Thought, the Failure of Transition and the Rise of Institutional Instability in Post-Soviet Russia
Joachim Zweynert

When Ideas Fail

Economic Thought, the Failure of Transition and the Rise of Institutional Instability in Post-Soviet Russia

Joachim Zweynert

Routledge
Taylor & Francis Group
LONDON AND NEW YORK

First published 2018 by Routledge

2 Park Square, Milton Park, Abingdon, Oxfordshire OX14 4RN
52 Vanderbilt Avenue, New York, NY 10017

Routledge is an imprint of the Taylor & Francis Group, an informa business

First issued in paperback 2019

British Library Cataloguing-in-Publication Data
A catalogue record for this book is available from the British Library

Library of Congress Cataloging-in-Publication Data
A catalog record for this book has been requested

ISBN: 978-1-138-55927-1 (hbk)
ISBN: 978-0-367-89112-1 (pbk)

Typeset in Times New Roman
by Apex CoVantage, LLC

Contents

Tables

Preface

In 1987, the year that marks the starting point of the present study, then still being at high school, I travelled to the Soviet Union for the first time. It was mainly due to the impressions that I gained during this and a further trip to the Soviet Union that I decided to study economics. Ten years later, when I had finished my studies, two things had changed: First, not least as a result of further and partly prolonged stays in Russia, I had convinced myself that economics the way it was taught in the 1990s had severe difficulties grasping the problems of a society in which every single aspect of social life was turned upside down and which had been shaped by a history that diverged on several important aspects from that of the Western countries. Secondly, by the second half of the 1990s it was already clear that Russia's economic transition was a relative failure compared to that of Central Eastern European Countries and the former Soviet Republics Estonia, Latvia and Lithuania.

In search for explanations that went beyond the realm of economic factors and allowed for integrating the influence of the past, I came across Karl Pribram's (1983) ideas about the links between the history of economic ideas and processes of institutional change. Inspired by his *History of Economic Reasoning*, from 1997 to 1999 I settled in St. Petersburg and started to work on my PhD thesis on Russian economic thought in the 19th century. Immediately after I had finished that study, I started to work on the project that would finally lead me to write this book. Its main chapters are based on articles that have been published in *Russian History* (Zweynert 2014) and in *Europe-Asia Studies* (Zweynert 2006, 2007, 2010; Zweynert and Boldyrev 2017). The section about the Russian Stabilisation Fund in Chapter 6 is based on a paper written with Ewa Dabrowska that was published in *New Political Economy* in 2015.

Having been in progress for almost 15 years, the ideas contained in this book have been presented at numerous workshops and conferences and have benefitted significantly from comments and suggestions by so many people that I can't mention all of them here. I would, however, like to express my gratitude to my co-authors Ivan Boldyrev and Ewa Dabrowska. Ivan Boldyrev has kindly read and commented on an earlier version of the manuscript, has helped me with some translations and last but not least suggested the title "When Ideas Fail". It is understood that all remaining mistakes are entirely my own. I am also grateful to my student assistants Ludwig Evers and Olivia Davis for their assistance in producing the final manuscript. In the context of a research network on "Institutions and Institutional Change in Post-Socialism", between 2010 and 2015 my work on the book has been supported by the German Ministry of Education and Science (BMBF). I happily take the opportunity here to express my gratitude particularly to our advisor in the Ministry Dr. Rolf Geserick for his friendly and encouraging support of our research activities. Where English translations of Russian texts were available, I refer to these translations. In all other cases, the translations are my own. Transliteration from Cyrillic follows the Modified Library of Congress system.

1 Introduction

This book develops and elaborates upon my monograph *Eine Geschichte des ökonomischen Denkens in Russland 1805–1905* (*A History of Russian Economic Reasoning 1805–1905*, 2002).[1] This book was meant both as a study of the history of economic ideas and as a contribution to research into the historical and cultural dimensions of post-socialist change. Following Karl Pribram's (1983: 40) assertion that "prerequisite to any change in social or economic institutions or organisations is a change of the prevailing pattern of reasoning which had provided the background to the predominant forms of social and economic life", I asked whether analysing the history of Russian economic reasoning might help us to understand why in post-Soviet Russia the implementation of a market economy after 1991 encountered so much resistance. In a greatly simplified and abbreviated form, my answer was that in the history of Russian economic ideas (and in Russian social philosophy in general), a peculiar mix of anthropocentrism and holism provided fertile breeding ground for patterns of thought that were in potential conflict with the market. These patterns, I argued, didn't render the emergence of capitalism in Russia impossible. But they entailed a deep intellectual division between adherents and fundamental opponents of Russia's capitalist transformation that made Russia's social evolution unstable and vulnerable to external shocks.

In taking up this question, the present book provides an in-depth analysis of the intellectual clashes on post-socialist reforms in the Russian economic discourse and asks how they relate to the ideational legacies of the past. My study is located at the intersection of area studies, the history of economic thought, and International Political Economy. Theoretically, it is closely related to the recent "idealist turn" (Blyth 1997) in the interdisciplinary research programme of new institutionalism. More and more scholars from political science, sociology and partly economics have now re-discovered the role of ideas as engines of institutional change (see e.g. Hall 1997; Campbell 1998; Blyth 2002; Hay 2006a; Schmidt 2008; Rodrik 2014; Blyth, Helgadottir and Kring 2016; for overviews see Gofas and Hay 2010; Béland and Cox 2011a).

Economic ideas play a prominent role in this literature. The shift from Keynesianism to Monetarism in many Western countries around 1980 especially is often referred to as a prime example of ideationally induced institutional change. Obviously, economic ideas played a crucial role in the breakdown of socialism and in the post-socialist reform processes all over the former Eastern block. Against this background, it is surprising that so far there has been relatively little research on ideas and institutional change in post-socialist Central Eastern and Eastern Europe.[2] The present book tries to fill this gap. I hope that applying the insights of the newer research on ideas and institutions[3] to the case of post-Soviet Russia will improve our understanding of the recent developments (both economic and political) in the Russian Federation. It is clear by now that Russia's transition into a democratic country with a market economy has provisionally failed. Unlike most Central Eastern European countries, Russia did not succeed in implementing macroeconomic and structural reforms, combating corruption, and democratising. Experts in Central Eastern and Eastern European area studies are still struggling to explain the differences in reform outcomes. My study puts an ideational explanation up to discussion. At the same time, I believe that this empirical case also bears important theoretical lessons for the general research on ideas and institutions.

As the title indicates, I claim that Russia's failed transition can meaningfully be described as a failure of ideas.[4] My central thesis is that after 1991 in Russian economics, instead of a "transition from one core belief to another" (Alston, Melo, Mueller and Pereira 2016: 10), there emerged a deep divide between two incompatible thought styles. As a first and very rough approximation these thought styles can be described as a traditional and inward-oriented "Russian" one and an outward oriented one that aimed at the re-integration of the Russian scientific community into the international discourse. The first of these strands was deeply embedded in certain specific Russian intellectual traditions, reflected a methodological position that dated back to before the marginal revolution and thus stood in irreconcilable contradiction to the international economics discourse to which the other part of the Russian scientific community tried to return. In this way, very much like in the second half of the 19th century, instead of a vastly shared interpretation of social reality there emerged a struggle between two thought collectives, the representatives of which had their roots in conflicting socio-philosophical frames and their respective normative orientations.

If Pribram's thesis about a fundamental shift in patterns of thought as prerequisite for social transformations is correct, the unresolved tension between two patterns of thought of roughly equal strength offers an explanation for instability and ambiguity of Russia's current social order. Today's Russian state capitalism can indeed be characterised as a hybrid order both in institutional and in ideational terms and it does not yet seem clear whether a stable equilibrium will emerge and what such an equilibrium would look like. To my knowledge, in this book I provide the first in-depth case study about the tensions that can emerge as a result of the import of economic ideas to a country: (1) the economists of which had not been part of the international scientific community; and in which (2) some of the deeper background ideas provided a problematic breeding ground for the imported ideas.

Put in a nutshell, my argument is that the case of Russia indicates that when it comes to the diffusion of economic ideas beyond the core group of Western developed countries, the relationship between imported (foreground) economic ideas and culturally and historically deeply rooted patterns of thought (background ideas) constitutes a major problem. I believe that this finding could, though it will take a specific form in every society, be relevant for other developing and emerging countries in which far-reaching reform processes are accompanied by the import of economic ideas. In this sense, I hope that the findings of my study might contribute to a better understanding of the current economic and political order in Russia, help us to better understand some of the problems that typically emerge during market reforms in developing and emerging societies, and last but not least contribute to the recent theorising about ideas and institutions.

I should like to state from the very beginning what I am doing and what I am not doing in this book: What I do is look at the academic (and partly, but only partly, also at the non-academic) economic discussions about economic reforms in Russia from 1987 to 2012 by qualitatively analysing the content of the Russian economics journals and selected academic monographs.[5] This focus rests on the conviction that the ideas of "academic scribblers" are of great importance for the successful implementation of economic reforms. Thus, analysing the ideas circulating and prevailing in the Russian economics community provides us with an important piece of the puzzle in understanding the ideational dimension of Russian post-Soviet institutional change. At the same time, I am aware that in order to gain a fuller picture other elite groups and the attitudes of broader strata of the population would have to be included, something I do *not* do. Also, and in contrast to much of the ideas and institutions literature, in this book I do not systematically look into the concrete links between economic ideas and economic reforms.[6] What I am mainly interested in are the broader pre-analytical visions (Schumpeter [1954] 1967), the thought styles, the *Gestaltvorstellungen* of Russian economists. This reflects my conviction that when it comes to a fundamental transformation of society, it is these broader visions, or, in the terminology of Pribram, patterns of thought, we should concentrate on.

Before I start my analysis of the Soviet and Post-Soviet Russian reform debates, in the next chapter I will elaborate on the theoretical foundations of my study and in particular on the question of how it relates to the recent theorising on ideas and institutions in the social sciences. Chapters 3 to 7 then provide a detailed analysis of the Brezhnev years (chapter 3), perestroika and the breakthrough of neo-liberal ideas (chapter 4), the 1990s (chapter 5), the first half of the 2000s (Chapter 6) and finally of the recent debate on innovation and modernisation (Chapter 7), before a rather short final chapter wherein I summarize my main findings. As most readers of this book will not be familiar with most of the Russian economists this book is dealing with, I have added a biographical index of the most important protagonists of my story.[7] Authors that are included in this index are marked with an asterisk at their first mentioning.

Notes

1 A Russian translation was published in 2007 by the publishing house of the Higher Schol of Economics, Moscow.

2 The literature that does exist operates with categories much too large, such as "neo-liberalism", "shock therapy" or "gradualism" and often lacks a sound theoretical and empirical foundation. For this critique see Dawisha and Ganev (2005). For a good

account of the influence of neoliberal ideas in post-Soviet Russia see Rutland (2013). At the time of writing this book, Vladimir Gel'man's, Dmitry Travin's and Otar Marganiia's book *Reexamining Economic and Political Reforms in Russia, 1985–2000* was published (2014), focusing on ideas and intergenerational conflicts among the elite in explaining the course of post-socialist reforms in Russia. Though the book offers important insights, it does not use the analytical instruments recently developed in the theorising on ideas and institutions as much as it might. The classification of individual persons into the two analysed generations of *shestidesiatniki* (people of the 1960s) and *semidesiatniki* (people of the 1970s) in some cases appears rather arbitrary.

3 In the following, I refer to this research as "constructivist institutionalism". This is a pragmatic decision made in order to avoid lengthy expressions like "research on ideas and institutions". I myself do not have strong preferences regarding the issues on whether an ideational version of institutionalism should be added to the three other institutionalisms (historical, sociological, rational choice) and if so, what the best label for this fourth branch should be. Again, I choose the term "constructivist institutionalism" for the purpose of convenience alone.

4 To be very clear, what I argue is not that this is the only possible explanation but that it is one of the various meaningful perspectives which will hopefully contribute to a better understanding of the problem of the relative failure of the Russian post-socialist transition process.

5 I also look partly at the general interest press, political speeches and internet sources, but the focus is on academic writings by Russian economists.

6 However, in Chapter 6 I use the example of the Russian Stabilisation Fund to illustrate how the ideational tension between the two thought collectives in Russian economics translates into incoherent economic reforms.

7 These short biographies intend to provide the reader with very basic information about my protagonists. Readers interested in more biographical information may find Robert Campbell's *A Biographical Dictionary of Russian and Soviet Economists* (2012) helpful (of the 50 authors covered in my biographical index, 31 are included in it).

2 The role of ideas in great transformations

In this chapter, I provide the theoretical foundations of my study. I will start by clarifying what I understand under the term transition throughout this book. Thereafter, I will provide a brief introduction into the recent discussion on ideas and institutional change. This overview is not meant to be complete and highlights those aspects that are relevant for my case. In a third step, I discuss three features I believe to be specific for the case of post-Soviet Russia, namely the lack of liberal underground discourses, the ideological divide between the two strands of economic thought and the role that deep background ideas have been playing in the Russian debates over economic reforms in the last thirty years.

Transition as functional differentiation

I believe that most mainstream economists tend to understand the phenomenon in a way that reflects both their upbringing in modern, capitalist societies and their socialisation as economists, but fails to capture its essence. For example, in Paul R. Gregory's and Robert C. Stuart's (1998: 18) standard work on "Russian and Soviet Economic Performance and Structure" we find the following definition:

> Generally interpreted as the replacement of one economic system by another economic system; in the 1990s, the replacement of the planned socialist economic system of the former Soviet Union and the countries of Eastern Europe with market economies.

In my view, the underlying idea that both in capitalist and socialist societies there existed "economic systems" and that, accordingly, transition was basically about changing the economic system of the socialist society, is utterly mistaken. I believe that the paradigm of functional differentiation offers a better foundation for understanding what post-socialist change was all about. A useful starting point for this is Karl Polanyi's description of capitalism:

> A self-regulating market demands nothing less than the institutional separation into an economic and political sphere. Such a dichotomy is, in effect,

> merely the restatement, from the point of view of society as a whole, of the existence of a self-regulating market. It might be argued that the separateness of the two spheres obtains in every type of society at all times. Such an inference, however, would be based on a fallacy . . . Neither under tribal, nor feudal, nor mercantile conditions was there . . . a separate economic system in society.
>
> (Polanyi [1944] 2001: 74)[1]

The decisive point that follows from this is that in socialism, as in all other non-capitalist societies, there was no such a thing as an economic system that was clearly distinguishable from the rest of society. What socialism as an ideology is all about is the demand to re-integrate the economic "value sphere"[2] (Max Weber) into society by subordinating it to politics. Where such attempts are successful, the system border (to borrow Luhmann's term) between the economy and the other parts of society disappears, and the economic system ceases to exist as a system in the full sense of the word.

As Karl Marx illustrated with his formula M – C – M', the self-regulating character of the capitalist economy is based on a specific motivation that is vastly detached from the satisfaction of wants as the final aim of economic activity and from other non-economic motivations. This isolation of economic motives (which finds a theoretical expression in the figure of the *homo oeconomicus*) reflects the relative autonomy of the economic system in capitalist society. Marx's observation about the connection between profit seeking and self-regulation of the economic system leads to the question about economic motivations in a socialist economy. This much-discussed problem has been addressed by Russian economist Iurii Aleksandrov in a particular instructive way:

> If one may imagine a market economy as deliquescing water, continually filling all lower points, a planned economy is something like a swamp, where the water is standing and therefore moulders. This system can only be set into motion by a forceful infusion of resources. From here stem the periodical efforts to force a jerk in one or the other direction, that at a certain point in time were regarded as the "basic link", being able to take along the whole chain: "virgin soil", "big chemical industry", "acceleration" and so forth.
>
> (Aleksandrov 1999: 66)

The metaphor of the swamp illustrates that where a purely economic motivation is missing, the economic system is not self-regulating and has to be set in motion by the infusion of ideology. This, however, is just another way of saying that the Soviet planned "economy" in the end was an appendix of the political system. Hence, and this is the decisive point, the task of transition was not about *transforming* an economic system but about providing the institutional prerequisites of the *emergence* of an economic system, that is, a system which is clearly separated from the other parts of society by a system border[3] and thus is enabled to develop its own functional rationality.

At the heart of the Russian debates on capitalism (both in the 19th/early 20th and in the late 20th/early 21st centuries) was precisely the issue of whether a functional separation of an economic sphere was desirable or whether the "autonomy" of the economic sphere represented a threat to social cohesion and should thus be prevented. This problem is difficult to theorize in terms of Western economics, which by its very nature is a science about functionally differentiated economic systems. Therefore, it tends to take for granted the institutional structure, the *creation* of which is the major problem of transition.

Constructivist institutionalism and the structure/agency-problem

The empirical cases which constructivist institutionalism has been dealing with so far are (1) usually located within the Western, industrialised countries, are (2) "success stories", that is, they tell stories of how shifts in ideas have indeed led to lasting changes in institutions, and (3) about changes of a small to medium range. The first mentioned characteristic is mainly due to the fact that the recent "ideational turn" took its beginnings in historical institutionalism, which traditionally focuses on Western welfare states (Farrell and Finnemore 2016: 573). The second and third reflect the fact that the ideational research programme was set up as a counter project against the more structuralist and thus "sticky" versions of historical institutionalism. As such, its aim was to "unstick institutions and to unfix preferences and norms" (Schmidt 2008: 313) and to demonstrate the possibility of "radical change as a response to new perceptions and ways of thinking" (Béland and Cox 2011b: 11).

As is typical for counter projects, constructivist institutionalism shares some basic features with the research programme it was directed against. Most importantly, it starts from a punctuated equilibrium approach according to which longer periods of stasis are from time to time interrupted by critical junctures that lead societies from one institutional equilibrium to another (see e.g. Capoccia and Kelemen 2007). In its most basic form, the ideational/constructivist explanation of institutional change goes as follows (e.g. Blyth 2002: chapter 2)[4]: In periods of "normal historical development" (that is, in periods of incremental, path dependent institutional change) there is usually a basic correspondence of (formal and informal) institutions and ideas in which they are embedded (see Hall 1993: 279). From an ideational perspective, the relative stability of periods of "normal history" is due to the stability of underlying ideas, more precisely of shared[5] interpretations of the relevant causal relationships and normative orientations. However, if institutions disappoint the expectations linked to them for a significant period of time, this will sooner or later lead to a perception of "crisis" and to a delegitimisation of the ideas underlying the relevant institutional setting. A "separation of ideas from their current institutional moorings" (Blyth 2002: 27) will then result in a relatively short period of "unsettled times" (Swidler 1986: 278) in which a comparatively unbound search for new ideas will take place. Like in a Kuhnian paradigm shift, sooner or later one set of ideas which is clearly distinguishable from the previous one will gain dominance and eventually find expression in a new set of institutions, thus creating a new period of path-dependent and incremental change.

This basic scenario can be illustrated by the example of the transition from Keynesianism to Monetarism around 1980. The phenomenon of stagflation that occurred in the developed capitalist countries in the 1970s could not be convincingly explained in terms of the analytical framework provided by Keynesianism[6], and thus undermined its authority. In contrast, neoliberal ideas, which for decades had lived in the shadow of the dominant Keynesian paradigm, could both explain stagflation and make concrete proposals how to overcome the dual problem of low growth rates and high inflation. As a result, they quickly gained popularity both within the scientific and the political realm and initiated a far-reaching reversal not only in the way economic policy was conducted but also in the way millions of people judged the relationship between state and society and social justice.

As the last mentioned point makes especially clear, different levels of ideas are involved in processes of institutional change. A particularly important distinction lies between foreground and background ideas (see e.g. Campbell 2002; Schmidt 2008). Foreground ideas are ideas about causes and effects related to specific policy measures. Whether anti-cyclical deficit spending leads to reduced unemployment (Keynesianism) or to the crowding-out of private enterprise (Monetarism) is one of the foreground questions Keynesians and Monetarists had different opinions on. This foreground question is embedded in the background question about the proper relationship between state and economy: Is the private sector potentially unstable and thus in need of regulation or is it the state that tends to destabilise the inherently stable private sector? This latter question is less concrete, less about causal mechanisms, less of a pure expert issue and to a higher degree ideologically charged. When dealing with it, people are likely to be heavily influenced by values and norms they have internalised throughout their socialisation. These pre-existing ideas are often embedded in "deeper" ideational backgrounds such as cultural norms and religious legacies. These deep ideational backgrounds are of decisive importance for my explanation of how institutional instability emerged in post-Soviet Russia.

The standard ideational/constructivist explanation of institutional change as outlined above is based on a punctuated equilibrium approach. In historical institutionalism, this approach has recently been increasingly criticised for neglecting the wide field between the poles of stasis and abrupt change. Recent contributions try to improve the critical juncture approach by "embed[ding] critical junctures in a richly detailed context" (Falleti and Lynch 2009: 1155), by considering "critical antecedents" (Slater and Simmons 2010) and by highlighting "productive conditions" (in addition to "permissive conditions") (Soifer 2012) that account for institutional change in critical junctures.

The problem of contextualising critical junctures is extremely relevant for the case of Russia; Reforms in post-Soviet Russia were an extreme case of reforms informed by imported ideas which in their countries of origin were embedded in ideational backgrounds that significantly differed from the Russian one. Related to this, Russian post-socialist reforms have to be seen in the context of a long history of Westernising reforms which time and again led to severe tensions between imported policy ideas and domestic ideational backgrounds. My main thesis regarding the empirical case of Russia is that the clash between imported foreground ideas and deeply rooted domestic background ideas held by a significant portion of Russian intellectuals explains the emergence of an ideational division among the elite of the country which became a main obstacle to the provision of coherent economic reforms. Instead of a shift from one to another equilibrium, what happened in Russia was a transition from a situation with one set of dominant core beliefs[7] to one marked by an ideational stalemate between two almost diametrically opposed sets of core beliefs. The ideational division translated into incoherent policy measures, the emergence of institutional hybrids and thus, all in all, into institutional instability. My hypothesis is that this problem of an ideational/ideological division is not a specific Russian phenomenon (though, as always when deep-seated ideational backgrounds are involved, it does have a specific dimension) but one that can emerge whenever reforms in non-Western and less developed countries are based on imported, Western ideas. Therefore, the case of post-Soviet Russia might comprise lessons for other emerging and developing countries.

The recent attempts to more systematically include contexts into the analysis of critical junctures are closely related to the structure/agency problem which has been in the centre of a recent debate among historical and constructivist institutionalists (see Hay 2006a; Schmidt 2008; Bell 2011; Schmidt 2012; Bell 2012). According to its constructivist critics, historical institutionalism, especially in its more "sticky" versions (e.g. Pierson 2000), generally underrates agency and hence the relevance of discontinuity and novelty in institutional change. As the constructivists concede (Hay 2006a: 61–62), in its more flexible version (e.g. Mahoney and Thelen 2010), historical institutionalism is less pre-occupied with structure and stability, gives more weight to agency and regularly deals with ideas. However, they argue that even this version of historical institutionalism is only able to describe, rather than explain, institutional change (Blyth 2002: 17; Hay 2006a: 62; Schmidt 2012: 709) because it lacks a clearly identifiable endogenous trigger of change. Historical institutionalists, on their part, criticise the constructivists for overstressing agency and the degree of unboundedness of actors in "unsettled times" (Jacobsen 1995: 297; Bell 2011: 87). Constructivists sometimes admit the danger of falling into "voluntarist idealism" (Hay 2006b: 93) and stress that they, very much like the representatives of the more flexible version of historical institutionalism, are aware of the interdependence between structure and agency, so that the difference "is at most one of emphasis" (Hay 2006a: 63).

In terms of ideas, the decisive question seems to be what relative weight an author attributes to foreground and background ideas: If one is convinced that for certain processes of institutional change a shift of foreground ideas is sufficient, there are good reasons to believe that a "separation of ideas from their current institutional moorings" can be relatively easily achieved, so that agency and radical change are possible. On the contrary, the more an author is convinced that ideational backgrounds are involved, the more will she emphasize the importance of structure and the less will she believe in the possibility of swift ideational and, accordingly, institutional change. As I shall argue in the following, if one looks at the diffusion of ideas beyond the realm of Western, developed countries, deeply established background ideas are decisively more important than in cases of policy diffusion within a group of relatively similar countries that form a common space of intense communication. Accordingly, the main theoretical challenge the case of Russia poses for constructivist institutionalism is the question of relevance of these ideational backgrounds.

What is specific about Russia?

The design of economic reforms in Central Eastern and Eastern Europe reflected a firm belief in the possibility of re-designing society according to theoretical blueprints.[8] The reality of reform processes, however, was a powerful reminder of the "limits of design" (Pierson 2000). Indeed, the lesson that not all "unsettled times" necessarily result in clear breaks with the past and in radically new institutions possibly had a stake in the rise of the concept of path dependence in the social sciences in the 1990s. Given this background, it is not overtly surprising that constructivist institutionalists weren't too keen to engage in empirical research on ideas and institutional change in the former Eastern block. The constructivists' eagerness to demonstrate the role of ideas as endogenous triggers of institutional change has led in general to a certain bias of their empirical work in favour of "success stories", that is, of cases in which shifts in ideas in fact led to rather radical and lasting institutional change. Even constructivists themselves concede that studies of "counterfactual cases" or "near misses" would be highly desirable (see Béland and Cox 2011b: 13; Capoccia and Ziblat 2010: 943–944). To provide an in-depth analysis of a counterfactual case is one of the contributions this book makes to the recent theorising of ideas and institutions.

What is specific about Russia I: lack of liberal underground discourses

In periods of crises new ideas usually do not emerge out of the blue, though they sometimes appear to.[9] Rather, the search for new solutions leads to the ascent of formerly "heretical" ideas that had been held by a minority of researchers challenging the mainstream views of their scientific community. The transition from Keynesianism to Monetarism is again a good example: Milton Friedman and Friedrich August von Hayek (who of course was not a monetarist) had developed their ideas in the 1940s and 1950s, and were both key players in the Montpelerin Society (see Mirowski and Plehwe 2009), an "epistemic community"[10] which saw itself in explicit opposition to the Keynesian mainstream. Such side discourses facilitate the flexibility of reasoning in at least four ways: First, they put into question the very basic postulates a dominating paradigm rests on and in this way remind the scientific community of the fact that scientific paradigms are not engraved in stone. Second, they also challenge some of the background ideas in which the current dominant shared interpretation of social reality is embedded. Third, the members of the heterodox community are ready to take over the various positions in academia and policy consulting previously reserved for the members of the old paradigm. Last but not least, they provide a ready-made alternative for those adherents of the old paradigm who are ready to shift to a new set of ideas. Both in a "permissive" as well as "productive" respect, the existence of such side discourses is a decisive prerequisite for "successful" critical junctures, that is, critical junctures that relatively smoothly and quickly lead to a new dominant shared belief which offers a focal point for a new institutional equilibrium. Points one and two are important permissive conditions as they contribute to separating both foreground and background ideas "from their current institutional moorings", whereas points three and four ensure that the resulting ideational vacuum can quickly be filled with new content.

These considerations are highly relevant for understanding the differences between many Central Eastern European countries and Russia. It can be shown how the existence of liberal underground discourses, as e.g. in Poland, Hungary and the Czech Republic, promoted both a smoother transition of economic ideas and resulted in better economic policies.[11] Their familiarity with Western economic ideas enabled domestic politicians and economic advisors to critically access the recommendations of Western consultants and to adapt policy measures to specific circumstances they were better informed about than their Western counterparts. However, the liberal underground discourses did not only challenge Marxist economic ideas but also some of the background ideas Marxism rested on. In contrast to most countries in Central Eastern Europe, in Soviet Russia there had not been liberal discourses of significant strength prior to the beginning of perestroika and glasnost.[12] Though, as I will show in the third chapter, the reformist thinking that spread all over Central Eastern and Eastern Europe in the 1960s took its beginning in Soviet Russia, in contrast to most countries in Central Eastern Europe the Brezhnev regime was successful in depriving reformist economic thinking of its most "subversive" content and re-channeling the discussions in a way that made it inoffensive to those in power.

What is specific about Russia II: the struggle between two thought collectives

In order to understand the emergence of the divide between two opposed thought collectives in Russian economic science after 1990, we have to go back a bit further into the general history of economic ideas and into the history of

Russian economic thought. The decisive revolution in the history of economic ideas after Adam Smith was the transition from classical political economy (to which Marxism is closely related) to neoclassical economics. The main difference is that the classical political economists, though they also described and analysed the "iron laws" of economic processes, saw economic phenomena as embedded in political and social phenomena and processes.[13] In other words, classical political economy was both interested in the processes *within* the economic system of society (as this perspective abstracts from the embeddedness of the economic system, in the following I call this an "isolated" perspective) and in the question of how the economic system *relates* to the other parts of society (I call this the "contextual" perspective).[14] With the breakthrough of marginalism, the core idea of neoclassical economics, weights decisively shifted in the direction of a thoroughly mathematised analysis of the processes within the economic subsystem which was increasingly modelled as an isolated system. Accordingly, the problem of the embeddedness of the economy, the question how the economic system interacted with the other parts of society and how it related to changes in human nature, was more and more excluded from the economic discourse and soon taken up by sociology (and later by political science).

It was especially in the late-coming nations, as in Germany and Russia (but also Italy or Japan), where the transition from political economy to neoclassical economics met with the resistance from parts of the scientific community (see Grimmer-Solem and Romani 1998). This is no coincidence; the idea of an economic system as a clearly identifiable sub-system of society guided by its own causal laws reflects the social reality of modern capitalist societies with their clear functional differentiation between polity and economy. In "developing" countries, the process of separation of the economic sub-system from the rest of society is still under way and the links between polity and economy are much tighter. This leads to the question: to what degree does neoclassical economics fit their social reality?

Though Russia had belonged to those countries in which the neoclassical revolution met with severe resistance and asserted itself only with some delay, the first third of the 20th century saw a bloom of economic theory in Russia with Russian economists making a number of path-breaking contributions to modern, neoclassical economics. This bloom continued through the first decade after the October Revolution. Only after the rise of Stalin did those economists who emanated from the premise of "objective" economic laws stand in the way of Stalinist ideology which claimed that the government was able to redesign society at will (so-called "subjectivity" of economic laws, see next chapter) and were eventually either repressed or forced into exile or inner emigration.

Even after the ideological pressure was weakened following 1953, Soviet economists remained much more isolated from the international discourse than their counterparts in Central Eastern Europe. After the reformist thinking of the 1950s and 1960s had been successfully suppressed following the 24th party congress in 1971 (see next chapter), Soviet Political Economy[15] essentially became a mere play with words that had more in common with medieval scholastics than with modern science (Sutela 1991: 53, 114). In the terminology just introduced, Soviet Political Economy of Socialism was an extreme form of contextual economics, so extreme indeed that it left little if not no space for the analysis of purely economic laws. This methodological orientation went hand in hand with a normative attitude that was hostile towards the most fundamental postulates of Western economics, as e.g. methodological individualism, and towards the very idea of a specific economic sphere of society.[16]

In order to understand what happened after 1990, it is important to note that the two major political interferences (the rise of Stalin around 1930 and the 24th party congress in 1971) did more than just isolate Soviet economic science from the marginalist mainstream. As I shall demonstrate in the next chapter, during the 1970s, in Soviet social thought there was an "idealist turn". As a result, in Soviet Political Economy conspicuous parallels to ideas and topics of the Slavophile and "populist" (*narodnicheskii*) tradition of Russian pre-revolutionary economic thought emerged. These parallels partly explain why, when Russian economists were searching for a new orientation after 1990, many adherents of Soviet Political Economy found it easier to return to Russian traditional ideas than to (re-)enter into the international discourse.

When, in the second half of the 1980s, Western economic ideas started considerably flowing in, there emerged a great divide within the scientific community between those who tried to re-integrate into the international scientific community and those who condemned Western mainstream economics wholesale and revived different versions of political economy which often consisted of a mix of Soviet and older, often nationalist, influences. The following table provides a rough characterisation of the basic methodological ideas and *Gestaltvorstellungen* typical of the representatives of the two thought collectives:

Table 2.1 Gestaltvorstellungen: political economy versus economics

	Political Economy	*Economics*
Methodology 1	Methodological collectivism/ holism	Methodological individualism
Methodology 2	Economics as a social science, dialectics	Economics as a science of the economic laws of society, isolating abstraction
Purpose/aim of economic activity	Various kinds of social missions: Classless society/post-industrial society, Russia's return as a world power	Material well-being of the individuals
State/Economy relationship	Economic system as subordinated to the state and its purposes (see above)	Economic system as a relatively autonomous sphere of society

For the sake of simplicity, in the following I will refer to the Marxian/traditional pattern as the "political economy camp" and to the camp that aims at integration into the international mainstream as the "economics" camp. This terminology emphasizes the fact that the first camp follows a methodology that dates back before the marginal revolution (as a result of which the term "economics" emerged), and this is also the term the representatives of this thought collective use to refer to themselves. In order to avoid confusion, when I refer to the Russian scientific community in general, I will avoid the term "economics" and "economists" but will use paraphrases like "Russian economic science". However, it must not be forgotten that we are not dealing with two distinct groups of scholars but with two broad patterns of thought or thought styles that each can be differentiated into various subgroups.

The adherents of political economy were either sticking to Soviet Political Economy or revived traditional Russian ideas. However, it would be exaggerating to say that this camp (which was far from homogenous) completely immunised itself against Western influences. Its representatives often integrated some Keynesian and institutionalist (usually stemming from the original institutionalists) ideas into their thinking. This, however, did not change the nature of the socio-philosophical patterns their economic thinking was embedded in. Despite all differences within this camp, its adherents usually shared a holistic and teleological understanding of social and economic development, rejected individualist social philosophy and saw the economy as something that had to serve society's path into a bright future. In contrast, the "economists" tried to adapt to Western economics. However, hardly surprisingly this adaptation did not work smoothly. Having been out of touch with the development of Western economics for six decades, in the beginning the reception of Western mainstream ideas remained rather superficial. As a result of their insufficient familiarity with Western mainstream economics, in the early period of post-socialist change, the adherents of this camp were ill-prepared to creatively relate to the inflowing ideas and their policy implications.

The main problem of the Russian economic discourse today is the ongoing tension between conflicting patterns of thought which does not, and this is the decisive point, only reflect disagreements about certain postulates of theory within a common body of economic science. Rather, the tensions reflect fundamentally different patterns of thought or *thought styles*, a term that was introduced by Ludwik Fleck in his 1935 work *Genesis of a Scientific Fact*:

> If we define "thought collective" as a community of persons mutually exchanging ideas or maintaining intellectual interaction, we will find by implication that it also provides the special "carrier" for the historical development of any field of thought, as well as for the given stock of knowledge and level of culture. This we have designated thought style.
>
> (Fleck [1935] 1979: 39)

Fleck's term "thought style" has much in common with Kuhn's paradigms (a term Kuhn indeed took over from Fleck). Thought styles are *Gestalten* into which scientific theories are embedded and which determine what questions are relevant for a certain thought collective:

> One can never say the same thought is true for A and false for B. If A and B belong to the same thought collective, the thought will be either true or false for both. But if they belong to different thought collectives, it will just *not be the same thought*! (ibid.: 100) . . . The greater the difference between two thought styles, the more inhibited will be the communication of ideas. . . . The alien way of thought seems like mysticism. The questions it rejects will often be regarded as the most important ones, its explanations as proving nothing or as missing the point, its problems as often unimportant or meaningless trivialities.
>
> (ibid.: 109)

The second part of this quotation is a rather perfect description of the state of affairs of Russian economic science today. It is marked by two different thought collectives with entirely different thought styles according to which the respective opposing camp seems to pose completely irrelevant questions and to be engaged in mysticism rather than science.

One may object that, as the example of Keynesianism and Monetarism shows, there are also fundamental theoretical and ideological divisions within Western economics. In order to make the difference as clear as possible, let us consider a current example of conflicting views within Western economic discourse. At present, we witness a debate about the European debt crisis with an increasing number of economists challenging the common wisdom of austerity and confronting it with a Keynesian vision of anti-cyclical deficit spending. Behind this discussion are different macroeconomic visions and normative orientations as to what role the state should play in the economy. However, these discussions take place within the common mainstream canon of modern economic theory as it took shape after the marginal revolution. Indeed, economic theory has been more successful[17] than any other social science to integrate seemingly revolutionary ideas and side discourses into its mainstream.[18]

In contrast to this, the discussions between the Russian adherents of political economy on the one hand and economics on the other resemble clashes between representatives of different scientific disciplines. A scholar who rejects methodological individualism, sees herself in the tradition of Hegelian dialectics and is mainly interested in economic development which she interprets as a teleological process, and someone who regards herself as a modern mainstream economist indeed have fairly little to say to each other.[19] In today's Russia, two thought collectives that do not only have different ideological orientations but start from entirely different *Gestaltvorstellungen* share the space of a single academic discipline. In this situation, it is almost impossible to develop interpretations of social reality that are shared by the majority of the scientific community.

What is specific about Russia III: deep ideational backgrounds

Turning now to the significance of deep ideational backgrounds, let me return to Karl Pribram's (1983: 40) central assertion that "prerequisite to any change in social or economic institutions or organisations is a change of the prevailing pattern of reasoning which had provided the background to the predominant forms of social and economic life". Interpreted in terms of constructivist institutionalism, Pribram argues that a fundamental change in background ideas is a prerequisite of institutional change. It is important to note that the processes of change Pribram is concerned with are the great upheavals in history as between the Middle Ages and the Renaissance and between mercantilism and capitalism.

The recent literature on ideas and institutions so far has not been dealing with as far-reaching processes of institutional change. This also holds true for Mark Blyth's seminal book *Great Transformations: Economic Ideas and Institutional Change in the Twentieth Century*. To repeat, according to Polanyi, a great transformation occurs if in a society which had previously not yet known such a separation, there emerges an institutional border between polity and economy.[20] The policy shift from Keynesianism to Monetarism, one of the cases Blyth is dealing with in his study, certainly was a process of more than superficial change. But it took place within stable societies that were democracies with market economies beforehand and afterwards.[21] The first challenge the Russian case poses to constructivist institutionalism, then, is that we are dealing not with a process of change *within* a capitalist order but indeed with a process of transformation in Polanyi's sense, or more precisely, with an attempt at a great transformation.

A further problem of the existing literature on ideas and institutions is that its empirical focus is on the Western, developed countries. There are two problems with this: first, Western Europe and the United States of America form a common cultural space marked by a common history and a common dominant religion. These countries are hence relatively homogenous regarding ideational backgrounds; and second, and related to this, Western Europe and the USA share a common space of scientific communication. As a result, as soon as a new economic idea comes up, it will quickly spread within this common space. This has been well documented for the case of "Keynesianism across nations" (Hall 1989).

Though I strongly disagree with the thesis of Russia's cultural and historical "uniqueness" (*samobytnost'*), I concede that Russia was and is a country at the periphery of Europe which did not fully participate in some of the key historical events that shaped what is usually referred to as the "Western world". The main point that marks a certain divide between Russia and the West is the legacy of Russian Orthodoxy characterised by a peculiar symbiosis of holism and anthropocentrism.[22] Up to the 18th century the Russian church authorities again and again defended the ideal of a unity between belief and thought, individual and society, state and church against the rationalistic "fragmentation" of Western societies. Both holism and anthropocentrism had been a central element of the original Christian dogma. Yet whereas in the Western versions of Christianity they had lost their original significance by and by, they had been preserved in the Eastern dogma. In Russian intellectual history, holism and anthropocentrism formed a symbiosis: the holistic criticism of the "fragmentation" or "atomisation" of society is always justified by the necessity of ensuring an extensive and complete development of the human personality. As the argument goes, social differentiation – as for example the division of labour – conceals the danger of "fragmentation" of individuals as well, which hinders their all-around development. The hostile attitude of many Russian intellectuals towards capitalism was traditionally based on this holistic-anthropocentric legacy.[23] This was especially true for the members of the left-wing intelligentsia, whose members conspicuously often had pronounced regional backgrounds and in a number of cases had been members of the seminary before pursuing careers as revolutionaries (see fundamentally Berdiaev [1937] 1990).

As is well known, in the middle of the 19th century, when Russia started to intensify her economic catch-up development, there emerged two opposed currents of Russian social thought: Slavophiles and Westernisers. The Slavophiles postulated a basic cultural difference between Western Europe and Russia. As both cultures were incomprehensible, they called to follow a "Russian path" of social development, characterised by the maintenance of the unity of society (see in detail Walicki [1975] 1989). The Westernisers, in contrast, denied that Russian culture was in principle different from that of Western Europe. Rather, they regarded the cultural differences between Russia and Western Europe as an expression of Russia's economic and cultural "backwardness". The debate between the two camps culminated in the course of an intense controversy over capitalism in the 1890s (see Walicki [1969] 1989). What this discussion was all about, can be illustrated by two key quotations. The leader of the so called *narodniki* (from people = *narod*), who tied in with the ideas of the Slavophiles, Nikolai K. Mikhailovskii, summarised his anti-capitalist attitude in a famous formula of progress:

> Progress is the gradual approach to the individual, to the fullest possible and the most diversified division of labour among man's organs and the least possible division of labour among men. . . . Everything that diminishes the heterogeneity of society and thereby increases the heterogeneity of its members is moral, just, reasonable and beneficial.
>
> (Mikhailovskii [1869] 1911, vol. 1: 159, translation according to: Walicki [1969] 1989: 53)

Directly reacting to this integralist vision of social progress, the intellectual leader of the Western camp, the liberal economist and politician Piotr B. Struve argued that "in an undifferentiated world, the individual is 'harmoniously whole' . . . in its monotony and shapelessness" (Struve 1894: 38). Russian intellectuals should thus, he concluded, admit their "lack of culture and enroll in the school of capitalism" (ibid.: 288).

The two key questions of Russian pre-revolutionary social thought – of whether the country should develop according to Western patterns or follow her own way, and whether functional differentiation should be admitted or the unity of society should be maintained – are inseparably connected to each other. The Slavophiles' rejection of the "Western way" always resulted from the desire to prevent the process of functional differentiation and protect the unity of society and the prevailing status quo. Similarly, the Westernisers' wish to share the historical fate of the West always included the demand to adopt the Western European path of the functional differentiation of society. These "eternal" questions of Russian social thought returned to the centre of attention in the 1990s, when Russia undertook another attempt at capitalist transformation.

It is important to note that the holistic-anthropocentric legacy of Russian Orthodoxy, which formed (and, as we will see, still forms) the ideational background of anti-capitalism in Russia, was by no means a static "cultural heritage" impeding Russia's capitalist transformation. And of course Russia was not the only country in the world where catch-up development led to severe ideological tensions. My argument, thus, is not that the holistic-anthropocentric legacy of Orthodoxy *caused* the protest against capitalism in Russia but rather that it *amplified* anti-capitalist sentiments of the Slavophile camp in their struggle with the Westernizers. And this, I argue, made Russia particularly vulnerable to external political shocks. To briefly illustrate this point: From the times of Peter the Great at latest, Russia developed with close interaction and in close competition with Western Europe, which imposed a permanent pressure of convergence. Despite the severe ideological tensions that accompanied its "great transformation", at the eve of the outbreak of the First World War everything spoke in favour of Russia becoming a "normal" European country ("normal" meaning that the country was about to develop its own variety of European modernity). The First World War, however, offered a window of opportunity for the Bolshevist political entrepreneurs who managed to revive the traditional ideal of the "holistic society" under the banner of Marxism-Leninism. In this context it is important to understand that in a way Marxism "only 'reminded' the popular Russian consciousness of its traditional way" (Zilberman 1977: 363). It shall not be denied here that the Soviet Union saw a kind of modernisation. However, this modernisation process took place on the basis of traditional, collectivist institutions (Mironov 2000: 333). At the micro-level, the planned economy, with its permanent shortage of goods, re-produced "primitive", deeply personalised relationships of reciprocal exchange and re-distribution known as *blat* (Ledeneva 1998). With regard to national identity too, the Bolshevists achieved a *Gestalt* switch that reconstructed the antagonism between Russia and the West and in a way revived the old story of Moscow as the Third Rome (see e.g. Duncan 2000). However, as we will see in the next chapter, especially after Stalin's death, the CPSU failed in its attempt to enforce a generally-binding interpretation of social reality, and the 1960s in particular were marked by severe ideological struggles, before the *politburo* in the early 1970s again strengthened its pressure on the intellectual life of society.

Notes

1 It shall not go without notice here that there is some discussion about whether Polanyi himself interpreted capitalism as a social order in which there really was an institutional separation between polity and economy or whether he saw it as a system that strived for the *utopian* ideal of such a separation (see e.g. Block 2001: xxiv–xxv).

2 The term nicely expresses the idea that in capitalism the economic system follows its own functional laws.

3 It is understood that the system border between polity and economy is always permeable; what is decisive here is only that in a functionally differentiated society can the economic and the political "value spheres" be clearly distinguished (though, of course, in functionally differentiated societies too there are fields of intersection where this distinction might be not so clear).

4 It shall not go without notice that in his later works Blyth further developed his basic concept. For example, his 2006 paper on "Great Punctuations" can already be interpreted as a "tipping-point story" (for this interpretation Mukherji 2013: 369) which pays much more attention to what Soifer later referred to as "productive conditions".

5 It is very important to note that the relevant "shared interpretation" needs *not* be shared *by anyone*. However, in order to become the basis for institutional stability, a certain interpretation needs to possess clear dominance over rival interpretations.

6 One should keep in mind that we are speaking of Keynesianism as a "policy paradigm" (Hall 1993), that is, of a strongly simplified (and arguably distorted) version of Keynes' ideas. The core idea of this simplified Keynesianism was the Phillips curve.

7 It should not be forgotten here that the hegemony of official Soviet ideology was maintained by the oppression of deviating ideas.

8 This belief was especially strong in the economics profession and found expression in the Washington consensus (Williamson 1990).

9 One of the shortcomings of the clear-cut distinction between periods of path dependence and critical junctures is that it tends to overemphasize the degree of consensus in periods of "normal history" (for a critique see Lieberman 2002: 700–701). As a result, the significance of heterodox ideas is also potentially being neglected.

10 "An epistemic community is a network of professionals with recognised expertise and competence in a particular domain and an authoritative claim to policy-relevant knowledge within that domain or issue-area", the members of which "have (1) a shared set of normative and principled beliefs, which provide a value-based rationale for the social action of community members; (2) shared causal beliefs, which are derived from their analysis of practices leading or contributing to a central set of problems . . . (3) shared notions of validity. . . . (4) a common policy enterprise" (Haas 1992: 3).

11 Johanna Bockman and Gil Eyal (2002) have convincingly shown how in the 1960s to 1980s "Eastern Europe" served as a laboratory for the development of Western neoliberal ideas and that there were close ties between Western and Eastern European liberal/libertarian economists. However, in my view their study suffers from too undifferentiated a notion of "Eastern Europe" and an overestimation of the presence of Russian scientists in this transnational enterprise. In his comparison between Polish and Russian liberal underground discourses, Jan Kubik comes to the conclusion that Russian liberalism "has never acquired the status of a socially influential discourse" (2003: 335). Similarly, Peter Rutland (2013: 337) argues that "there was no epistemic community of 'market fundamentalists' in Russia prior to 1989, just a handful of thinkers edging towards market solutions . . . Most of the indigenous advocates of neoliberalism in the 1990s were recent converts with little professional training in free market economics".

12 To avoid misunderstanding, of course there was oppositional thought in the Soviet Union, but it was dominated by socialist and nationalist, not liberal ideas.

13 It was no coincidence that the key figures of political economy – Adam Smith, John Stuart Mill and Karl Marx – were philosophers and economists rather than "only"

economic thinkers, while the Ricardian system, as abstract as it might seem, was also deeply rooted in the economic policy contexts of his times.

14 In more detail about this distinction see Goldschmidt, Grimmer-Solem and Zweynert (2016).

15 Besides the dominating Political Economy of Socialism, there was also a much smaller mathematical current in Soviet economics (see Sutela 1991, chapter 2). However, it focused so exclusively on mathematical problems that in the West its representatives would have been classified as operations researchers rather than economists (Brue and MacPhee 1995: 184).

16 Worse still, while providing and sustaining an ideological framework, Soviet political economists had little contact with the international critical thought or radical economics, as well as to some "milder" heterodox approaches in economics (such as Post-Keynesianism). Thus, those approaches that were critical of the dominant neoclassical mainstream and which could have served as a foundation for a well-informed critique of Western textbook wisdom evaded them as well.

17 "More successful" should not be interpreted here as an approving evaluation but as a mere contestation of the fact that challenges to the hard core of the neoclassical canon have repeatedly been integrated into this mainstream. This is one of the meanings Fourcade, Ollion and Algan (2015) also have in mind when calling economics (and economists) "superior" to other social sciences.

18 Keynesianism is the best example of this. Whereas Keynes himself had developed ideas that were opposed to the basic neoclassical assumptions of human behavior (e.g., Keynes had very much questioned the rationality of economic actors), already his first major recipient, John R. Hicks, deprived Keynes' analysis of these "heretic" elements and, together with Paul A. Samuelson, laid the foundation of the so called "neoclassical synthesis" firmly integrating Keynes' ideas into the mainstream of economic thought. Milton Friedman's famous sentence, "We are all Keynesians now", gives clear evidence of the degree to which the adherents of the different theoretical and ideological camps stand on common ground.

19 Communication is often additionally hampered by the fact that the two camps have incompatible definitions of terms. For example, in the recent Russian debate on modernisation (see Chapter 7) a lot of confusion emerged from the fact that economists and the adherents of political economy used the term "modernisation" in completely different, often opposed, ways.

20 The reverse process of a re-integration of the economy into the political system (a socialist transformation) also would be a great transformation according to Polanyi.

21 Though the relationship between polity and economy changed significantly after 1980, in the Keynesian welfare state it was also clearly possible to distinguish between the political and the economic sphere of society.

22 This is a thesis I developed in my 2002 book in some detail (for a summary in English see Zweynert 2004). My account of the history of Russian social philosophy closely follows Zen'kovsky ([1948] 2003).

23 This is absolutely comprehensible: Not only is the characteristic feature of capitalism an institutional separation between the state and the economy. Also the growing division of labour necessarily bears the risk of a one-sided development of individual skills, a problem that has been vastly discussed also in Western economic literature and found its most forceful expression in Marx's teaching about alienation.

3 The legacy of the Brezhnev period: 1971–1986

Why deal with the Brezhnev period?

The Brezhnev years are highly relevant for two reasons for what happened later. First, the reform concepts of the people of the sixties (*shestidesiatniki*), which have their roots in this period, provided the background to Gorbachev's reforms and later to the opposition of a then older generation of economists against Western mainstream economics. In other words, the ideas of one of the two thought collectives in today's Russian economic science can be directly traced back to this period. Secondly, in order to comprehend the thesis that – not only in ideational terms – the country today is approaching a kind of "neo-*zastoi*" (standstill), it is important to be familiar with the ideational foundations of the Soviet order of the 1960s to early 1980s. Both the political ideology of the Brezhnev period, in the centre of which stood the notion of "developed socialism" (see e.g. Evans 1977; Kelley 1977; Sandle 2002) and the development of Soviet economic thought in the 1960s to 1980s are relatively well researched topics (Sutela 1991, 2008; Sutela and Mau 1998), but to my knowledge no systematic research has yet been done into the relationships between economic ideas and the political doctrine behind what has later been labelled the period of *zastoi*.[1]

It is important to note that the idea of developed socialism and its economic counterpart, the concept of "perfectioning of the economic mechanism", were by no means inventions of the Soviet politburo. Both had their origin in the context of reformist thinking in Central Eastern Europe, from where they were imported into the Soviet Union. The Soviet versions of the two above-mentioned concepts, as introduced into the official discourse by Leonid Brezhnev in his speech at the 24th Communist Party Congress in 1971, took up key reformist topics (and thus seemingly made concessions to the critics of over-centralisation), yet at the same time decisively tightened the borders within which these topics could be discussed.

What happened here can best be described in terms of Imre Lakatos' (1965) theory of scientific research programmes. According to Lakatos, these research programmes consist of two parts: some very general theoretical hypotheses form the "hard core". The second part, the so-called "protective belt", consists of auxiliary hypotheses that supplement the hard core, and of assumptions that are basic to the initial conditions and observational hypotheses. The crux of Lakatos' theory is that the hard core of the programme "is 'irrefutable' by the methodological decision of its protagonists" (Lakatos 1965: 135). If the programme is challenged by phenomena it cannot explain, for a considerable time its adherents will do everything possible to protect the hard core of the programme and permit changes only within the protective belt. Only if these rescue attempts lastingly fail will the hard core and thus the research programme be given up and replaced with a new one. Formulated in terms of this concept, it can be argued that the politburo successfully fought off ideas that were increasingly challenging the foundations of the Soviet order by admitting a freer discussion of elements of the protective belt (e.g. the management methods of state enterprises) around the hard core (the primacy of state planning and collective property)[2] of Soviet ideology, while at the same time this core was declared to be a taboo subject for scientific debate.[3]

In the Soviet Union, this strategy proved to be successful. In the 1970s, the economic debates shifted from topics dangerously close (from the point of view of the political leaders) to the hard core of Soviet ideology into the extended protective belt, and, in striking contrast to Central Eastern Europe, no liberal-bourgeois underground economic discourses of considerable strength emerged. As is typical for the generation of Soviet *shestidesiatniki*, the "progressive" economists of the 1970s and early '80s managed to convince themselves and others that they were engaged in a serious reform discourse. In fact, however, playing according to the rules of the game meant discussing questions of secondary importance relatively freely, but systematically leaving the most fundamental issues out of consideration and ignoring important aspects of empirical reality. The somewhat virtual nature of the Soviet economic reform discourse that took place in the context of the dogma of developed socialism can be seen as one of the main reasons why its key figures failed so disastrously when it later came to the task of applying their ideas to reality in the late 1980s.

The chapter is organised as follows: the next section offers a basic analysis of how the concept of developed socialism relates to the evolution of the Soviet economy. The third section takes a closer look at the origin of the dogma of developed socialism, the economic ideas that developed in its context and some key topics within the moderately reformist debates in the "political economy of socialism". The conclusion discusses the relevance of the political economy of socialism as it developed in the Brezhnev years for the further development of Russian economic science and the discussions on post-Soviet economic reforms.

Self-organisation versus mobilisation

As I argued in the previous chapter, a "socialist economic system" cannot be regarded as a system, for it is unable to develop its own economic dynamics; this "system" is set into motion (mobilised) by political targets, and the most important infusions of energy into the economy are of an ideological nature. Exactly because planned "economies" are subordinated to politics, they are superior to market economies when it comes to focusing all resources on attaining an overriding goal, e.g. fighting a war or, as in the case of the Soviet Union, rapid catch-up modernisation. To once more refer to Iurii Aleksandrov's metaphor of the swamp: It was only after the overriding goals of industrialisation (in the Soviet Union) and post-war reconstruction (both in the Soviet Union and in Central Eastern Europe) had been achieved that the planned "economies" turned into mouldering swamps and that at the same time the question of demand satisfaction became more and more urgent. The idea of market socialism, which came up in Central Eastern Europe in the early 1960s, promised to establish an economic system that would, due to the interplay of demand and supply, become self-organising and, at the same time, remain socialist.[4]

From about the middle of the 1960s onward, this discourse was increasingly imported into the Soviet Union[5] and caused "a real revolution" (Campbell 1974) in Soviet economic thought, which led to a rapidly increasing public interest in economic issues. Between 1964 and 1971 in *Novyi mir*, a growing number of articles on various aspects of the theory and practice of economic reforms was published. Among the authors of these articles were academic economists like Aleksandr Birman, Nikolai Petrakov*and Leonid Abalkin*, and journalists like Otto R. Latsis*, Vasilii Seliunin* and Genadii Lisichkin*. The most radical statements in favour of market socialism were put forth by the journalists, among whom Lisichkin was the outstanding figure. In his 1966 book *Plan and Market*, he directly questioned the hard core of Soviet ideology when characterising economic laws as an "objective factor, functioning outside the sphere of our will" (Lisichkin 1966: 266). Accordingly, in his view the Soviet experience confirmed

> the invalidity. . . of any principle of distribution other than one based on commensurability of what is contributed to society and what is received from it, that is, on buying and selling. This basic feature of the law of value is ignored, and it takes its revenge in the low level of efficiency in our use of technology and the high cost of what we produce.
>
> (Lisichkin 1966: 60)

From the very beginning, the theoretical problem of the "subjectivity" or "objectivity" of economic laws under socialism represented a major challenge for the Soviet rulers. If there were really "objective" economic laws, then there still existed something like a specific subsystem within society which resisted the socialist will to shape and transform things. The fact that Karl Marx had regarded the law of value as something like a natural (and thus "objective") law could hardly be denied, yet it could be questioned whether this would remain true in a socialist society. Many of the controversies in Soviet economics of the 1920s and 1930s dealt with this question, and the decision to produce an "official" textbook of the political economy of socialism that was taken in the middle of the 1930s reflected the need to clarify the party line regarding this issue (Sutela 1991: 15–18). The textbook, finally published in 1954 (Ostrovitianov 1954), in effect (though not explicitly) denied the objectivity of economic laws by arguing that the government was able to annul disagreeable laws using political methods.

What happened in the Eastern block from the late 1950s onward was quite a radical backswing of the pendulum from the notion of subjectivity to that of objectivity in economic laws under socialism. This shift in economic thought was inextricably linked with political de-Stalinisation. In its radical form, as formulated by Lisichkin and others, the notion that the "iron" law of supply and demand existed independently of the political order challenged the party's hegemony over all aspects of social life. Indeed, the idea of placing the economic system in service of the consumers and their needs on the basis of supply and demand would in the final analysis have meant establishing something like a systems border between polity and economy – something that was entirely against the nature of the Soviet system.

In official Soviet discourse the term "developed socialism" appeared for the first time (in a rather fuzzy form) in a speech Leonid Brezhnev delivered on the occasion of the 50th anniversary of the October Revolution in 1967 (Brezhnev 1967) and was then developed in more detail in his speech at the 24th Party Congress in March 1971 (Materialy 1971). The term made significant concessions to the reformist thought of the 1960s by admitting that the organizational structure of the planned economy did not meet the challenges of the second industrial revolution and that the time had come to align economic activity more closely to the needs of the consumers. At the same time, Brezhnev explicitly underlined that "our economy at that time [the late 1930s, J.Z.] and our modern economy are based on one and the same type of relationships of production, on the same economic laws – the laws of socialism" (Materialy 1971). In other words, changes in the organisational structure of the economy, including increasing use of money-commodity relations and more autonomy for production units, were acceptable as long as this did not challenge the primacy of state planning and collective property.

If interpreted in terms of Aleksandrov's comparison between planned and market economies, in its official Soviet version, "developed socialism" was nothing other than a perfect recipe for *zastoi*. On the one hand, it argued in favour of orientating production towards consumer preferences, on the other it fully suppressed the price mechanism, which is the only possible basis for this kind of economic self-organisation. Sticking to the organisational foundations of a mobilised society in this way, and proclaiming demand satisfaction as the final economic goal, it abstained from infusing any mobilising political energy into the system. It is no accident that all the "basic links" Aleksandrov mentions refer to the time either before or after Brezhnev – the standstill of developed socialism was indeed inherent in the very concept (more precisely, in its official Soviet version).

The economics of developed socialism

The origins of the concept

The usual interpretation of "developed socialism" sees it mainly as an attempt to silently abandon Nikita Khrushchev's ambitious timetable for the transition into Communism by introducing a further transitional period of more or less indefinite duration. This interpretation is certainly not entirely wrong, but as Mark Sandle (2002) has shown, the contrast between Khrushchev's understanding of Communism and Brezhnev's version of "developed socialism" should not be exaggerated. More important than the buying of time was the problem of coping with the reformist debates which, especially in Central Eastern Europe, fundamentally questioned more and more the social order which the Soviet Union had obtruded on its satellites. As Sarah M. Terry has demonstrated, the term "developed socialism" was by no means invented by the Soviet politburo but had been central to the demand to adapt economic institutions to the social reality of the highly developed and highly diversified economies of Central Eastern Europe. As Terry (1984: 225) shows,

> the term was introduced by the Czechoslovak party at its June 1960 Central Committee plenum, more than seven years before Brezhnev's first documented reference or attempts on the part of Soviet scholars to apply the term to the Soviet system itself; and the Czech example was shortly followed by the Hungarian, East German, and Bulgarian parties.

It is telling that in Soviet print the term appeared for the first time in a documentation of an international meeting of "communist and workers' parties" that had taken place in Moscow in 1960. Possibly due to the ideologically sensitive issues that were at stake, this documentation was published only in 1964. Interestingly, the term "construction of a developed socialist society" is here attributed to the countries of Central Eastern Europe:

> The Soviet Union successfully realises an unfolded construction of a communist society. Other countries of the socialist camp have successfully laid the foundations of socialism, yet some of them have already entered the period of construction of a developed socialist society.
>
> (quoted after Kozlov 1977: 14)

Apart from channelling these debates, in its official Soviet version the term could be used to deal with one of the fundamental problems of every Soviet government: on the one hand, stick to the basic promise of Marxism-Leninism that even the socialist state was only a transitional stage on the road to Communism, but at the same time justify the existing institutions and power relations. Now, a society cannot at the same time develop and be developed. The formula "developed socialism" did much more than expand the timetable; it shifted this trade-off in favour of the justification of the present state of affairs to a degree that came very close to abandoning the idea of development itself. The following definition by the philosopher and then deputy chairman of the Academy of Sciences Piotr N. Fedoseev (1974; quoted after Sandle 2002: 166) makes this plainly clear:

> Developed socialist society is not considered by us as something midway between socialism and communism . . . It is a socialist society attaining a

> developed condition, characterised by the all-round disclosure of the advantages of socialism.[6]

Although in almost every definition of the concept lip-service was paid to its character as a "a natural stage in the progress of the first phase of the communist mode of production", in the end it was declared to be "a relatively independent stage with its own specific features and attributes" (Abalkin 1981: 66). The notion that at different stages of the building of Communism different economic laws applied had (again, especially in the further developed countries of Central Eastern Europe) been at the heart of the pre-1968 reform debate. However, this notion had been explicitly refuted by Leonid Brezhnev in his 1971 speech underlining that the same basic economic laws applied to all periods on the road to Communism. Here we see most clearly how the concept of "developed socialism" took up key elements of reformist thought but at the same time tried to defend the hard core of the ideological paradigm on which the Soviet state rested. In an article on "The highest goal of social production under socialism" Galina Latysheva and Aleksei Sergeev (1978: 105) formulated this almost in Lakatosian terms when noting that the "basic law of socialism" represented the "core of the comprehensive function of the economic laws under socialism" from which the "specific economic laws" of different periods should be carefully distinguished.[7]

The crux of "developed socialism" is that it is neither arch-conservative, nor, as Sandle (2002: 165) has recently argued, "far more progressive" than previously thought, but that it managed to take the sting out of the reformist concepts of the 1960s and integrate them into mainstream discourse in such a way that they no longer represented a threat to the political leadership. On the one hand, it turned the hard core of the Soviet social order, state property and the priority of the central plan, into taboo subjects. On the other, by declaring "developed socialism" to be a specific period with specific features and attributes, the economists willing to play according to the rules of the game were offered a new and enlarged playing field. In the following sections I will demonstrate how these toothless reform discourses looked using the example of the debate over the reform of the economic mechanism, the discussion on the relationship between base and superstructure and on the role of commodity-monetary relations.

The economic mechanism

The history of the concept of the economic mechanism reveals striking parallels to that of "developed socialism". The term was introduced into the official political discourse in the same speech by Brezhnev at the 24th Party Congress, in which "developed socialism" also started its official career,[8] and a reference to this speech became more or less mandatory in publications dedicated to the "perfection" of the economic mechanism.[9] However, very much as in the case of "developed socialism", this standard reference should not belie the fact that the term had its roots in Central Eastern Europe, especially Hungary and Czechoslovakia, where it had been at the centre of the economic reform debates. Not only these debates, but also the reforms in which these debates resulted, went further than the Kosygin reforms of 1965 (Denton 1971; Eddie 1996; King 1979). In 1967 (Czechoslovakia) and 1968 (Hungary), "new economic mechanisms" had been implemented that saw at least a modest role for market price formation. Whereas directly after 1968 it had not been immediately clear whether the Soviet invasion of Czechoslovakia would also put an end to economic reforms, by 1970–71 it was obvious that re-centralisation would follow.

The Soviet discourse on the economic mechanism is inseparably connected with the name of Leonid Abalkin, who more so than any other stands for the continuity between the Brezhnev period and perestroika. In 1988, he became Gorbachev's economic advisor (and in 1989 Deputy Prime Minister) and up to the 2000s played an important role in Russian economic science. In an autobiographical sketch, Abalkin (1997, quoted after Kuznetsova 2000: 9, fn.) explicitly defined himself as *shestidesiatnik*:

> Let us remember the September Plenum 1953 – that was the most radical turning point in all sorts of notions – about the economic model, about the situation of the farmers, finally on the necessity to break with the attempts to support the economy and to live on the deprivation and the strangling of the farmers . . . It was a gulp of fresh air. Moreover these were not only words – things really began to change . . . There also began colossal changes in intellectual life, when there could appear and publish not dissidents, but Voznesenskii and Evtushenko.

In 1973, Abalkin published his book *The Economic Mechanism of Developed Socialist Society*, which can be seen as a perfect manifestation of the Soviet "mainstream reform economics" (Sutela and Mau 1998: 53) of the 1970s. Abalkin starts with the mantra of all reform economists of the 1960s: the structure of planning, as it had developed in the 1930s, no longer matched the productive forces. However, as he is quick to remark, the necessary changes in the relations of production (read: decentralization) should leave the forms of property relations (read: state property) unaltered (Abalkin 1973: 13). In similar fashion, he (ibid.: 98) discusses the reforms of the 1960s (and explicitly also refers to the reforms in Central Eastern Europe) with obvious sympathy, but also explicitly notes,

> that to go beyond certain borders leads to the undermining of central administration, to the full "autonomy" of the economic entities and in the end to the unleashing of the spontaneous forces of anarchy and competition.

Without directly mentioning Lisichkin and the other more radical participants of the Soviet reform debates, Abalkin urgently warned against the "fetishisation of economic laws" (Abalkin 1973: 26). In his version, the concept of the economic mechanism offered a compromise between the "subjectivity" and "objectivity" of economic laws. As economic performance depended on technological and economic, and on socio-political, juridical and ideological factors, the economic mechanism could, Abalkin argued, be attributed unequivocally to neither the base nor to the superstructure, to the realm of neither objective nor subjective factors (Abalkin 1973: 9). In fact, as is shown by Abalkin's definition of the economic mechanism as a "mode of organisation of social production with the forms and methods characteristic for it, like economic incentives and legal norms" (ibid.: 10), it dealt with the interplay between base and superstructure and thus also with the interplay between "objective" and "subjective" laws.

In principle, this compromise formula would have been flexible enough to continue the discussion of some of the key reformist topics of the 1960s. Abalkin himself indicated this by devoting considerable space to the issue of the relative autonomy of the socialist enterprises in the context of which he even directly mentioned the Hungarian "new economic mechanism" (Abalkin 1973: 112).[10] However, what his book mainly stands for is a fundamental shift of the economic discourse from the "objective" to the "subjective" or from base to superstructure. Indeed, if economic laws were regarded as the complex outcome of human interaction including social and political factors, it also made sense analytically to go beyond the border of pure economics and to pay attention to the issue of the social embeddedness of economic interaction. In particular, Abalkin highlighted the importance of social psychology for economic reforms. It could often be observed, he noted, how economically rational reform measures failed because social consciousness had not yet reached the necessary degree of maturity (Abalkin 1973: 212–219).

The question of to what degree economics should pay attention to the social context of economic activity is an "eternal" methodological problem of economics and has been intensely discussed, especially in the so-called *methodenstreit* between the Austrian and the younger historical schools in economics in the late 19th and early 20th centuries (for a recent account see Louzek 2011). Without going into detail, the main advantage of a more contextual approach as favoured by Abalkin is certainly that it lowers the level of abstraction and does more justice to the complexity of social life. Yet, if the existence of objective economic laws is generally questioned this can all too easily lead to a negligence of economic theory by economists themselves, and this is what had happened in German "historical" economics in the late 19th century and in Soviet economics in the 1970s. These are not merely methodological problems, for historical experience shows that economists who deny the existence of economic laws that are valid independently of the conditions of time and space and of human consciousness regularly fail as policy advisors.[11]

Base and superstructure

For Marxist observers, it should have been no surprise that the necessity to adapt the socialist economies to the second industrial revolution within the Eastern block was first recognised in countries like Czechoslovakia and Hungary, which were better equipped with physical and human capital than the Soviet Union. By taking up a strongly revised version of the concept of "developed socialism", the

Soviet leaders also reinforced their aspiration for hegemony over the satellite states (Sandle 2002: 172). After 1971, the claim that the Soviet Union was the only country thus far that had reached the stage of "developed socialism" became a standard notion in the relevant literature.

As has been shown in the last section, the idea of objective economic laws represented a permanent challenge to the Soviet leaders. Now whereas the static law of supply and demand was at the heart of the Soviet and Central Eastern European reform discourse, Western convergence theory challenged Soviet ideology on the field of the long-term developmental laws, something on which Marxists had had a de facto monopoly since the times of the German historical schools and American original institutionalism (in the tradition of which stood John Kenneth Galbraith). Of the convergence theorists, Galbraith was by far the most influential figure in the Soviet Union. His *New Industrial Society* had been translated in 1969, and in Soviet social science journals there were quite a number of reactions to Galbraith, who was acknowledged as the creator of the "most sophisticated bourgeois economic theory of socialism" (Dvorkin 1970: 67), and as an author who in his works at least came closer to the reality of monopoly capitalism than most neo-classical and Keynesian authors (Mileikovskii 1975: 80); later, in 1988, he was awarded an honorary doctorate by the faculty of economics of Lomonosov University, Moscow. In view of perestroika and the market reforms of the 1990s, the main impact of the convergence theorists was that they "almost succeeded in convincing a generation of Soviet economists that the market economy belongs to the past" (Sutela and Mau 1998: 72). For the economic discourse of the 1970s, however, it was much more important that it challenged the claim that the development of the productive forces would inevitably lead to increasing centralisation and predicted the emergence of mixed economies in both the West and the East. It is one of the finest ironies in the history of Soviet economic thought that in the 1970s Galbraith and other convergence theorists were repeatedly accused of "one-sided materialism" by Soviet economists, who reminded their bourgeois counterparts that technological changes alone would not automatically lead to changes in the relations of production (Ignatovskii 1974: 70; Khavina 1977: 114; Kozlov 1977: 82; Safarov 1983: 14).

Even though the increasing influence of the superstructure on the economic base was declared to be the decisive "specific feature" of "developed socialism", this, like every major ideological shift, called for a justification in the works of the classics of Marxism-Leninism. In this context it became standard to refer to Engels' letter to Joseph Bloch (Engels 1967), in which he clarified that his and Marx's sometimes rather one-sided emphasis on the impact of the economic base on the superstructure had mainly been a counter-reaction to the contemporary dominance of idealism. In fact, Engels wrote, they had always been aware of the mutual influence of base and superstructure.

The (politically demanded) re-orientation from the "objective" to the "subjective" went hand-in-hand with what in the context of Marxist-Leninism could be labelled as a fairly radical idealist turn; the problem of the influence of the superstructure on the economic basis was now declared to be the all-decisive problem, and sometimes the superstructure was even declared to be "relatively independent" (Kuz'minov 1975: 26) of the economic base. Quite tellingly, books on "developed socialism" sometimes included subtitles such as "Issues of the formation of social consciousness" (Medved'ev 1980) or "The influence of superstructural factors on the economy" (Safarov 1983). In the (even mainstream reformist) official discourse it became a common idea that with the growing "maturity" of socialist society the influence of "spiritual-ideological" factors on economic development would grow until man would finally become the "creator of the entire social life" (Medved'ev 1980: 25). This, however, demanded that human consciousness, including the evolution of preferences, should be carefully guided by the state (Kozlov 1973; Medved'ev 1980; Sergeev 1974).

It can again very clearly be seen here how "developed socialism" took up themes from the reform discourse but in the final analysis turned them into their opposite. The Central Eastern European reform discourses had taken the satisfaction of individual needs as their starting-point, accepting these needs, in typical "bourgeois" manner, and demanded that production be adapted to them. On the one hand, the official discourse under Brezhnev took up this goal, but on the other, tied it to the communist pretension of making the individual needs subject of state planning.

Commodity-money relations

Even though Soviet economic thought of the 1970s was marked by an overall shift from the "objective" to the "subjective", the 24th Party Congress had also explicitly called for finding "the most effective forms and methods of utilising the objective economic laws for the management practice of the national economy" (Materialy 1971: 70). In a fairly dialectical manner, the consolidation of the hard core of ideology at the same time expanded the possibilities of discussing the use of what in the Soviet Union was called commodity-money relations, within strictly defined borders.

Regarding the relationship between commodity-money relations and the central plan, it was again Abalkin who offered a compromise formula that became widely accepted in the political economy of socialist discourse. Instead of confronting the two principles, commodity-money relations should, Abalkin noted, be seen as an inherent component of the plan (Abalkin 1973: 35–36). As Genrikh A. Kozlov added, if one postulated that commodity-money relations existed outside of the plan, this was to acknowledge that non-socialist relations still existed in Soviet society. The key point was to understand, Kozlov (and others) argued, that "under the unrestricted reign of the socialist order, those relations remaining of earlier formations both in their form and their content undergo a fundamental transformation" (Kozlov 1977: 26). This notion, which was inseparably connected with the "historical" distinction between the "basic socialist law" and "specific features" of different periods, made it possible to discuss fairly "conspicuous" topics as long it was sufficiently emphasised that under collective property and a planned economy, commodity-money relations had taken on a genuinely socialist character.

However, since here we are dealings with exactly – if there was such a thing – the most "progressive" side of "developed socialism", it is these debates (and perhaps most obviously those about "socialist competition" [*sorevnovanie*]) that also most clearly reveal the toothlessness of the moderate reformist debates of the 1970s and early '80s. The reason for this is not only that the issue of property relations was banned from the discussion. The dogma that in socialism commodity-money relations would fundamentally change their character in the end deprived them of their content. Market relations can only be meaningfully analysed when they are treated as natural laws (that is "objectively") and in relative isolation from the complexity of other social relations, and in particular the issue of human consciousness (that is "subjectivity"). A "subjective" and "complex" treatment, according to which there is an undefined degree to which individuals (or society in general) are able to subordinate economic laws to their purposeful interference, is destined to fail because it systematically overtaxes human cognitive capacities. Precisely because commodity-money relations can only be meaningfully analysed "objectively", this label became something of a symbol reflecting reformist ideas that hinted at the 1960s, but did not itself become a subject of scientific analysis.

Conclusion

In the previous sections I have shown that "developed socialism" can mainly be seen as a reaction of the Soviet leadership to the Central Eastern European and Soviet reform discourses of the 1960s. By taking over key concepts from the reform debates but filling them with new content, the politburo strengthened the hard core of Soviet ideology by widening the protective belt around it. The Soviet economists followed the intentions of the political leadership when they turned from the "objective" commodity-money relations to the "subjective" interplay between economic and non-economic factors, a shift that went hand in hand with an increasing negligence of economic theory. Put polemically, one might speak of a win-win constellation here: the political leadership got rid of debates challenging their power position, whereas the economists could engage in "progressive" debates without risking their social privileges. However, I do not wish to deny that the *shestidesiatnikis*' idealism was often a serious expression of concern about the living and working conditions of their fellow citizens. This is especially true for those rather critical intellectuals who, like Abel Aganbegian* or Tatiana Zaslavskaia*, since the early 1980s had emphasised the role of the "human factor" in the development prospects of the Soviet Union. However, whether consciously or not, these authors still very much played according to the rules of "developed socialism" when they raised issues regarding how the planned economy was managed instead of challenging the "objective" factors causing the social grievances. What proved to be much more problematic was that even after the political pressure had been lifted, the reformist mainstream economists of the Brezhnev period proved unable to cast off the mental imprinting they had received in the Brezhnev era; when in the perestroika period authors like Abalkin and Medved'ev discussed topics that previously had been taboo, like property or market relations, they did so in a way still resembling the political economy of socialism discourses of the Brezhnev era. Further still, throughout the 1990s, this generation of economists would, on the basis of their ideas about socialism with a human face, oppose liberal reforms and Western mainstream economics.

At the same time, it should not be overlooked that the ideas of the *shestidesiatniki* also influenced the policy-oriented economists of the *semidesiatniki* (1970s) generation, such as Egor Gaidar*, Vitaly Naishul* and others. For understandable reasons and certainly also as a result of a typical generational conflict, these authors radically distanced themselves from the idealism of the *shestidesiatniki* and contrasted it with a purely economic and markedly "objectivist" understanding of social relations.[12] In my view, the radical departure from *shestidesiatniki* ideology proved to be almost as problematic as the utopianism of the Abalkin generation. It was the Russian transition experience that reminded economists all over the world that "subjective" factors do matter in processes of institutional change, a problem the *shestidesiatniki* had paid much attention to.

Notes

1 On the emergence of the term, see e.g. Iurchak (2005: 7).

2 In the next chapter, I will refine my definition of Soviet ideology. I will argue that the primacy of state planning and collective property were embedded into a Soviet telos of long term development towards a "holistic society".

3 As Hans-Jürgen Wagener (1998b: 12) aptly puts it: "What prevented a sovereign intellectual activity were the taboos which had to be respected: the core of the paradigm, especially questions of ownership, the principle of planning and the predominant role of the party (the primacy of politics) were not to be touched upon. Economists who conformed to these rules could themselves identify as being sovereign, but in fact they submitted to the argument from authority".

4 The much-debated question as to whether a socialist market is possible or not is irrelevant to my topic, so it will not be considered here. For comprehensive accounts of the reformist discourses in socialist Central Europe see Wagener (1998a, chs. 3–5).

5 More precisely, re-imported in a radicalised form, for the Central Eastern European debates had been strongly inspired by Soviet authors, especially by Liberman's 1956 article on "Means to Raise the Profitability of the Socialistic Enterprises".

6 For similar definitions of the term see Abalkin (1981), Cherkovets (1973), Glezerman (1981).

7 The semantic differentiation between the two categories of "laws" brought Soviet social scientists considerable headaches before they finally agreed on concepts such as "specific features" [*spetsificheskie cherty*]. One author (Bzhilianski 1973, 1975), for example, dedicated two full-length papers to the proposal to distinguish between "economic laws" [*zakony*] and "regularities" [*zakonomersti*].

8 This passage reads as follows: "The political side of the question is also very important. The smooth functioning of the economic mechanism helps to provide a good, active climate in the country, helps to increase the working activity of the broad masses, as people see that their work brings the expected fruits, that it benefits the people, benefits the whole society" (Materialy xxiv. s'ezda kpss, 66).

9 Mau (1995: 11, fn.) provides a list of the most important publications on the "economic mechanism".

10 In this context, in a typical "read between the lines" fashion he (ibid.: 106) noted that the question of the socialist enterprise was still relatively poorly researched and referred

to a 1966 book on this topic by Vadim Medved'ev*, besides Abalkin the key mainstream reformist economist of the Brezhnev era.

11 In Germany, the representatives of the younger historical school failed to explain the inflation after World War One, and this failure caused a decisive loss of scientific reputation. However, an important difference between the German historical school and Soviet political economy of socialism of the 1970s should not be overlooked. In contrast to the representatives of the German historical school, the Soviet scholars of the 1970s were unable to make an independent decision about their methodological position. It was under severe political pressure that they decided more or less to abandon research into "objective" economic laws and turn to the issue of the social embeddedness of the economy instead.

12 For a detailed analysis of this intergenerational conflict see Gel'man, Marganiia and Travin 2014.

4 Cracking the protective belt: 1987–1992

Back to the 1960s and taking it further

This chapter deals with the economic debates around perestroika, the decline of the political economy of socialism and the following rapid inflow of Western, liberal ideas. What happened in the five years between 1987 and 1992 can be seen as a direct continuation of the discussion of the 1960s. The concept of perestroika was not only based on the ideas of the *shestidesiatniki* generation, it was also a pattern familiar from the 1960s that economic journalists and free thinkers were clearly ahead of the academic economists[1] in challenging the old ideological taboos. As a result, very much as in the 1960s,

> [t]he readers' interest today has to a considerable degree shifted in the direction of socio-political journals. Articles by M. Antonov, S. Andreev, S. Zalygin, V. Seliunin are read and discussed more than works by economic scholars.
>
> (Miasoedov and Lobova [1989] 1990: 80)

During the years of 1987–1992, acrid self-criticism and urgent appeals to re-integrate into the international scientific community were typical for the self-reflection of Russian economists. In a programmatic editorial, "The Journal – for Perestroika" Gavriil Popov* (1988: 4), the then new chief editor of *Voprosy ekonomiki* noted that "the years of zastoi have negatively affected the progress of theory", as "scholasticism, effectless pondering and ruthless adulation of any single practical measure of the leadership, which were praised as highest theoretical achievements", had become main features of Soviet economic science. As today, he continued, "even new ideas are drowning in standard phrases" and demanded "a brave exchange of opinions" which should not care about "the mourners over the fate of socialism". Fully acknowledging the allegation of "scholasticism, dogmatism and apologetics", Alexander Auzan* (1989: 5) noted that mainly due to "a lack of civic courage and scientific objectivity which would have been needed to formulate dangerously critical conclusions about the condition and the development trends of the socialist economy", Soviet political economists "knew only little more than the rest of society about the conditions and the real history of the economy".

In line with this, Oleg Anan'in (1988: 70) drew a direct line between the inability of political economy of socialism to provide answers to the concrete problems of perestroika and its pronounced disinterest in empirical questions. Advancing a particularly nuanced position, on the one hand he urgently called for a re-integration of Russian economics into the international scientific community and demanded the banning of the hitherto ubiquitous phrase in Soviet dissertations: "this study is mainly based on national literature". This phrase had expressed nothing, he pointed out, but complete isolation from the international discourse (Anan'in 1992: 98; see similarly also Maiminas 1992: 520 and Kuz'minov1992: 50–51). On the other hand, he questioned the unconditional applicability of general equilibrium theory, with its "extrapolation of Western behavioural stereotypes" (Anan'in 1992: 92) to Russia. The fact that Russia was somehow different did not, he explicitly argued, mean that Western theories were inappropriate for her ("Russia is different, but every country is different"), but if Russian economics wanted to make itself heard again, it should also refer to its own tradition (ibid.: 97). These considerations already anticipated the discussions that came up in the middle of the 1990s and which will be dealt with in the next chapter.

The main focus of this chapter is the decline of Soviet ideology and its replacement with imported liberal ideas. In order to better understand this process, I first will go a bit deeper into the issue of what Soviet ideology was all about. Further elaborating on my application of Imre Lakatos' theory of scientific research programmes, I will argue that the hard core of Soviet ideology was the idea that the country was on an historical road to a holistic society, an ideal that, as I have shown in the introduction, was not only taken over from Marx, but had deep roots in Russian religious thought. I will interpret perestroika as the last attempt to save the hard core of Soviet ideology by making far-reaching adjustments in the protective belt. However, the obvious failure of the ideas of the *shestidesiatniki* generation to stop the decline of the Soviet economy, led, in combination with the new freedom of scientific debate, to their delegitimisation, until finally the very idea that history could be interpreted as an evolution towards the holistic society (and thus the hard core of the ideological programme) was discarded.

What was Soviet ideology?

According to a common view, Soviet ideology rested on three pillars: on the belief that Marxism-Leninism offered a "true" interpretation of social reality, on "democratic centralism" (read: the dictatorship of the CPSU), and on central planning (e.g. Schull 1992).Though there is no doubt that these concepts were part of the hard core of Soviet ideology, throughout the history of the Soviet Union, particularly the concepts of "central planning" and "democratic centralism" underwent frequent reinterpretations that filled them with a wide range of meanings. Hence, if these were the central elements of Soviet ideology, it would be extremely difficult to define its content precisely (Armstrong 1978: 50).[2] Neil Robinson (1995: 20) has therefore suggested a different definition of Soviet ideology. He argues that at the heart of Soviet ideology was a peculiar interpretation of history:

> [T]he coherence in Soviet ideology derived from the idea of the telos of communism. As a part of the content of ideology, the concept of telos, the idea that the USSR was on a specific course of development, structured ideology because it shaped the party's ontology.

Though fully agreeing with Robinson in all other respects, I think that it would be more precise to speak not of a Communist, but of a Soviet telos here. Marxism was hardly the only source of the conviction that the Soviet Union was ahead of the Western countries on a historically pre-determined developmental path. Rather, its roots reach far back into the country's religious and intellectual history. As I argued in the second chapter, in Russian intellectual history a vision of a "holistic society" can be detected which was in potential conflict with the Western European patterns of life and thought (see also Buss 2003). I also argued that Marxism proved so fruitful in Russia because it was highly compatible with the Russian intellectual traditions shaped by the legacy of Orthodox Christianity.

In terms of Imre Lakatos' concept of scientific research programmes, the teleological interpretation of history as a path towards the holistic society can be seen as the deepest stratum of the hard core of the Soviet ideological programme. According to this interpretation, central planning and "democratic socialism" can still be regarded as elements of the hard core of the ideological programme, but they are political expressions of the "deeper" idea of the Soviet telos. The issue of the right means to cover the distance from the "fragmented" or "alienated" world to the holistic society could be debated, but the idea that this was the direction world history was taking, could not.[3]

In the 1960s and then again in the second half of the 1980s, the growing awareness of the contradictions between empirical reality and the official dogma resulted in attempts at economic decentralisation within the system of planned economy. Now, did such debates and reforms not directly contradict the Soviet telos, according to which history was characterised by an ever-growing homogeneity of society? They certainly did, but here an important element of the protective belt came to the rescue of official ideology: the dialectic method. According to this, all development can be attributed to the movement of antipodal forces. Applied to the developmental laws, this means that under certain circumstances, decentralisation could be regarded as the right means to stimulate centralisation (Sutela 1991: 60). This was indeed the line of argumentation adopted by the adherents of perestroika (see e.g. Abalkin 1987: 10).

Perestroika and the Soviet telos

At its June plenum of 1987, the General Secretary of the Central Committee of the CPSU declared the economy to be at the "front line of perestroika" (Gorbachev 1987: 27). In his speech, Mikhail Gorbachev outlined his plan for a "fundamental reconstruction of economic governance", motivated by the increasing scientific and technical backwardness of the Soviet Union compared to the Western industrial countries. While the latter had already "begun a structural perestroika of the economy . . . in our country scientific-technical progress has been frozen in" (Gorbachev 1987: 27). The cause of this phenomenon had already been outlined in a "Project of a New Edition" of the party manifesto (CPSU 1985) and was well known from the 1960s: Contradictions between productive forces and the relations of production could not only emerge in capitalist, but also in socialist societies. The dogma that Soviet society had already achieved harmony between the productive forces and the relations of production, first formulated in the 1940s, had to be given up. As Soviet society was still on the road to Communism, the productive forces were still in motion. Yet the rigid organisation of the relations of production had held back their evolution.

In order to overcome stagnation, Gorbachev called for a "transition from mainly administrative to mainly economic methods of management at all levels, for a broad democratisation of governance, an all-embracing activation of the human factor".[4] This included the exploitation of "commodity-monetary relations" and the implementation of "economic competition". Gorbachev (1987: 29) himself raised the question of whether the economic programme of perestroika marked a break with Soviet ideology, and there is no reason to doubt the sincerity of his answer:

> [W]hat we are already doing and what we intend to do should enhance socialism, it should remove everything that stands in the way of the development of socialism and checks its progress, open up its enormous potential on behalf of the people, bring into action all the advantages of our social organisation [*stroi*], and give socialism a modern face.

Early debates in Voprosy ekonomiki, and the new textbook on political economy

In the years between 1986 and 1987, most Soviet economists were still true servants of politics. This was not so much a result of political pressure (which, however, might have had its share) but of patterns of behaviour and thought institutionalised over the decades of Soviet rule. Consequently, the Party theses on the "fundamental reconstruction of economic governance" pre-determined the issues to be discussed by the economic profession. What was the nature of the basic contradictions in socialism and how could they be resolved? What lessons could be drawn from recent developments in the capitalist countries? What would be the right relationship between administrative and economic methods of governance?

Immediately after the "Project of a New Edition of the Programme of the CPSU" had been published, a discussion on "The Economic Contradictions of Socialism" (Kulikov 1986) was set off in the leading Soviet economic journal *Voprosy ekonomiki*. In the course of the debate no less than twenty-two articles on this topic were published.[5] On the one hand the intensity with which the scientific community made use of the chance to exchange views on a topic that had been taboo for decades demonstrated their eagerness to overcome the ideological barriers of the past. On the other hand, the discussion also provided sad evidence that, as Leonid Abalkin (1987: 5), one of the initiators of the debate, wrote in a disappointed résumé, "games with words and definitions" had become the main occupation of the Soviet economists. To give the reader a brief impression of this, I quote a statement from the discussion on price formation (see below) which illustrates the point:

> This way, the means to increase the efficacy of the price mechanism cannot be found in itself, but beyond its borders. It should be based on the general functional laws inherent to prices and incorporated into social and economic relationships and, by means of influencing social, collective and individual interests actively develop them into the necessary direction. Throughout its [the price mechanism, JZ] development concrete aims and tasks [should be realized, JZ]: a significant increase of the quality and effectiveness of new technology; its quicker transition into serial production; a general development of a regime of economy and others.
>
> (Tropin 1987: 115–116)

In this sense, the debate on the inherent contradictions clearly confirmed, as Aleksandr I. Anchishkin had put it in 1987, "that economic science . . . proved not to be ready to answer the questions that were posed by the XXVII Congress, the January Plenum and by the whole of our development " (quoted after Sutela 1991: 3). Nevertheless, over the course of this debate, for the first time since the 1960s the suspicion was voiced that the problems of the Soviet economy might have their roots in a conflict between its bureaucratic organisation and some "natural" economic laws.[6] Boris V. Rakitskii ([1987] 1988: 22) even launched an attack on the heart of the Soviet telos: "It is indispensable to overcome the metaphysical notion of the nature of development, the idea that in its essence it is a process of overcoming contradictions". This was indeed an attack on the holiest of the holy, and – for that – an extremely untypical statement in 1987.[7]

The ambition to turn from philosophical debates to the country's concrete economic problems manifested itself in a discussion on "The Complex Solution of the Problem of Planned Price Formation" that was opened by a contribution of Nikolai Petrakov (1987), one of the *shestidesiatniki* heavyweights who also played a key role among Gorbachev's advisors, in *Voprosy ekonomiki* in 1987. The way in which he introduced ideological novelties was typical of the first two years of perestroika: Marx had already argued that social wants (demand) determined the amount of social work to be spent on the production of a product. Hence, the Soviet economists who had ignored the demand side could be accused of having dissented from the true dogma.[8] Nevertheless, the discussion was still about the "perfection of the calculation of planned production expenditures" (Petrakov 1987: 51), not about a transition to market prices.[9] It was therefore rather misleading that economists frequently laid claim to the attribute "radical", even though at the time they still believed that adequate administrative measures were sufficient to achieve a more rational allocation of the factors of production. Some authors, however, did at least indicate the consequences of a demand-based price formation. One discussant, for example, stated that in a planned economy the prices could not fulfil their most important task – to "exclude the less effective producers from the sphere of the creation of social products" (Efremov 1987: 53). Another bluntly accused a conservative colleague – who had warned that liberalisation of retail prices would endanger the equilibrium of the plan – of obviously being more concerned about the balance of the plan than about market equilibrium (Borozdin 1987: 69).

The discussion on price formation provoked sharp reactions from the conservative camp. One author ardently defended the dogma that prices in socialism reflected nothing but "socially necessary labour time"; he consequently perceived the whole debate as "invented" (Kondrashev 1988: 96). Hardly surprising, many economists, especially *Gosplan* economists, making full use of their own journal *Planovoe khoziaistvo*, fiercely resisted a reform of price formation. It was also no coincidence that at the exact moment that the debate on prices began in the then "progressive" *Voprosy ekonomiki*, Anatolii Deriabin (1987: 81), the conservative former Department Chief of the Institute of Economics of the Academy of Sciences appealed for "preserving the achievements of the Soviet price system".

The economic debates received a new stimulus when the new official textbook of political economy, written by a team of authors under the direction of Vadim A. Medved'ev (Sutela 1991: 97–98) in close co-operation with Abalkin and Aganbegian, was introduced in February 1988. At the very beginning of this 700-page volume, the reader learns that the main task of political economy was to reveal the developmental laws of society (Medved'ev 1988: 21) and that the negation of such laws could be "equated with a negation of science, its ability to discover behind the chaos of phenomena their coherence and logic" (ibid.: 60). For all their "progressiveness", to these authors it was still self-evident that history was a "movement towards socialism", or in other words that social development was always characterised by the "growing wholeness" [*tselostnost'*] of society (ibid.: 731).[10] However, it would hardly be justified to classify the book as conservative. Despite its explicit defence of the hard core of Soviet ideology, it broke with a number of the dogmas forming its protective belt. Special attention was paid to the problem of "socialist property".

In the same issue of *Voprosy ekonomiki*, in which the structure of the new textbook had been outlined, a discussion was started on this question. In the bold article opening this debate, Gennadii Gorlanov (1988) equated the institution of public property with *biurokratizm*, which had led to alienation within socialism. This argument was supported by Gavriil Popov (1988: 4):

> [I]n practice, the workers' sense of ownership [*chuvstvo khoziaina*] did not sufficiently compensate the abolished personal interest. There emerged, therefore, a situation, in which socialist property did not have a real owner – neither in the person of the worker, or in that of the apparatus. This became the basic contradiction of the new organisational structure [*stroi*]

If state property was the main cause of the contradictions in socialist society, the attempts to carry out far-reaching economic reforms without changing the basic structure of property had been an "illusion" (Kulikov 1989: 53). The majority of Soviet economists, however, still believed that "socialist alienation" could be overcome by a reform of socialist property. Yet the demand to implement a "system of all-people (*obshchenarodnyi*) property" that would "not oppress the personality of the worker" (Abalkin [1989] 1990: 85), was not usually accompanied by concrete proposals for achieving this. By the second half of 1988, the contradictions between such ethical demands and the rapid decline of the Soviet economy were hard to ignore. However, before dealing with the final breakdown of Soviet economic ideology, we shall look at how the ideology that was soon to replace the Marxist dogma entered Soviet economic discourse.

The inflow of Western liberal ideas

Liberal ideas were introduced into Soviet economic thought mainly through two channels: first, through a discussion on the structural changes in the capitalist economies in the academic journal *Mirovaia ekonomika i mezhdunarodnye otnosheniia* (World Economy and International Relations, hereafter MEiMO), and second, through the general interest newspapers and journals such as *Literaturnaia gazeta* and *Novyi mir*.

The MEiMO *debate on Western reforms*

MEiMO was (and still is) published by the Institute of World Economy and International Relations of the Soviet (now Russian) Academy of Sciences. Established in 1956, during the Brezhnev years, it provided a niche for scholars at odds with official Soviet economics.[11] The main task of the institute, to observe the economic development of the capitalist countries, offered the opportunity to deal with topics and literature that were otherwise strictly taboo.[12] In October 1986, the pages of *MEiMO* became the scene of a discussion on "State Regulation and Private Business in the Capitalist Countries: The Evolution of Mutual Relations", which was to last two and a half years. In a short prologue, Viktor Kuznetsov defined the problem to be discussed: since the early 1980s a wave of privatisation could be observed in the Western world, which had obviously enabled these countries to revive economic growth. In unmistakable fashion, he demanded that Soviet economists should not "shirk the new facts" and that "it would be a mistake to force these facts into theoretical schemes which are able to explain them only partially or in an unsatisfying manner" (Kuznetsov 1986: 87).

In the course of this debate, the central principles of Soviet ideology came under fire from all sides for the first time. The wave of re-privatisation caused "theoretical discomfort" (Kapeliushnikov 1987: 71) to those who believed in the correctness of Marx's prognosis (and that of Western convergence theorists), and had until the end of the 1970s felt themselves vindicated by the increasing state intervention in the Western capitalist countries. The controversy centred on the issue of whether re-privatisation was a short-term phenomenon reflecting a neo-conservative wave of fashion, or whether it reflected "objective" reasons inherent in the capitalist economic system. The majority of the *MEiMO* authors understood re-privatisation as "the most natural" (Osadchaia 1986: 101; similarly Kollontai 1987: 81) solution to the capitalist countries' problems caused by the full employment policy of the 1970s. "The previous call for nationalisation", Iakov Pevzner* (1987: 60) argued, had been "of a temporary character and caused by fashion, whereas the current reversal is based on a deeper assessment of reality". Challenges of this kind did not remain unanswered by the conservative camp. A number of authors explicitly denied that massive re-privatisation had taken place in the Western countries (Shapiro 1987; Mochernyi 1987) or emphasised its temporary character (Pan'kov 1987; Gnatovskaia 1987).

A discussion of the structural changes in the Western economies had the advantage that the problems of the Soviet economy could be elaborated under the disguise of a critique of Western "state monopolistic" capitalism. This is particularly evident from Viktor Studentsov's article on "Bourgeois nationalisation and privatisation in the mechanism of state-monopolistic capitalism" that opened up the debate. It had to be recognised, Studentsov (1986: 93) argued, that even self-financing of the state enterprises was unlikely to end permanent state intervention because it was "unrealistic" to hope that this would diminish political interference in the nationalised sector. In his preliminary résumé of the discussion, published in the January 1989 issue of *MEiMO*, Studentsov raised the key issue of the 1960s again, that of the objectivity or subjectivity of economic laws. His answer to "political power or economic law" (which is just another way of putting the objectivity/subjectivity question) reads as follows:

> State regulation is effective only when it corrects, but by no means ignores or spurns the motives of the market agents . . . If state measures contradict the interests of the economic agents, the latter either ignore them or search for ways of avoidance.
>
> (Studentsov 1989: 16)

The debates in the general interest press

As already mentioned, one of the parallels between the discussions of the 1960s (up to 1968) and of the late 1980s was that economic journalists and free thinkers where way ahead of their academic colleagues in asking radically new questions and in giving no less radical new answers. As early as May 1987, on the eve of the June plenum, a sensational letter to the editor was published in the weekly journal *Novyi mir*. Under the provocative title "Where are the Pirogi meatier?" and needing little more than two pages, Larisa [Popkova-]Piiasheva*,[13] refuted all the ideological pillars on which the concept of perestroika rested:

> I have a certain amount of experience studying the 'third path' along which West European social democrats have tried to lead their countries in the

> post-war decades. The 'social democratic decade' has most graphically confirmed Lenin's conviction that there is no third path. One cannot be a little pregnant. Either the plan or the market, either the directive or competition.
>
> (Popkova [1987] 1988: 45)

Yet even where "third paths" were practised, as in some of the socialist countries, it could be observed: "Where there is more market, the pirogi are meatier". Consequently, the Soviet Union had been on the wrong historical track, and capitalism had not even reached full bloom yet:

> Both Western socialists and our 'commodityists' believe that the age of the pure market economy belongs irrevocably to the past. But I sometimes think that the Western world is still merely on its threshold, at the very beginning of the road. Free enterprise was for a long time stifled by the vestiges of feudalism and the activity of utopians of every ilk, as a result of which the twentieth century proved to be so bloody. It was stifled, but it seems to me that it was not smothered and that it has a serious future whether we like it or not. We must look the realities straight in the eye.
>
> (Popkova[-Piiasheva] 1987: 48)[14]

It is a fine irony of history that the book *Economic Neo-Conservatism: Theory and International Practice*, jointly written by Piiasheva and her husband Boris Pinsker, was published in the book series "Critique of Bourgeois Ideology and Revisionism". What was in fact criticised in a remarkable enumeration were "national socialism", "social-reformism", "German social market economy", as well as all other forms of social organisation that in one way or another had allegedly constrained full economic freedom ([Popkova-]Piiasheva and Pinsker 1988: 4; shortened English translation: 1989).[15] In a number of articles published between 1988 and 1990, Piiasheva and Pinsker demanded radical economic reforms and drew a bright picture of Russia's capitalist future (Pinsker and [Popkova-]Piiasheva 1989). Part of this picture was that "someone will, for example, print and edit literature on economic liberalism – books of authors like F. Hayek and M. Friedman and the textbook by Paul Samuelson" ([Popkova-]Piiasheva 1990: 10).[16] The political recommendations that followed from this attitude were concretised by Pinsker in 1990:

> Therefore the simultaneous liberalisation of all prices and massive privatisation, i.e. the forced release of 60–70% of the productive property [*proizvoditel'naia sobstvennost'*] in the first months of reforms is the only chance of improvement with minimal danger for the social and political equilibrium.
>
> (Pinsker 1990: 11)

[Popkova-]Piiasheva's and Pinsker's central theses regarding the principal incompatibility between the market and the plan lay at the heart of the liberal discourse in the general-interest journals (see e.g. Levikov 1988; Seliunin 1989, 1990). In an article on "Advances and Debts" that was published in June 1987, Nikolai Shmelev* even argued that the violation of economic laws "is just as impermissible as the violation of the laws of the Chernobyl nuclear reactor" (Shmelev [1987] 1988: 40). Especially in view of the discussions about Russia's specificity and the related problem of the applicability of Western economic theories that came up in the middle of the 1990s, it is important to see that Shmelev ([1989] 2006: 64) explicitly emphasised the general nature of economic laws:

> And haven't we yet sufficiently convinced ourselves of the fact that the stimuli to diligent, creative work are the same all over the world, whether in America, in Japan or the Solomon Islands? Yes, yes – the same!

It is interesting that in an attack on the dogma of full employment, Shmelev referred to Milton Friedman's concept of the "natural rate of unemployment", but wrongly interpreted it as the number of those "who are seeking to change jobs" (Shmelev [1987] 1988: 21).[17] This article is also a striking example of how Marxist terminology kept creeping into the early Russian neo-liberal writings. Shmelev argued that a "relatively small reserve army of labour" was necessary in order to raise labour efficiency.

The decline of Soviet ideology

In the years 1989 and 1990, three factors finally paved the way to the decline of Soviet ideology: the increasing symptoms of crisis within the Soviet economy, the influence of Western neo-liberal ideas and the peaceful revolutions in the Central Eastern European countries and in the GDR.[18] In 1989, it became clear that perestroika had not fulfilled its promise to raise the standard of living of the population.[19] Severe shortages of consumer goods as well as other performance problems led to the implementation of emergency measures. Some administrative controls were re-established, the state augmented its power over consumer prices and wages and an unsuccessful attempt was made to tighten financial discipline. The economic decline was water on the mills of those who had argued that the plan and the market were incompatible. Especially the re-introduction of administrative controls raised the apprehension that perestroika would share the fate of the Kosygin reforms of the 1960s (Shmelev 1990: 29).

As mentioned above, a special chapter in the new textbook of 1988 had been devoted to the "socialist market". This subject was first discussed in *Voprosy ekonomiki* in July of the same year. In a rather conservative essay, Aleksei Emel'ianov (1988; English translation 1989) emphasised that market elements always had to be subordinated to the institutions of central planning. His paper received much disfavour in two articles in *MEiMO*, (Pevzner 1988; Sheinis 1988), the authors of which had already done without the adjective "socialist" when discussing the market and one of whom praised the market as "one of the greatest achievements of human civilisation" (Sheinis 1988: 16). In an important article on "New Thinking and the need of new approaches in political economy" that was published in *MEiMo* in 1988, Iakov Pevzner (1988: 15) expressed his conviction, "that not much time will pass until the necessity of the market mechanism will turn into a truism" and criticised his colleagues for hiding behind terms like "market socialism" or "exchange approaches". One of the most visible figures of the early liberal discourse, the journalist Vasilii Seliunin*, in an article published in October 1989 in *Novyi mir*, found the clearest words on the term "socialist market":

> Let's train a little to pronounce the word 'market economy'. . . The market is a thing like that: it either exists or it doesn't, and it doesn't happen to be socialist, capitalist or grey-brown-rasperry-coloured.
>
> (Seliunin 1989: 172)

It is no exaggeration to say that Leonid Abalkin intoned the swan song of the ideology of perestroika when he outlined the future of the socialist economy in an article tellingly entitled "The market in the economic system of socialism":

> The economic system that should form as a result of perestroika must combine: the highest effectiveness of production with the humanistic goals of its development . . . the rebirth of the co-operative system and the broad development of the public sector of the society; the formation of the socialist market; the intensification of its impact on production coupled with improvement of centralised planned management techniques.
>
> (Abalkin [1989] 1990: 6–7)

As convincing as such demands may have sounded in the more or less stable situation of the preceding years, in 1989 it had become obvious that the country was at the threshold of severe crisis, which could not be overcome by political slogans. In this situation, Evgenii Iasin's* article "The Socialist Market or a Fair of Illusions?", published in October 1989, provided a blunt answer to Abalkin and Petrakov:

> The time has come to shed illusions: there is no easy road to solving the economic problems confronting the nation. We have reached the point where decisive, even if painful and unpopular, measures are needed, where their execution can no longer be postponed because any delay will only complicate the operation.
>
> (Iasin [1989] 1990: 25)

The measures proposed by Abalkin and Petrakov, he argued, were insufficient, for "we are missing the key that would combine everything into a whole programme" (Iasin [1989] 1990: 27). This key was free prices: "Free prices coupled with the independence of enterprises and direct economic relations are the minimum from which the market begins" (ibid.: 28). In a further article, published in *Voprosy ekonomiki*, Iasin (1990: 3) bluntly stated that it should have become clear by then "that the planned and the market economy are antipodes". This way, the core point of the liberal journalistic discourse, that the plan and the market were incompatible, had finally made it into a leading academic journal.

Another taboo was debased when Al'bert Ryvkin attacked the intellectual fathers of the Kosygin reforms of the 1960s to whom not only Gorbachev (1987: 28) but also the leading perestroika economists Aganbegian, Abalkin and Petrakov had referred to repeatedly. Ryvkin argued that Kantorovich's, Nemchinov's and Novozhilov's adamant faith in the possibility to "optimize" the socialist economy by introducing methods of linear programming was a highly questionable attempt at "social engineering" (Ryvkin 1989). He argued that this belief, while it had been typical not only of the Soviet economists but also of some influential Western economists such as Paul Samuelson, had been taken to the extreme by the Soviet "economic-mathematical school" (Ryvkin 1989: 141). The author's insistence on the impossibility of constructing a perfect social mechanism clearly reflected the ideas of Popper and Hayek, although Ryvkin did not explicitly refer to the latter.

In the same article Al'bert Ryvkin (1989: 130) also explicitly noted that in Soviet economics there no longer existed "a uniform theory, on which all economists agree". One year before, in the above-mentioned article, Viktor Sheinis had already called for a "new general theoretical paradigm" which would allow one to see the world "as it is, to imagine how it might become tomorrow, and to acknowledge how it will certainly not become either tomorrow, or the day after tomorrow" (Sheinis 1988: 15). His words indicate that the reason for the growing divergence of theoretical views and political recommendations laid in the different possible interpretations of the course of history. This was summed up most aptly by Vadim Radaev* and Aleksandr Auzan in September 1989:

> Figuratively speaking, the road that has been travelled by socialism can be depicted as a straight line, as a zigzag, and as a blind alley. The strategy for overcoming the crisis is therefore also different: the extension, the 'improvement' of elements of positive experience accumulated in preceding phases; recognition of results of movement and rejection of methods of attaining them in the new forms of development; 'backsliding' and the search for a new road from the old historic 'fork'.
>
> (Vad. Radaev and Auzan [1989] 1990: 71)

If Soviet history could be interpreted "as a straight line, as a zigzag, and as a blind alley", this was to say that the hard core of Soviet ideology was finally cracked.

Paradigm shift or continuity?

From 1989 onwards, the leading economic thinkers whose works had provided the intellectual background to the neo-conservative revolution in Great Britain and in the USA eventually entered the Soviet economic journals. Friedrich

August von Hayek's ideas were reviewed with much sympathy by Natal'ia Makasheva (1989) in *Voprosy ekonomiki*, and a translation of his "Competition as a Discovery Procedure" was published in the December issue of *MEiMO*.[20] Simultaneously, Gavriil Popov gave a short introduction to the ideas of Milton Friedman (in *Voprosy ekonomiki*), which was followed by an anonymous, highly favourable review of "The Essence of Milton Friedman", and in July 1990 *Novyi mir* printed the first part of a Russian translation of Hayek's *Road to Serfdom*.[21] In 1991, S. Alekseev critically described the prevailing mood among Russian intellectuals as follows:

> Above all I am concerned that the word 'market' has become a fashionable political symbol, even a stereotype. You want to be regarded as up to date and progressive? Nothing easier than that – call yourself a 'marketer', or even better 'pure marketer'. And everything will be all right. In the name of the market you can even argue the need to constrain democracy, to establish an authoritarian government, to enhance 'order and discipline' in the most totalitarian way.
>
> (Alekseev 1991: 10)

Obviously, in Soviet economic thought the old dogmas had been "replaced in whole or in part by an incompatible new one" (Kuhn 1962: 92). This is evident not only from the content of the major Soviet economic journals. In 1992, Vincent Barnett published an instructive survey about attitudes towards the market among Soviet and British economists. His study shows that at this time even more Soviet economists than their British colleagues (95%–66%) fully or partly agreed with the statement "the market is the best mechanism to regulate economic life", and they were also more supportive towards radical privatisation (Barnett 1992: 1094).

However, in my view, although there had definitely been a fundamental shift, it can be shown even at this early stage and at the peak of the popularity of neoliberalism that revolution and ideational continuity are not necessarily mutually exclusive. Gavriil Popov's above-mentioned appraisal of Milton Friedman can be seen as typical of the reception of monetarism by Russian liberal economists in the last years of the Soviet Union. The first key element of this interpretation was the thesis that in the 1970s, the capitalist and the socialist economies had encountered essentially the same problems and that monetarism provided the solution to these problems:

> This school [the monetarist, JZ], which initially seemed utterly 'fossilised', 'paternalistic', and 'nostalgic', began attracting more and more attention as the unquestionable limits to centralised management of human society and the contradictions, dangers, and dead-end streets of centralism in both social systems – capitalist and socialist – became increasingly apparent toward the end of the twentieth century.
>
> (Popov [1989] 1990: 100)

The second key element was the conviction that monetarism contained the right interpretation of the historical laws determining the fate of mankind:

> Beyond a doubt, many years of discussions between 'Keynesians' and the 'Chicago school' have a direct bearing on many problems of our perestroika and the measures that are proposed today to solve these problems. In the foreword to *Capital* K., Marx said to the German reader concerning the English foundation of his theoretical conclusions: 'Is this not our history?' And added: 'A country that is industrially more developed shows the less developed country only the picture of its own future'.
>
> (Popov [1989] 1990: 103)

The message of the Russian neo-liberals can be summarised as follows: the market economy is the natural organisation of economic affairs. Both in the Soviet Union and in Western countries, this natural order had been disabled by socialists and social democrats, and in both East and West this had led to stagnation by the end of the 1970s. Yet while in Western Europe and in the USA the neo-conservative revolution had restored the right order and brought society back on the natural road of historical development, the Soviet leaders and their economic advisors still dreamed about "socialism with a human face".

Whether this was an apt interpretation of monetarism or not, the Russian neo-liberals certainly contributed much to the eventual collapse of Soviet ideology. At the same time, however, neo-liberal ideas were first of all received as an anti-ideology against the Marxist-Leninist dogma. As an anti-telos, this liberalism was deeply influenced by the very ideology it opposed. The Russian liberals were just as convinced of being the bearers of an absolute truth, and in the end their liberalism was no less utopian than the vulgarised Marxism of their opponents. There certainly was a break with Soviet ideology, but there was no clear break with the methods of reasoning this ideology had been resting on. In the last years of the Soviet Union, the hard core of Soviet ideology – that the country had been on the holy road to the holistic society – was replaced by the conviction that it had, in fact, been moving towards a dead end. What was not altered, however, was the notion of history being a purposeful process. The Soviet telos was replaced by a liberal telos.

Notes

1 This term here denotes both the economists working in the Academy of Sciences and at the universities.

2 This problem becomes evident in the following statement: "There is, however, another side to the unavowed flexibility of Marxist-Leninist doctrine. Because the basic tenets are actually subject to revision, there is no dogma in the true sense of the word. The dominant element in the Communist Party determines what is orthodox; those who cling to another interpretation, even one undisputed in earlier years, become heretics, and no exegetical appeal to the 'classics' can save them" (Armstrong 1978: 50).

3 However, this hard core of the Soviet ideological programme was not only defended by pain of penalties. Since it related to the future, it could not be exposed to empirical

verification. Any criticism based on the gap between ideal and reality was easily refuted by the argument that reality was necessarily imperfect but that society was at least moving in the right direction.

4 The reference to the "human factor" was maybe the clearest indicator of how strongly Gorbachev's idea of perestroika was influenced by the ideas of the *shestidesiatniki.* In September 1986, a sensational article by the famous Soviet sociologist Tatiana Zaslavskaia (1927–2013), "Social Justice and the Human Factor in Economic Development", was published in *Kommunist.*

5 Number 4, 1987, of *Voprosy ekonomiki* (pp. 80–92) even contains an overview of the materials that were sent to the redaction in the course of the discussion.

6 For example, Iurii Pakhomov and Vitalii Vrublevskii (1987: 90) argued with reference to the experience of the 1970s and 1980s that "if economic laws are ignored, they take 'revenge' – with disastrous socio- economic consequences".

7 Rakitskii's article provoked a sharp reaction by Kaisin A. Khubiev (1988), who defended the 1954 Stalinist textbook.

8 In similar fashion: Gatovskii (1987), Borozdin (1987).

9 And instead of making concrete proposals as to how to reform price formation, some authors formulated such vague ethical demands as the "democratisation of the order of price formation"; see Komin (1987: 114).

10 This passage reads as follows: "The science of political economy allows not only to reveal the inner logic of the historical process, but also to advance into the secrets of economic life, to understand its driving forces . . . The dialectics of this process is such that the very increase of the number of varieties of national and regional developments in countries and peoples in the end 'works' in the direction of the consolidation of the wholeness of the world, in direction of an increasing mutual dependency".

11 On the history of the institute see Cherkasov (2004).

12 As an excellent command of foreign languages was required for employment at the Institute of World Economy, its members were not only much more familiar with the Western economic systems, but also with Western economic literature than the average member of the Academy of Sciences.

13 Larisa Piiasheva published articles under the pseudonym Popkova, her true name Piiasheva, and sometimes under the name Popkova-Piiasheva. This has occasionally caused confusion. One of her critics (Veber 1989) tried hard to bring out the fine differences between the views held by Popkova and by Piiasheva.

14 (Popkova[-Piiasheva] 1987: 48). In a joint article, Piiasheva and her husband Boris Pinsker formulated the same idea as follows: "In the mid-1970s the old verdict concerning the deepening general crisis of capitalism became justified. However, the crisis was by no means generated by the anarchy of competition but by the growth of state expenditures and the increasing role of the state in social and economic life" (Pinsker and Piiasheva 1989: 187, quoted in Ianowitch 1991: 135).

15 This enumeration makes it easy to guess by whom Piiasheva and Pinsker were inspired. Indeed, in an interview with Philip Hanson in 1990, they said that they had been Hayekians since first having come across his works (Hanson 2003: 3).

16 She seemed to not have been informed that an – albeit much abbreviated – translation of Samuelson's *Economics* had been published in the Soviet Union in 1964; see Gerschenkron (1978), Wagener (1998b: 19). Besides that, it is quite strange to see Samuelson, a supporter of the mixed economy, in this list with his two main intellectual opponents.

17 This is the definition of frictional unemployment, only forming a part of the NAIRU.

18 In March 1988, on the eve of the peaceful revolutions in Central Europe, an important conference on "Alternative Models of Socialist Economic Systems" took place in Győr (Hungary). The conference, attended by Western (including emigrants from Central and Eastern Europe), Central European and Soviet economists, focused on the shortcomings of reforms within socialism. Philip Hanson, who reports on the conference in his

book (Hanson 2003: 214) emphasises the role of this event for the growing disillusionment with the idea of market socialism in the Soviet Union.

19 According to the CIA (1990), in the years 1986, 1987 and 1988, the Soviet Union had seen a modest growth in GNP and even a significant improvement in labour productivity. In 1989, however, both indicators turned negative.

20 It was supplemented by an article by Rostislav Kapeliushnikov (1989) on "Hayek's Philosophy of the Market".

21 Hayek's "Preface to the Russian Edition" mentions that a first Russian edition of the work had already been published in 1982. However, I was not able to discover any more details about this edition.

5 Towards a precarious consensus: 1993–1998

Western textbooks, Russian reality

As I have shown in the last chapter, between 1990 and 1992 in Russian economic science there was a general striving toward a return to the international scientific community. Indeed, the years between 1992 and 1995 saw a rapidly increasing number of Russian editions of Western, mainly American, economic textbooks[1] and the exploration of a range of different subjects drawn from Western literature. However, the liberal heyday proved to be rather short-lived.[2] By 1993 it was obvious that Russia was in a deep transitional crisis. A key characteristic of a utopian ideology is its being related to the future, so for it to be sustained "it is of crucial importance that reality should at least develop in the right direction" (Gerner and Hedlund 1989: 20). Once it turned out that the road to recovery was much more painful and tedious than predicted not only by the Russian, but also by the Western neo-liberal experts, the excitement for liberal ideas gave way to a re-consideration of Russian reality. In line with this, in his speech at the 7th Congress of the People's Deputies, held in December 1992, President El'tsin announced "that the time has come for a reversal of our whole policy . . . with the face to Russia, to her traditions, to her very history, presence and future" (cited in Kul'kov 1993: 15).

In the centre of this second phase of the transition debate soon stood the traditional Russian question of the applicability of Western ideas to Russian reality, and a nationalist turn occurred in the more conservative camp of Russian economic science. In 1995 Vadim Radaev, pointing to a coalition of "slightly painted socialists", "pochvenniki (returners to the soil) of various sorts", "economists of the neo-Keynesian mold", intellectuals who called for "ideas of religious, imperial and even monarchic renewal" and "new right and new Eurasianists" stated that "the conservative turn has already been completed" (Vad. Radaev 1995: 37).

The intensity of the inter-enterprise debt-crisis in particular (Ickes and Ryterman 1993)[3] raised the question of whether the Russian economic agents showed "normal" reactions to economic incentives or whether their behavior reflected specific traits which deviated from the standard assumptions of economic theory (see e.g. Iavlinskii 1993: 117; Diskin 1997: 148). If this was the case, it was obviously highly questionable whether mainstream economics provided a suitable foundation for reform concepts. The appropriateness of monetarist-liberal ideas was also questioned by a group of economists related to the Academy of Sciences and mostly belonging to the *shestidesiatniki* generation. This group demanded a state-led reform strategy prioritising the stabilisation of production over macroeconomic stability. This challenge led to an intense debate between liberals and *gosudarstvenniki*.[4]

By the middle of the 1990s, it had become clear to more and more essentially liberal and Western-minded economists that mainstream textbook economics (and it was mainly the standard textbook version of Western mainstream economics the Russian economists at this stage were familiar with) had its shortcomings when it came to dealing with post-socialist economic change. This led to a search for "some kind of common vector, an effective and viable synthesis of the general laws of progress and of what is in fact possible in our concrete Russian conditions" (Shmelev 1996: 17). In the context of this search, Russian institutionalism emerged which also seemed to offer possibilities to bridge the gap between the liberals and those conservatives who emphasised Russia's cultural and historical specificity. By the end of the 1990s it looked indeed as though a consensus was within reach.

The intellectual background to shock therapy

While perestroika set in thirty years after Liberman, Kantorovich and others had advanced their ideas on "perfecting" socialism by combining it with market elements, "shock therapy came as a shock to many Russian economists" (Avtonomov et al. 2001: 85). Had Leonid Abalkin been the key economist both of the Brezhnev period and of perestroika, Egor Gaidar was – both intellectually and politically – the central figure of shock therapy. Therefore, in order to understand the ideas that became dominant in the early 1990s, as a first step we should take a look into his book *State and Evolution: Russia's Search for a Free Market* (Russian original 1994, English edition 2003), which provides insights into the mindsets of the "young reformers".

Gaidar's analysis rests on a comparison between "Eastern" and "Western" societies. The key difference between these ideal types lies in the structure of property relations. In Eastern societies "a bureaucracy rules both economic and political life", so that "property is, after all, merely an attribute of political power" (Gaidar 2003: 5–6). By contrast, in Western societies the institution of private property protects the economy from state intervention (ibid.: 9). With regard to Russia, his central thesis is that her "Easternisation" was due to historical misfortune. The Tatar yoke, he argues, turned Russia into an Eastern-type society, just when she started to approach the Western pattern of development (Gaidar 2003: 26). And at the very time when Russia had again come close to transforming into a Western society in the later decades of the nineteenth century, the October Revolution turned property ownership into "a function of political authority" (ibid.: 53). Gaidar takes the "fundamental laws of economic rational behavior" for granted in all places and at all times, so the question of the possible role of Russian specificity does not enter his mind (Gaidar 1994: 10). For him transition is "a matter of socio-economic structure" alone (ibid.: 107). Providing the "conditions for stabilising property ownership" will breed "a change in the very structure of our society, the long awaited birth of a middle class", which will not only "create true markets, dynamic industry, economic growth", but also set Russia back on the "Western" track of social development (ibid.: 104). To Gaidar, it is self-evident that "Russia today has a unique opportunity to change her entire historical orientation, her social, political, economic orientation, to become a republic in the Western sense of that term" (ibid.: 116).

The contrast between Gaidar and the economists of the *shestidesiatniki* generation couldn't be sharper. As illustrated in the third chapter, the latter had intensely dealt with the impact of social psychology on economic processes (as part of the superstructure) and had even accused Western convergence theorists of "one-sided materialism". Gaidar, in contrast, argues in strictly materialist terms. Indeed, in a two-part article jointly written with Vladimir Mau* and published in 2004, Gaidar explicitly confessed to historical materialism and to what he and his co-author referred to as "liberal Marxism" (Gaidar and Mau 2004). However, for all the differences between Gaidar and Abalkin to both of them economic reforms were ultimately to serve a historical mission: for the *shestidesiatniki* this superior goal was to accomplish "socialism with a human face" and thereby to prove the superiority of Soviet socialism to Western capitalism.[5] By contrast, the *semidesiatniki*, in the tradition of the pre-revolutionary Westernisers, wanted to realign Russia with the Western path of social development. In other words, it was the old debate between Slavophiles and Westernisers that flared up again in the discussions of the 1990s.[6]

Post-industrial society and the comeback of Slavophile ideas

At the beginning of the radical market reforms, the majority of Russian economists shared the enthusiasm of most intellectuals about the departure into a new era of Russian history. Yet, while for the liberal *semidesiatniki* this departure meant a convergence towards Western patterns of social development, for many of their colleagues it had a much "deeper" meaning. Very soon after having given up the dream of building "socialism with a human face", they discovered a new utopia.[7] The very same hopes that had formerly been connected with the dream of humanising socialism were now projected onto transition to "post-industrial society":

> Post-industrial society forms creative man who plays a leading role in the functioning and the development of society. Under these conditions, the political economy of social richness should be replaced with a political economy of man.
>
> (Val. Radaev 1992b: 117)[8]

The bridge that led from "developed socialism" to "post-industrial society" is particularly evident in an article by Oleg Bogomolov* from 1989 (1990: 18, emphasis added). The developmental tendencies of "developed capitalism" (!), he argued,

> show that not only are the material prerequisites for the transition to a qualitatively different phase of development *that we call socialistic and that the West calls "post-industrial"* accumulating within the framework of contemporary capitalistic society, but that new social relations are also being generated.

For those trained in the Marxian theory of social development, the thesis that the Western countries were about to enter an age "that we call socialistic and that the West calls post-industrial" led to a question which had occupied Russian economic thinkers since the middle of the nineteenth century: was it possible for a backward country like Russia to leap over certain stages of development and – making use of the historical experience of the West – directly enter the most "progressive" stage?[9] Furthermore, why should Russia, at the very moment when the Western countries developed "in the direction of overall historical progress" (Eremin 1992: 46), characterised by the "gradual transition of the whole society into a homogenous organism" (Val. Radaev 1992a: 75), go through capitalism instead of directly harvesting the fruits of post-industrialism?

The question of how Russia could regain her status as a leading power in the world was present from the very beginning of the reform debate and formed an important ingredient to the discussion about post-industrial society. Only by joining the worldwide direction of social development could Russia remain (or again become) one of the "leaders of world-wide progress", Iurii V. Iakovets* (1994: 83) argued. More than that, the very fact that she had entered the period of painful "transition of the whole human community" earlier than the other major countries (ibid.: 77), gave her the chance to play "not the smallest role in overcoming the difficulties that are awaiting mankind" (similarly se Moiseev 1998: 79; Kurishchak 1995: 21; Kushlin 1997: 9). As Abalkin emphasised, it was especially Russia's status as a great power that imposed on her the moral responsibility "for the destiny of the world community" (Abalkin 1994: 12).

Besides being a perfect substitute for "socialism with a human face", the idea of post-industrial society also provided a comforting perspective, for it meant that not only the post-socialist countries, but the whole world was about to begin a painful fundamental reorientation of all aspects of social life, including science (see e.g. Iakovets 1994: 77). In fact, if not only the Marxist current, but the social sciences throughout the world experience a crisis, this called "for a critical analysis of the whole potential of the social sciences, for a search for fundamentally new answers to the problems of humanistic knowledge" Medved'ev (1993: 22) argued (similar see Abalkin 1993: 4; Buzgalin 1993: 44). More than that, Iakovets (1999: 103) argued, this way Russia could become the "epicenter of the development of a post-industrial paradigm" and regain intellectual leadership.

All too soon, however, it became clear that Russia had missed the "great leap" into post-industrialism and had ended in "wild capitalism" instead (Medved'ev 1995: 28). The disappointing results of the economic reforms raised – yet again – the continually recurring question of Russian social philosophy: was capitalism actually possible, and if so, was it suitable for Russia? Although as early as 1986 there had been single attempts to revive Slavophile ideas in economics (Sutela 1991: 154–155), the conservative turn of many Russian intellectuals started in 1993. It was not only a reaction to the disappointed hopes of the early 1990s, but also a result of the fact that the conflict between Western liberalism and the traditional Russian patterns of thought could only be covered up in a short-lived phase of "market-romantic enthusiasm" (Pakhomov 2000: 5).

In his 1993 book *The Russian Way in the Economy* [*Russkii put' v ekonomike*], Oleg A. Platonov outlined the basic pillars of the new economic nationalism, which took up ideas of 19th century Slavophilism but often also tried to affiliate itself with elements of current ecological and post-modern ideas. As he argued,

> Western criteria of economic development cannot serve as criterion for the Russian economy. In the race which the Western world conducts, based on the unequal exchange with the raw material delivering countries, our place could only be among the exploited. Furthermore, the Western race for consumption under the conditions of declining resources leads mankind into a dead end. The Russian model of the economy which is oriented towards a reasonable prosperity and able of self-restraint, offers mankind a possible way of survival.
> (Platonov 1993: 36)

It was the leading Russian economic journal, *Voprosy ekonomiki*, that picked up the subject in its August 1993 edition. Titles such as "The economic system and ethnos" (Ol'sevich 1992), "Economic problems and national self-identity" (Goricheva 1993) and "Russian Orthodoxy and its economic possibilities" (Platonov 1993) clearly indicate that an old question had again entered the agenda of Russian economic thought: "who are we and what are our roots?" (Zaitseva 1994: 95).

According to V.M. Kul'kov (1993) the main feature of "The Russian social tradition" had to be seen in a "materialist interpretation of the Trinity", according to which "an organic unity of the economic, the social and the spiritual sides" (ibid.: 16) was regarded as a social ideal. The social structure of the Soviet Union had not only been a reflection of this tradition, but the "dictate of the political-ideological side over the economic" could also be traced back to the traditional "primacy of spirituality over materiality" (ibid.: 20) of Russian culture. Very much in this sense, Aleksandr Buzgalin* (1995: 19) saw the main mistake of the liberal reform strategy in the attempt to "artificially separate this [the economic, J.Z.] sphere of social life and somehow isolate it from all others". Here we have two of the clearest manifestations of how the holistic tradition of one of the two thought collectives in Russian social philosophy could be turned against the idea of establishing a market economy as a relatively independent sub-system of society. Other authors traced Russian specificity back not only to cultural legacies, but also to her geopolitical conditions. This argument is well known from the history of Russian thought and suggests that the lack of natural borders had traditionally required a strong state (Seleznev 1994: 49).[10]

The economists quoted here agreed that it was necessary to "acknowledge the specific path of Russia's development, which does not fit into any commonly known mould" (Petrov 1995: 4).[11] Hence, the simple imitation of Western reform models was condemned to failure, and only the consideration of Russian history could provide the basis for a reform strategy that was in accordance with her unique traditions. It was less clear, however, what political conclusions were to be drawn from this basic postulate. The moderate voices emphasised that a Russian market economy was possible, but that it would be very much different from the Western types. Since the Slavophiles regarded Russia as an Asian rather than as a European country, Japan was regularly mentioned as a model (Basina and Shereveva 1993: 37; Kul'kov 1993: 21; Seleznev 1994: 51). In a much more radical manner, authors like V.K. Petrov or Dmitrii S. L'vov*, who is the most striking example of a communist turned Slavophile, adopted the old thesis that, due to Russia's cultural specificity, capitalism had always been and would always remain impossible for her (Petrov 1995: 8; L'vov 1997: 11).

Regulation, economic security, and the 'Russian economic school'

In the Soviet Union, the Russian Academy of Sciences was strictly separated from the universities. This was not only due to a longstanding tradition of Russian science, but also because it secured control of the intellectual life of the country. Only the small group of researchers at the Academy of Sciences had almost full access to foreign literature, whereas university professors were largely cut off from international discourse. For two reasons, after 1991 this relationship started to reverse. First, the students pressed their teachers to acquaint them with the international standard of economic knowledge, whereas the Academy researchers lacked such a stimulus (Avtonomov et al. 2001: 87). Second, those who wanted to build a career in the Academy not only had to show a distinguished scientific performance, but were also expected to be especially loyal to the Marxist dogma. Therefore, in the 1990s the academicians were less "vulnerable" to "infiltration" with liberal ideas than the university professors.

In this light, it did not come as a surprise that the academicians were the first to fight back fiercely against the market reforms.[12] In two articles, both published in February 1994 – one in *Voprosy ekonomiki* and one in the newspaper *Rabochaia tribuna*, the organ of the Central Committee of the Communist Party – the authors demanded a renunciation of the neo-liberal reform strategy. The first sentence of the article published in *Voprosy ekonomiki* reveals that the critique of the liberal reforms was not motivated by economic arguments alone:

> The socio-economic situation which has emerged in Russia as a result of two years of a policy of "shock therapy" is characterised by a previously unknown decline of production, mass impoverishment of the population, a loss of social ideals and the destruction of the moral pillars of society.
>
> (Abalkin, Petrakov and Shatalin 1994a: 126)

Since the authors were as concerned with "social ideals" and "moral pillars" as with economic problems, it comes as no surprise that to them the final target of economic reforms was Russia's "renaissance as a great power" (Abalkin et al. 1994a: 126). The core of the programme was the idea of "selective support for the most important [*prioritetnye*] branches of production" in accordance with Russia's "national interests", which were to be laid down in a national developmental strategy (Abalkin et al. 1994a: 132, 143). Apart from support for strategic branches, the academicians also generally called for a looser monetary policy in order to stop the overall decline in production (ibid.: 140). The question of how an active structural and social policy was compatible with the demand of a "further decrease of budgetary expenditures" (ibid.: 140), remained unanswered, however.

The economic department of the Russian Academy of Sciences and the *Reforma* foundation presented their views much more radically in a jointly written newspaper article that was serialised in February 1994 in *Rabochaia tribuna*. The central demand put forward by the authors, Leonid Abalkin, Nikolai Petrakov and Stanislav Shatalin*, was that in order to achieve its "rational" reconstruction, the whole economy "should be put back on state-regulated tracks". As inflation was mainly caused by structural (monopolistic) distortions, a reduction in the money supply would only "deprive the whole economy of the chance to achieve rational structural changes". According to the authors, investment activity could be stimulated only by the state "by changing the price relations of basic products and resources". In practice, "with the help of a certain set of instruments, including administrative measures, a certain rational relation of prices has to be fixed", around which afterwards "the whole system of economic regulators will be built" (Abalkin et al. 1994b, part 1: 4–5).

The advance of Abalkin and colleagues triggered an intense debate on regulation. However, the discussion suffered from the fact that the adherents of the opposed camps all too often talked at cross-purposes. Although its participants regularly referred to Friedman or Keynes, it had little in common with the debates on Keynesianism versus Monetarism in Western economics in the 1970s and 1980s. In this discussion, it became obvious for the first time that the Russian controversies over economic policy did not reflect disagreements within the common methodological and theoretical body of a single scientific discipline, but between scholars who belonged to different thought collectives and who were thus divided by a wide gap of fundamentally conflicting thought styles. The decisive point was that in contrast to Western Keynesians, to the Russian *gosudarstvenniki*, regulation did not mean exerting an influence on a system that in principle was acknowledged to be self-regulating, but rather to subordinate it to the logic of the political system. For the *akademiki* a "rational" economic system was not one which made the most efficient use of scarce resources, but one that followed a political logic. This idea was absolutely coherent if one started from the assumption that the economic system was subordinated to the nation state and had to serve its interests, but it is incompatible with the socio-philosophical ideas modern (Western) economics is based on. In this context, it is revealing that an author reporting on a conference on "State regulation of the economy" held in Moscow in 1996 enumerated a whole list of Russian participants in whose presentations "the idea of the inseparability of the state and the economy" had been the *leitmotiv* (Shvyrkov 1996: 35).

The standard reaction of the liberal camp to the reproaches of the *akademiki* was the argument that there had never been true shock therapy in Russia. Those countries where radical reforms had been implemented rigorously and coherently had already achieved some stability, they argued (Gaidar 2003: 97; Illarionov 1995: 46; Mau 1999: 11). The assessment of this argument depends very much on how the term "shock therapy" is defined, and this was therefore more a discussion of words than of facts. However, the whole debate also suffered from the fact that both camps paid little attention to Russian reality. As Aleksandr D. Nekipelov aptly put it in 2002, the discussion between Keynesian and monetarist concepts, "when applied mechanically to our soil, . . . is turned into a caricature" (Nekipelov 2002: 20–21).

In a situation where by far the majority of property was still in the hands of the state, and where there was consequently almost no competition at all, it was by no means easy to comprehend what the liberals' belief in economic self-regulation was based upon. Yet the adherents of regulation too all too often failed to provide anything more than slogans. One author, for example, called for the replacement of the slogan "market and plan are incompatible" with "a civilised, socially oriented market is incompatible with spontaneity [*stikhiia*] and anarchy in society" (Bachurin 1993: 6). Another author from the regulation camp admitted that efficient regulation in Russia was impossible as there was still nothing to regulate, as the market sphere was not yet sufficiently developed. He hastened to add, however, that in principle, it would be desirable to have increased regulation by a strong government, since this was practised internationally in all of the more developed market economies (Stepanov 1993: 15).

As Vladimir Gutnik* (1996: 10) argued, this kind of ideological reasoning was clearly a reflection of the habits of thought Russian economists had acquired during the Soviet period:

> In the period of transition, [in Russia, JZ] economic theory has changed its complexion, but not its methodology. Theory, as it exists today in Russia, does not start from abstract ("exact") models and not from real facts, but from political decisions and slogans (the latter usually have their roots in Western images of market economy and a democratic state, but they lack the according content and play . . . a purely decorative role).[13]

The central idea of the *gosudarstvenniki*, that the economy should serve the "national interests", was also expressed – and more radically – in a further debate over "economic security".[14] As was often the case, the subject was put onto the agenda by *Voprosy ekonomiki*, which dedicated its December 1994 issue to this topic.[15] How tightly this matter was connected with that of regulation becomes clear from the fact that in February of the same year, at the very moment when the *akademiki* put forward their notorious theses, Abalkin published an article "on the national [*natsional'no-gosudarstvennye*] interests of Russia" (Abalkin 1994). The discussion about "economic security" produced strange results. Not only was there a fairly wide range of definitions of the term,[16] but for a short period it even became fashionable to apply the concept to a diverse set of related subjects, so that terms such as "regional economic security", "economic security of the enterprise" and even "economic security of the personality" emerged (Afontsev 2002: 32). Sergei A. Afontsev, who critically reviewed the discussion in an article that was published in *MEiMO* in 2002, pointed to the fact the Russian adherents of the concept of economic security almost never referred to the international literature that existed on the topic. Even more revealing is the fact that the Western discourse (for an overview see e.g. Cable 1995) is one clearly dominated by political scientists, experts of international law and partly strategic management; in other words, there is no such a thing as a discourse on economic security in international economics.

At the methodological level, the concept clearly reflected the holistic tradition of Russian social thought. For example, Viacheslav V. Sokolov criticised the liberals for understanding national interest as "the sum of individual interests, as far removed from state control as possible" and contrasted it with a definition of the "national economy" as a "holistic organism" (Sokolov 1996: 9–10). Iurii Ol'sevich*, too, emphasised that the interpretation of the nation as a "living organism" was central to the concept of "national economic interests" (1996: 119). Regarding the problem of how to define generally binding national interests independently from individual preferences, he made the memorable statement that "a person putting her or his interests above the interests of the nation is simply beyond the nation" (ibid.). This was the case, he clarified, especially for "a certain part of the 'new Russians'", whom he characterised as "international vagabonds".

The rise of Russian institutionalism

From roughly the mid-1990s onwards, an increasing number of voices demanded a new focus on the analysis of Russian reality (Grishin and Stepanov 1994: 35; Khavina 1994: 89; Auktsionek 1996: 12; Diskin 1997: 147). The growing awareness that the structural and institutional conditions of the Russian economy had been severely neglected in the previous debates marked the beginning of an intense discussion on the peculiarities of the "economy in transition". The discrepancy between the world described in the translated American textbooks and Russian economic reality, Rustem Nureev and Iuriii V. Latov (2001: 90) argued, was at least as wide as that between Soviet reality and its description in the Marxist-Leninist textbooks. As these authors put it, as their education was by then almost entirely based on American textbooks, the alumni of the Russian economic faculties were likely to have a far better knowledge of the functioning of the New York stock exchange than of the vegetable market around the corner (ibid.: 104).

From the middle of the 1990s onwards, a growing number of Russian textbooks appeared that increasingly often contained special sections on the problem of transition.[17] In the economic journals too, a rising number of publications were dedicated to the features of the Russian transitional economy (Vad. Radaev, Auzan, Gerasimenko, Krasnikova, Shastitko and Shekht 1994; Kuznetsov 1994; Kolganov 1995), and in 1995 the first Russian textbooks on this problem were published (Buzgalin 1995; Val. Radaev and Buzgalin 1995; Auktsionek 1995; Murav'ev 1995). The turn towards the structural characteristics of the transition economy was closely linked with the rise of institutional economics in Russia. At its beginning stood the

> acknowledgement of the fact that the reforms that were accomplished in the Russian economy did not take into account the readiness of the Russian society as a whole to the top-down introduced institutional restructuring.
> (Zotov, Presniakov and Rozental 2001: 52)

In the mid-1990s, a number of essays criticising the neoclassical paradigm and recommending institutionalism as the adequate approach for dealing with Russia's economic problems appeared, along with translations of institutionalist literature (Shastitko*1995, 1997, 1999; Bondarenko 1995; Gutnik 1995; Levita 1996).[18] These were soon followed by the first Russian institutionalist textbooks (Shastitko 1998; Kuz'minov 1999; Kuz'minov and Iudkevich 2000; Oleinik 2000). Right from the start, Russian institutional economics fulfilled the function of a mediator between the different ideological camps that also disagreed over the degree to which Western economic standard theory could be applied to Russian reality. The compromise offered by institutional economics was aptly formulated by Vladimir S. Avtonomov* (1996: 15):

> The consideration of different currents of economic theory and their approach to the problems of the transition economy provides evidence . . . that theoretical treatment of these problems is possible, albeit likely to be less strict in character than the implications of formal neoclassical theory. Therefore . . . there is no need to reinvent the wheel and to appeal to the intangible 'Russian soul'. Yet at the same time . . . it is necessary to take account of the methodological principles of these approaches and their applicability to Russian institutional reality (including the peculiarities of ethnos and mentality).

However, Russian institutionalism is not a homogenous movement. Although it definitely led to a certain convergence of methodological positions and facilitated the exchange of ideas, the divide between the two thought collectives also made itself felt within the institutional current of Russian economics. Some radical opponents of the liberal reforms, as for example Ol'sevich and L'vov, now regularly referred to institutionalist ideas to argue their case (L'vov 1994: 8; Ol'sevich 1999: 39). "Institutionalism" of this sort was little more than an attempt to sell conservative ideas under reference to a "progressive" current of Western economics. Where such attempts can lead is most clearly shown by Abalkin's contribution to a conference volume in which the author stated in earnest that the "corner stone of evolutionary economics" was the assumption about "the unity of blood and belief, culture and customs of the population, the system of norms and institutions", and that therefore the "renaissance of Russian economy . . . is inseparably connected with the reconstruction of the historical memory of the people . . ." (Abalkin 2000a: 12). An even more conservative representative of this current is Viktor Volkonskii*, who glorifies the Chinese economic reforms and the Soviet workers' collective (see e.g.Volkonskii 1998, 1999, 2000). Besides Leonid Abalkin, Volkonskii is perhaps the best example of an author who in Soviet times belonged to the most "progressive" of economists (Sutela and Mau 1998: 49), but whose views in the second half of the 1990s looked anything but progressive. However, more moderate critics of the liberal reforms also perceived in institutionalism a new foundation for their critique of Western mainstream economics (Buzgalin and Kolganov 1998). These authors, who often belonged to the *shestidesiatniki* generation, preferred the institutionalist paradigm to the neoclassical one because of its allegedly collectivist orientation and organismic understanding of society, assuming the "primacy of the whole over the sum of the parts" (Zotov, Presniakov and Rozental' 1998: 5). A particularly striking example of ideational and semantic continuity is Iurii Ol'sevich's (1999: 39) call for an "institutionalism with a human face".

The clearest manifestation of what one might call *shestidesiatniki*-institutionalism can be found in the textbook written by Valerii V. Radaev* and Alexander V. Buzgalin (1995). The authors, emphasising that they were following the institutional approach but tellingly referring mainly to authors like Thorstein Veblen, Werner Sombart, Joseph A. Schumpeter and John Hobson instead of to the representatives of the New Institutional Economics (such as Coase, Williamson or North), put forward the full programme of *shestidesiatniki* ideology. Taking as their starting-point a stage theory of social development, they postulated that Russia's transition into the post-industrial society was imminent. Although a "regressive movement" back to capitalism was inevitable, the main aim was to move as soon as possible to a stage where the merits of the post-industrial society would be enjoyed, and in which alienation would eventually be overcome (Val. Radaev and Buzgalin 1995: 9, 32, 42, 300, 414). A couple of years earlier, in an article "On the Criteria of Social Development", Valerii Radaev (1992a: 78) made it explicitly clear that to him "progress" meant the "gradual conversion of society into a unified holistic [*edinyi tselostnoi*] organism". When Radaev and Buzgalin argued that the persiting influence of the planned economy on economic behaviour and thought was a major problem of Russian transition and that both the nostalgia for the Soviet system and the radical attempts to minimise the role of the state in the economy needed be overcome, they did little more than put new wine into old bottles. However, at the same time they expressed concerns that were shared by many economists from both thought collectives in Russian economic science (Val. Radaev and Buzgalin 1995: 392).

The interplay between formal and informal institutions is the central subject of the modern current of Russian institutional economics.[19] Until the mid-1990s, the argument that economic reforms in Russia had met with a wide range of difficulties which could not be explained in the terms of neoclassical economics had been highlighted mainly by the Slavophiles, who exploited the "cultural" argument in favour of their ideological position. Unsurprisingly, given the quality of the Slavophile critique, the liberals ignored these arguments or – like Vladimir Mau in 1999 – withdrew to the position that the cultural argument was unscientific because it could not be empirically falsified (Mau 1999: 21).

Russian institutionalism bridged this gap by providing matter-of-fact analyses of the relations between formal institutional settings and the inertia of behavioural and cultural patterns in the process of transition (Oleinik 1997; Movsesian 1998; Nesterenko 2000). The discussion centred on the issue that had been the key problem of Russian history since the times of Peter the Great (Oleinik 1997, 1998), namely "the transplantation of economic institutions" (Polterovich 2001a). Could Western settings simply be transferred to Russia or would that lead to a "rejection" of the "institutional implant"? If such reactions had to be reckoned with, what were the prerequisites for a successful absorption of institutional arrangements? If, as the Russian transition experience suggested, the efficiency of formal arrangements depended largely on their compatibility with the prevailing informal institutions (Oleinik 1997: 23; Kleiner 2000: 15; see also Zotov et al.' 2001; Porokhovskii 2002), it followed that analysing the prevailing patterns of thought and behaviour was a prerequisite for successful economic reforms (Stepin 1995; Maiminas 1996; Sidorovich 2001).

In an important article, referring mainly to W. Brian Arthur (1988) and Douglass C. North (1990), Vladimir Polterovich* (2001b) explained some of the key problems of the Russian economy, such as barter, mutual arrears, tax evasion and corruption, by locating them in the conflict between formal and informal institutional settings. In the conclusion of the article he formulated the credo of modern Russian institutionalism:

> One should not think that a market institution could be effective regardless of culture and history. Naive attempts to imitate economic organisations of more developed countries result in institutional conflicts. Wise reform strategies would help economics find its own form of the invisible hand.
>
> (Polterovich 2001b: 112)

The theory of institutional transplantation indeed offered potential for a compromise between the different ideological camps. This became clear when Anton Oleinik* (1998: 26; similar Porokhovskii 2002: 35) recommended the "establishment of a national model of the market, which would significantly deviate from the classical Western model, which is based on market agreement". Even Egor Gaidar acknowledged in the 2003 foreword to the English edition of his *State and Evolution* (and it has to be emphasised that in the main text of the book, which originally dates from 1994, such statements are absent) that "a market is first and foremost a set of historical traditions, of established norms of behaviour; it does not spring out of nowhere" (Gaidar 2003: viii). Another Russian liberal of the early transition period, Evgenii Iasin, who, as illustrated in the fourth chapter of this book, around 1990 had been among the most exposed adherents of shock therapy, now acknowledged that the creation of a functioning market system presupposed "real changes in the system of values, of informal institutions, and of culture" (Iasin 2003: 7).[20] In 2006, he self-critically acknowledged that liberal reformers had over-estimated the possibilities to implement radical structural changes:

> Radical changes need an ideological foundation, and at some point reformers overstated the creative possibilities of the market mechanism, especially at the early stage of restructuring on the 'ruins' of the planned economy.
>
> (Iasin 2006: 12)

A new consensus?

At the turn of the twenty-first century there was a widespread consensus in Russia that dissent had to be overcome and that it was indispensable to find a future model of Russian society which the different ideological camps could agree on. In the words of Nikolai P. Shmelev:

> Russian society is tired of discord, it calls for unity, which is certainly possible in the economic and social spheres. More than that, not in words, but in actual fact it already exists, although consciously or unconsciously it is not always noted.
>
> (Shmelev 1999: 49)

Indeed, by the end of the 1990s it looked as though the previously hostile ideological camps of Slavophiles and Westernisers, and liberals and *gosudarstvenniki*, had brought their respective points of view much closer together (Mau 2001: 10). Now not only the major political parties, but also most Russian economists, agreed "that political consolidation and a strengthening of the government are the crucial factors for the backing of stable economic growth and social development", as the liberal Vladimir Mau put it (2000: 9). Also, the realisation that Western reform programmes could not simply be transferred to Russia, but had to be adapted to the historical and cultural traditions of the country, now became widely accepted. As Leonid Ia. Kosal (2000: 14) noted:

> the thesis on the influence of Russian peculiarities on the course and on the results of market reforms has become generally accepted; it is one of the most often made statements in economic and sociological literature, in journalism and in political programs.[21]

Yet a closer look reveals that the different camps had a fairly diverse understanding of these basic postulates. The liberals, referring to institutionalist ideas, called for a strong state that should control the rules of the game and free itself from the pressure of private interest groups, but not participate directly in the economic process (Uliukaev 1996: 7–8; Nesterenko 2000: 4–5; Aganbegian 2001: 15). In contrast, both the adherents of regulation and the Slavophiles demanded that the separation of the state from the economy be prevented, and they bemoaned the "atomisation of society" (Goricheva 2002: 81).

The same applies to the question of cultural traditions. The liberals turned to this problem because experience had shown that here was a factor which could decide the success or failure of future reforms. Yet this realisation did not mean a revision of their negative assessment of the role played by traditional Russian values in the reform process. Nowhere does this become clearer than in Iasin's essay on the "modernisation of the economy and the system of values" in which he calls for a change in the basic values of Russian society, values that in his view reflected the "relations and institutions of an archaic society and the hierarchic structure of authority and power within an agrarian – feudalist economy" (Iasin 2003: 123). The Slavophiles, by contrast, still tended to idealise the Russian cultural heritage and demanded that the reform strategy be fundamentally adapted to these traditions (Arkhipov 1999; Kniazev 2003).

Notes

1 The first foreign textbooks to be translated into Russian were: Heynes (first edition 1973), translated in 1991; Dolan and Lindsey (1974), translated in 1991; Pindyck and Rubinfeld (1989), translated in 1992; Fisher, Dornbusch and Schmalensee (1988), translated in 1993; Samuelson (1948), translated in 1994; and, last but not least, McConnell and Brue (1990), translated in 1992 – which for a couple of years was the leading textbook of economics at Russian universities (see Nureev and Latov 2001: 97).

2 In a paper, "A new ideology for Russia: a drama from contemporary history", that was published in *MEiMO* in 1993, the historian Vladimir Sorgin (1993: 16) explained the sudden shift from liberal enthusiasm to the search for a new, "Russian" ideology with "the obvious intellectual unwillingness of Russian society as a whole and the intelligentsia in particular to absorb and to adopt the new ideals. . . There is still not a single important Russian philosopher, sociologist, political scientist or economist, not to speak of theoretical currents, with a liberal-democratic orientation. The acquisition of liberal-democratic ideology in Russia took place in the form of a journalistic attack at the end of the 80s and 90s. Maybe this explains its utopism, eclecticism and its declarative and imitative character?"

3 This phenomenon could also be observed in other transition countries, yet nowhere did it reach the level it did in the Russian Federation. For an overview see Rostowski (1994).

4 Adherents of a strong state, from *gosudarstvo* = State.

5 With regard to the similarity of the Marxist and the liberal believing in historical progress in Russia, see also Sokolov (1997: 7).

6 In order to avoid too clear-cut a juxtaposition on the ideas that inspired perestroika and shock therapy, it should not go without notice that in the years 1990–92 there had already been single voices who argued that in the Western countries the market was deeply embedded into civil society (Alekseev 1991: 10), and that the task included overcoming the previous socio-pyschological imprints and ideas (Volkonskii 1990; Kuz'minov 1992) so that the task of establishing a market economy "goes far beyond the borders of a purely economic undertaking; it probably mainly . . . is a problem of the reform governance" (Gorodetskii 1990: 44).

7 See for example, Val. Radaev (1992b), Superfin (1993), Iakovets (1994), Kashin (1996), Inozemtsev (1997) and Vasil'chuk (1997).

8 Similarly see Superfin (1993), Iakovets (1994), Kashin (1996), Inozemtsev (1997), Vasil'chuk (1997). The anthropocentric orientation of the idea of post-industrial society

becomes even more articulate in Vadim A. Medved'ev's (1993: 24–25) statement that "in the centre of the new civilisation, man stands not only as a creator, but also as the aim of all activity. Therefore the transition to the new civilisation must be regarded above all as a process taking place on the basis of the whole intellectual and social progress of mankind".

9 This idea had first been developed by Piotr Chaadaev, Alexander Herzen and Nikolai Chernyshevskii and also played a decisive role in Lenin's thought.

10 Additionally, collectivism was often mentioned as a stubborn Russian tradition, contradicting the application of Western reform concepts to Russian reality (see Moiseev 1998: 78).

11 See also Khubiev (1993: 65).

12 Sorokin (2004: 68, fn.) provides a list of the central contributions of the economists from the Institute of Economics of the Russian Academy of Science to the debate on post-socialist reforms up to 2004.

13 Similarly see Iaremenko (1995: 60) who explicitly argued that the tendency to argue abstractly and "in principle" was a problem of the "thought style" of Russian economists.

14 For an overview see Sergei Afontsev (2002).

15 The titles of the articles in this special issue, such as "Elements of a concept of economic security" (Samsonov 1994), "Economic security: evaluations, problems, methods of maintenance" (Arkhipov 1994) or "The object of Russia's economic security" (Tambovtsev 1994), indicate that the main task was seen in outlining the problem methodologically. The concept was then further developed in countless articles and in the monographs of Sergei Iu. Glaz'ev (1996), V. Zagashvili (1997) and the collections of articles edited by Viacheslav K. Senchagov (1998) and by Shavaev (2001).

16 In their critical analysis of the concept of economic security, Aleksei A. Prokhozhev and M. Kornilov (2003: 225) found no less than thirty (!) different definitions of the concept.

17 See the list provided by Nureev and Latov (2001: 99, notes 10 and 11).

18 The Western works that were translated included Coase (1988), translated in 1991; Olson (1965, 1982), translated in 1995 and 1998, respectively; Williamson (1985), translated in 1996; Ménard (1990), translated in 1996; Buchanan (1962, 1975), both translated in 1997; North (1990), translated in 1997 (see Nureev and Latov 2001: 104–105).

19 Rostislav I. Kapeliushnikov (2001: 141) argued that it was mainly due to the fact that every formal rule that was applied to the Russian context immediately turned into informal relations and personal contacts that made it so urgently necessary to take informal institutions into account.

20 Iasin (2003: 7). It is a point in favour of Evgenii Iasin's great scientific honesty that he explicitly stressed, in his opening talk on the "Modernisation of Economy and Nurturing of Institutions" at the 2005 annual conference of the Moscow Higher School of Economics, that he had renounced his previous views. He had, said Iasin, underestimated the inertia of informal institutions in the early 1990s.

21 See also Nesterenko (2000: 6) and Volkonskii (2000: 124).

6 In search of a "Russian Way": 1999–2006

Taking stock of post-socialist reforms

The tenth anniversary of the beginning of market reforms in Russia gave occasion to take stock of post-socialist reforms. There was a broad consensus among Russian economists that the results were devastating both in economic and political terms. As Ivan D. Afanasenko (2001: 5) succinctly noted, "the failure of successive reforms . . . is not a subject of discussion any more". Vladimir Shemiatenkov's (2003: 10) characterisation of the present system as "a formless mixture of Soviet red-tapism, late socialist nepotism [*blatmeisterstvo*], the worst characteristics of Western 'wild' [*dikii*] capitalism and what in former times was often called 'aziatchina'" was certainly polemical, but it expressed a feeling that was shared by many (Akinin, Shevelev and Pochikovskaia 2004: 892). Worse still, there was a widely shared apprehension that the economic problems of the country bore a "systematic character" (Alekseev 2005: 53). The fact that more than a decade after the beginning of market reforms GDP had not even reached its pre-1992 level (Dynkin 2003: 50), made the high growth rates between 2000 and 2007[1] appear much less impressive, as recovery growth would come to a halt as soon as the pre-reform GDP was reached (Tsvetkov 2006: 23; Khanin 2007: 36). In this context, some authors arrived at the conclusion that when it came to the task of catching-up, Russia's post-socialist economic system proved to be even less efficient than that prior to reform (Ovsienko and Petrakov 2004: 72; Ovsienko 2005: 54). A further argument in support of the notion of the relative failure of reforms was to be found in Russia's poor transition performance compared to the countries of Central Eastern Europe (Radygin and Entov 2005: 15; Martynov 2003a: 27; Kudrov 2005: 3). For many Russian economists it was this somewhat humiliating experience in particular that raised doubts about whether the "Western" path of development was viable for Russia.[2]

The mix of fear of having missed the boat in comparison to other transition countries and that of having been betrayed by the West stood at the beginning of a new phase in the Russian political and economic discourses. From then on, two questions would stand at the centre of Russian economic debates. First, the feeling that the "Western way" hadn't worked out for Russia led to attempts to develop scientific arguments for Russia's specificity [*samobytnost'*] and to derive political and economic strategies that took this specificity into account. Connected to this nationalist turn was a widely shared nostalgia for the Soviet Empire, which was expressed also by President Putin, when in 2005 he called the collapse of the Soviet Union the "greatest geopolitical catastrophe of the century". From then on, the representatives of Soviet-style political economy in particular used the general ideological climate to argue their case that in economics too, the time had come to reconsider the achievements of the Soviet past. Secondly, the fear of permanently falling behind led to an intense search for a viable strategy for medium and long term development. In the context of this discussion, more and more authors demanded to "mobilise energy and political will in order to build a new Russian society" (Fedorenko 2003: 12), which was possible only on the basis of a unifying national idea.

The discussions about these two basic questions – Russian specificity and the need for a medium to long term development strategy – were developing in parallel, and there was frequent overlap between them. The need of a development strategy had been repeatedly articulated by the *akademiki* in their interventions from 1994 onward (see chapter 5); in the period under review here, it was raised by a group of conservative journalists in a prolific so called *Serafimovskii* manifesto (Leont'ev, Privalov, Sokolov and Fadeev 2003). However, the discussion about modernisation and innovation gained momentum only from 2007 onward and reached its peak in 2009 and 2010. Therefore, in this chapter I concentrate on the nationalist turn, whereas in the next chapter I will turn to the debate about development strategies.

With regard to the two thought collectives in Russian economic science, the tenth anniversary of the beginning of market reforms marks the end of convergence. The feeling that drastic changes were needed to halt the decline of the country led to a radicalisation of the discussion and accordingly to new clashes between liberals and *gosudarstvenniki*.[3] Much of the debate focused on the Stabilisation Fund (in the following SF) that was established in 2004 in order to sterilise a part of the oil and gas revenue and thus prevent inflation. This last important reform measure that clearly reflected liberal-monetarist ideas[4] caused another major debate on the orientation of Russian economic policy.

In 2007, it was decided to use the means of the SF partly to set up so called "institutions of development". This decision marked a clear victory of etatist over liberal ideas. Divergence and radicalisation also concerned the relationship to Western economics. Encouraged by the nationalist turn, parts of the conservative community now openly demanded the overcoming of the "pathological mimicry syndrome" [*patologicheskii sindrom podrazhatel'stva*] (Grinberg 2005: 3) and tried to establish a "Russian" school of post-Soviet political economy.

The discussion about the stabilisation fund

The story of the Russian SF is a striking case of an imported institution which in the Russian context of a growing influence of etatist and nationalist ideas turned from a liberal-monetarist instrument of macroeconomic stabilisation into an instrument of neo-Soviet industrial policy. As Ewa Dabrowska and I (2015) have dealt with this case in some detail in another study, I here confine myself to summarising the points that are relevant to the argument of the present book.

Around 2000, the neo-liberal idea of SFs was very much *en vogue* – between 1998 and 2000 no less than nine oil and gas exporting countries introduced SFs, among them the former Soviet Republics of Azerbaijan (1999) and Kazakhstan (2000). The idea of a Russian SF was first raised by the then vice-director of the IMF Stanley Fisher in 2000 (Vardul 2000). A year later, a policy proposal was worked out by the liberal Gaidar institute (Zolotareva, Drobyshevskii, Sinel'nikov and Kadochnikov [2001] 2002) which was supported by libertarian economist Andrei Illarionov, the then closest economic advisor to Vladimir Putin, and was implemented on 1 January 2004. From the beginning onward, there was a controversy about the right balance between the sterilisation and reserve function on the one hand, and using SF means for investments into infrastructure and industrial policy on the other. As a compromise, it was decided that in case the SF would exceed RUB 500 billion, the means could also be used for "other purposes" than sterilisation and reserve. When this compromise was made, hardly anyone expected the hike in oil prices, as a result of which the fund had reached this amount by the end of 2004.

The accumulation of vast financial means in the SF decisively aggravated the tensions between the two thought collectives. The main reason for this is that the SF most strongly symbolised the neo-liberal idea of isolating the economic sphere from all political "disturbances" and influences. Accordingly, to those who saw the unity of polity and economy as an ideal and hoped for the state as the decisive engine of economic modernisation, the SF caused massive cognitive discomfort. More than that, in the Soviet Union there had been a similar absorption mechanism which, however, aimed at using the extracted oil and gas revenue for the diversification of the economy.

The intense "development versus stabilisation" debate that took place between 2004 and 2006 accordingly focused mainly on the SF. In the political struggle, the stabilisation camp led by Minister of Finance Alexei Kudrin* (who holds a *kandidat* (roughly a PhD) in economics) came under increasing pressure from the development camp. The political leader of the latter was Andrei Belousov*, an economist trained in reformist Soviet macroeconomics (Belousov holds both a *kandidat* and a *doktor nauk* (equivalent of a German/Austrian Habilitation) in economics), who had been appointed Deputy Minister of Economic Development in 2006. In theoretical terms, the discussion focused on the causes of inflation. Whereas Kudrin (2007; HSE 2006) held a clearly monetarist view and argued that inflation in Russia was entirely due to too expansive a budgetary policy, Beolusov and other economists from the political economy camp saw the main causes of inflation as being on the supply side. The implementation of the SF, they argued, had only aggravated the problem of too small a money supply which resulted in a liquidity crisis of the enterprises and thus a decline in investment (Panova 2008; Fetisov 2007; Glaz'ev et al. 2011). With this narrative of the Russian macroeconomic problems being mainly a problem of insufficient money supply, they stood in the continuity of the 1994 interventions of Abalkin, Petrakov and Shatalin (1994a/b) (see Chapter 5).

The discussion about the SF is a prime example of how the two thought collectives in Russian economics developed two perspectives on an economic institution that were rooted in entirely different thought styles so that it was impossible to engage in a fruitful debate. The following table summarises these two perspectives:

Table 6.1 Gestaltvorstellungen and the stabilisation fund

	Neo-Soviet/Keynesian Interpretation	*Neo-liberal Interpretation*
Overall macroeconomic *Gestaltvorstellung*	Cycle	Supply/demand
Main macroeconomic priorities	Development	Stability
Relationship state/economy	Priority of the state, economy politically embedded	Clear functional differentiation between state and economy, depoliticisation of the economy desirable
Main engine of structural change	Industrial policy	Private investments
Main function of the SF	Reserve function	Stabilisation function
Nature of resource income	The 'oil rent' belongs to the people	Economically undeserved windfall profits

The political clash, and thus too the clash between the two shared interpretations of the function of the SF, found their peaks in June 2006, when Kudrin reacted to Prime Minister Mikhail Fradkov's remarks on industrial policy with the comment that "as long as inflation is higher than 3% all talk of innovation policy is nonsense (*boltovni*)" (quoted from Netreba 2006).

A year later the tension was resolved when the SF was split into a Reserve Fund and a so-called Fund of National Welfare. On the basis of a government decision taken on 11 October 2007, it was decided to use SF means partly for the capitalisation of so-called "institutions of development", above all for the capitalisation of the *Vneshekonombank*, which was turned into the main state development bank. This way, the clash between two conflicting patterns of thought found a manifestation in a reform of the SF that turned it into a hybrid and somewhat contradictory institution. An originally monetarist-liberal instrument of macroeconomic stabilisation was now partly used to revive the Soviet practice to use oil revenues for the diversification of the economy. It is telling that the first two projects that were financed by the SF were direct continuations of projects that had been started in Soviet times, namely the *Baguchany dam*, a large hydroelectric dam on the Angara River in Kodinsk, and the petro-chemical plant in *Nizhnekamsk* (Tatarstan), Russia's largest producer of synthetic rubber (Ekspert 2006).

The nationalist turn

The ideological climate of the years 2000–2006 was marked by growing nationalism. As we have seen in the previous chapter, the old Slavophile notion that Russian and Western cultures were incompatible had been present in Russian reform debates since the early 1990s, but neither the original Slavophiles nor the neo-Slavophiles had based their arguments on a coherent analytical framework. Such a framework was now provided by two economic sociologists from the Novosibirsk school – Olga Bessonova* and Svetlana Kirdina*. They developed a pseudo-theoretical explanation of Russian economic evolution in their works, which provided a scientific backing for the increasing sentiment of nationalism. They started to develop their ideas in 1996 (in a joint book with Ruth O'Sullivan[5] [Bessonova, Kirdina and O'Sullivan 1996)]), and it was mainly Bessonova (1997, 1998, 1999) who in a number of contributions developed the basic idea of Russia as a "redistributive" [*razdatochnoe*] economy standing in eternal contrast to Western-type market societies. However, only after the publication of Kirdina's *Institutional Matrices and Russia's Development* in 2000,[6] did their ideas find a wider audience.[7] For the sake of brevity, I will mainly follow the lines of Kirdina's book, which opens with a question that engaged Russian social scientists at the turn of the century like no other, namely why post-socialist reforms had been successful in Central Eastern Europe but much less so in Russia and the other CIS states (Kirdina 2001: 6). Her answer was that all national forms of social and economic organisation could be traced back to two ideal types, the so called X- and Y-matrices,[8] which Kirdina characterises as shown in Table 6.2 (Kirdina 2001: 113).

It is certainly up for discussion whether all historical forms of economic life can be described as varying compositions of some kind of polarity. However, the crux of Kirdina's argument is her claim that both types are incompatible, so that all mixed forms would, in the medium to long run, turn into one of the two types (Kirdina 2001: 7). Kirdina's second and crucial assumption is that institutional matrices form the "unchangeable base of human society" (Kirdina 2001: 6).[9] In other words, in her view, the X-organisation of the economy had been a recurrent theme throughout Russian history. From this perspective, Russian history since Peter the Great could be interpreted as a series of attempts to reform the country by applying Y-elements, all of which had failed – with the market reforms of the 1990s being only the latest example. The main implication of the concept was quite obvious: if the "institutional basis of a re-distributive economy . . . cannot be reformed even through the most elaborate plans of the most distinguished reformers" (Bessonova 2006: 106), it seemed futile to take on "Westernising" reforms.

Table 6.2 X- and Y-Matrices

X	*Y*
Public Property	Private Property
Redistribution	Exchange
Service Labour	Hired Labour
Coordination	Competition
Proportionality	Profit

Instead, Russia would have to find her own reform method within the framework of a "redistributive", "Eastern" or "X" society.

This key message, and in particular the assumption of the incompatibility of "Western" and "Eastern" societies, found a wide echo in Russian economic literature (Afanasenko 2001: 9; Kireeva 2003; Val. Radaev 2003: 14; Shkolnikova 2004: 654; Oleinikov 2006: 154). The search for a "national economic model" was now often based on the notion that "Russians cannot fully develop within the framework of a market economy" (Iasinskaia 2002: 292), as Russian values and traditions did not provide a fertile breeding ground for Western-style capitalism (Plotitsyna 2003: 472). One author even noted that the attempts to change the Russian mentality were amongst the "most catastrophic results" of market reforms, as the attempts to turn Russian man into economic man would mean "the end of Russian history" (Gel'vanovskii 2003: 377). A number of authors saw the decisive cultural feature of the country in the fact that "Russians cannot live without a greater goal [*sverkhzadacha*]", and that it therefore was necessary to find a generally binding ideology or "national idea" (Zalygina and Mel'nichuk 2003: 504; Rubanov 2004: 20; Novosel'skii 2005: 4). This notion has been part of the Russian debate on transition since the early 1990s. However, compared to earlier debates on this topic, it was now more and more often directed against the Western world, especially the USA. For example, D.I. Kokurin and O.K. Shalenkova (2003: 975) saw the Russian reforms as a

> realisation of the plans of Russia's external enemies whose target it is to destroy our country as an independent developed state, and, in the longer run, the Russians as a unified great people, the conversion of Russia into 'living space' and sphere of interest of other countries.

One should keep in mind that this quotation does not stem from a newspaper or a political pamphlet but from a paper that was published in a collection of scientific articles edited by a professor who regards himself as the leading economic philosopher of the country. Other authors argued that in its "mono-centric" form, globalisation mainly served the interests of the USA (Subetto 2003; Iur'ev 2003: 208; Baburin 2004: 181), represented a threat to Russian national culture and was the main cause of Russia's economic problems (Medved'ev 2004: 6; Gel'vanovskii 2003: 224). The failure to reform would certainly continue, Nosova (2004: 709) noted, "as long as we do not manage to free ourselves from the chains of Americanism".

At the same time, there was a certain revival of Eurasian ideas. Not all authors went as far as Mikhail I. Voeikov (2003: 99), who quoted Trubetskoi's classic Eurasian statement that the "Romance – Germanic world is . . . our worst enemy" and added:

> These words could be understood as exaggerated and polemic, if we had not seen the last decade of the 20th century, in which Western idols, ideals and prejudices were imposed on Russia almost with force.

The well-known Eurasian geopolitician Alexander Dugin (2003: 195) remarked that a key element of Eurasian ideology had always been an economy subordinated to the nation state, and that a violation of this eternal principle of Russian culture had been a main reason for the failure to reform. O. A. Sergeeva (2003: 572) was quite explicit about the motivation behind the revival of Eurasian ideas when stating that Russia could only hope to take on a leading role internationally as the leading nation of the Eurasian, but not as part of the Western, world.

In the first years of the new millennium, "culture" and "cultural change" became major topics in the writings of the "grand old man" of Russian economic liberalism, Evgenii Iasin, who opposed the widespread cultural fatalism by appealing for a modernisation of traditional Russian values as "a matter of survival", meaning that "we simply cannot allow ourselves to relax and not change" (Iasin 2006: 19; see also Iasin 2007: 24–29). This point of view was echoed in an article by I. Groshev and V. Iur'ev (2005: 221) on "Economic Reforms and Russian Mentality": "Russia's problem lies precisely in the necessity to transform the national psyche, broaden the spectrum of values by modes of the market while preventing a *mankurtizatsiia*[10] of the Russian people".

Other authors agreed that the main problem was to "adopt capitalism as a universal and impersonal system of formal rationality in its pure and accomplished form" (Belousov 2005: 126), and positioned themselves in between by stating that before any definite conclusions could be drawn, an in-depth analysis of the existing mentality and values was needed – a task that had thus far been utterly neglected (Balatskii 2007: 53; Plotitsyna 2003: 478).

Reappraisal of the planned economy

Encouraged by Putin's statement on the catastrophe of the collapse of the Soviet Union, and with a distance of fifteen years after the breakdown of the Soviet economy, parts of the Russian economics community came up with quite astonishing re-evaluations of the Soviet planned economy. A typical example reads as follows:

> The Soviet economy as the unified economic [*narodnokhoziaistvennyi*] complex of the Soviet Union was far better prepared for the challenges of the 21st century than the Western countries, as the social psychology, focused on the priority of the social over individual and collective interests offered possibilities to solve the problems the country is facing on a qualitatively higher level compared to the contemporary contractions of bourgeois society.
>
> (Iokhin 2006: 357)[11]

A number of authors claimed that Russian capitalism had not helped to construct anything, but rather it had only exhausted the resources that had been accumulated in Soviet times (Makarevich 2003: 35; Khanin 2003a: 78). Whilst an ultra-nationalist (if not fascist) book like *Forward into the USSR – 2* by the journalist Maksim Kalashnikov (a "programmatic" pseudonym of Vladimir A. Kucherenko) cannot be attributed to scientific discourse on economic reforms, two points deserve mentioning here: first, no less than 10,000 copies of this book were printed, suggesting that it aroused keen interest amongst readers; and second, when the author praised the Soviet Union as a "society of high culture, general education and distinguished technology" (Kalashnikov 2003: 7), he expressed the very sentiment that has now also made its way into the economic debates.

According to the supporters of the planned economy, experience showed that the market was unable "to serve the interests of the nation-state" (Smirnov 2006: 131), and in particular was not the right means for successful catch-up development (Grinberg et al. 2007: 34; Smirnov 2006: 131; Neshitoi 2007: 6). These authors claimed that in terms of qualitative growth, the Soviet planned economy had outperformed today's "wild capitalism". In sharp contrast to the current situation, they argued, the country had held a leading international position both in several scientific disciplines as well as in a number of high-tech industries. Technical progress had not only been achieved through the systematic support of science, but also by the ability of the government to control the balance between investment and consumption. This in turn had allegedly enabled the government to ensure permanent modernisation of the capital stock. Given that the planned economy had been such a success story, how could its decline be explained? On the one hand, most (but not all) admirers of the planned economy admitted that there had certainly been unfavourable developments and contradictions within the system which had slowed down its adaptability. On the other hand, in their view the breakdown of the Soviet Union had also been the result of the economic and military efforts of the Western powers, and in particular the United States of America, to conquer the Soviet Union (Ivanchenko and Ivanchenko 2005: 4; Senchagov 2007: 4–5).[12]

One would expect that the latter point of view would primarily be supported by former trusted Soviet economists. And indeed, the journal *Ekonomist*, which until 1991 had been published under the title *Planovoe khoziaistvo* (Planned Economy) as the official organ of *Gosplan*, was at the centre of the reappraisal of the Soviet economy (Vissarionov and Fedorova 2003; Plyshevskii 2004; Ivanchenko and Ivanchenko 2005; Popova 2007). However, even authors who had previously openly supported market reforms now rediscovered the planned economy as the solution to the problem of economic modernisation. The outstanding example of this is the editor of the journal *EKO* and acclaimed growth statistician Grigorii Khanin*. In the 1980s, Khanin published deeply provocative studies on economic growth in the Soviet Union, in comparison to which not only the official Soviet but also most Western analyses looked hopelessly optimistic (Khanin and Seliunin 1987; Khanin 1989, English version 1992). In the early 1990s, he had decidedly defended "the market and capitalism" as having been confirmed by "the whole of world experience" (Khanin 1992: 23). From 2003 onward, Khanin, remarking that the reform experience had disabused him (Khanin 2003a: 90),[13] came forth with a series of articles on the "Soviet economic miracle" (Khanin 2003b), in which he claimed that only a planned economy could set the country back on the track of modernisation. The current situation of the Russian economy, Khanin noted, was similar to that of the Soviet economy in the late 1920s; after a period of intense recovery growth the potential of the market forces had been exhausted, and a transition towards a mobilised economy was the only way to achieve sustained growth and catch-up modernisation. According to him, history had shown that all successful attempts at catch-up modernisation had relied on autocracy and mobilisation, whereas all failed attempts had been based on democracy and the market (Khanin 2005a: 97–98).

Even more surprisingly, for an intellectual having previously been highly critical of Soviet power, he went as far as to praise Stalin for being the only Russian statesman under whom the planned economy had worked properly (Khanin 2005b). Being fully aware of the political consequences of a return to the plan, he saw no alternative but to restrict individual liberty in order to achieve economic progress (Khanin 2004: 180). The last twenty years of reforms, he noted, had clearly shown what happened if one tried to pursue a policy contradicting the economic traditions of the country. It is exactly this type of historical fatalism which the reappraisal of the planned economy and the economic nationalism of Bessonova and Kirdina have in common.

Certainly, as Westernizers, the Russian liberal economists were now swimming against the tide of public sentiment, and they had difficulties having their voices heard. However, they were efficient in their division of labour; if Iasin had reacted to the spread of nationalism and cultural fatalism by making the case for a modernisation of the Russian system of values, it was the other "heavyweight" of Russian liberal economic thought, Egor Gaidar, who gave a clear answer to the nostalgia for the Soviet Union and the planned economy. In 2006, the former prime minister published his book, *Collapse of an Empire. Lessons for Modern Russia* (which was translated into English in 2007), in which he castigated the increasing "post-imperial nostalgia" as an "illness":

> Unfortunately, for the past few years Pandora's box has been left open for Russia. The appeals to post-imperial nostalgia, nationalistic xenophobia, the usual anti-Americanism, and even to a not quite habitual anti-Europeanism have become fashionable and might soon become the norm. It is important to realise how dangerous this is for the country and the world.
>
> (Gaidar 2007: xiv)

In his view, it was far more comfortable to believe that the collapse of the Soviet Union had not been the result of internal weakness but of a world conspiracy. It was an alarming sign, Gaidar wrote, that according to 2005 opinion poll figures, less than 30% of the population shared the view that the borders of the Russian Federation should remain as they were (2007: 259) and that approximately a quarter of the eligible voters stated that they would vote for Stalin were he among the candidates (ibid.: xvi). He concluded that there existed a popular myth, that after Russia had been brought to her knees by her foreign enemies and (with the help of the IMF and the World Bank) had been forced to adopt a policy serving Western interests, the government that came to power in 1999 would be able to restore Russia to her former status.

Indicative planning and mobilisation versus structural reforms

In the years under review here, state planning became a truly fashionable topic. Only a small minority, however, was in favour of a "neo-Soviet alternative" (Gubanov* 2005b) modelled on the example of Belarus (Cherkovets 2003). Instead, the concept of planning, which had been under a certain ideological ban for roughly a decade, was now discussed in the context of a state-regulated economy, one of the oldest topics of the Russian reform debate. Well trained dialecticians as they were, a number of authors argued that it was a strange twist of fate that the very country whose pioneering contributions to the theory and practice of planning that had inspired economic policy in many countries of the world had almost entirely disregarded its own planning experience during the transition period (Popova 2007: 4; Ignatovskii 2007: 13; Ivanchenko 2007; Glaz'ev 2007: 22). These authors regularly referred to France and Japan and their respective experiences with indicative planning.

As is common in Russian economic journals, the claim that "indicative planning" had been successful was never empirically underpinned. The degree to which academic debates still made use of buzzwords can also be illustrated in how "indicative planning" now became one of the dominating keywords of the debate on economic policy (Klotsvog and Chernova 2004: 62; Ivanov 2006: 56; Glaz'ev 2007: 24; Grinberg et al. 2007: 8) – although I could not find a single article in which there was a thorough explanation of how this system worked in general, or how it might be applied to Russia.

Sometimes explicitly referring to the example of Soviet industrial policy (Plyshevskii 2004), the supporters of "indicative planning" put forth the very same arguments that are well known from earlier regulation debates: only "indicative planning" could ensure that economic development would no longer follow the "anarchy of the market" but be geared towards the interests of the "whole of society" or the "interests of the nation state". More than fifteen years after the breakdown of the Soviet Union, these were (and up to the present still are) widely used terms in the Russian economic debate, although authors using them have almost never discussed the problem of how to define collective interests. For example, according to Kleiner* and Petrosian, "in its role as the official representative of the whole society" the state should "formulate (and to some degree also shape) economic, social, intellectual and other preferences [*potrebnosti*] of society, also taking into account the interests of future generations, and express these preferences in relevant economic and political programmes" (Kleiner and Petrosian 2005: 48–49). It should be noted that the authors were fully aware that the realisation of their proposal demanded "all-embracing social control and the formation of public opinion" (Petrosian 2007: 92). Here we have another example of how one of the thought collectives remained true to the ideas of the 1970s and early 1980s. The idea that the state could and should form peoples' preferences so that they accorded to the interests of "society as a whole" had been an important element in the ideas of the Soviet *shestdesiatniki* (see Chapter 3).

As in the previous regulation debates, the supporters of "indicative planning" and industrial policy insisted that the economic system should not be allowed to follow its own logic but should once more serve political goals. In the article "The Question of Economic Efficiency Criteria", Anatolii Ptushenko (2004: 157) wrote the following on the Russian economic policy of the 1990s:

> The mere fact that scientists did not [critically, JZ] react to the widespread opinion on the autonomy of economic life . . . [according to which, JZ] it was possible (and even necessary) 'to deal with business and leave politics to the politicians' proves the unwillingness to consider the unity of all spheres of life of society.

As I argued in Chapter 2, the image of society as an "organic whole" that should not be fragmented into distinguishable subspheres is deeply rooted in the traditions of Russian social philosophy and economic reasoning and can be seen as the decisive intellectual obstacle to implementing a functioning market economy in Russia. After what was considered to be a negative experience with imported functional differentiation of society, the idea of "unity" grew stronger again in the new millennium. As an alternative to the separation of economic and political life, a number of authors now explicitly asked for a return to a mobilised economy and thus for "vertical integration" to be applied to the economic sphere of society as well (Gubanov 2001, 2005a, 2005b; Zagladin 2005: 31; Kuznetsov 2005: 42). The increasing popularity of the idea that all parts of society should once more be subordinated to the will of political leadership also found expression in the style of Russian economic discourse. With Vladimir Putin in power, authors felt more and more the desire or need to pay tribute to the president (Kudrov 2005: 32; Simoniia 2003: 118; Makarevich 2003: 12), a Soviet habit that had almost ceased to exist from the late 1980s onwards.

Liberal reactions to increasing state interference

While the years 2000 to 2003 had, according to many observers, seen the most consistent liberal reforms since the early 1990s, the government not only started to increasingly interfere with the markets during Putin's second term, but the state became a decisive player in the economic sphere. In doing so, it violated the interests of private business with increasing frequency. As in the El'tsin era, the fundamental problem was the lack of a clear separation between state and economy. While El'tsin's second term had been marked by "state capture" (Hellman, Jones and Kaufmann 2003), "business capture" (Iakovlev 2006; Oleinik 2006) became the main feature of Putin's second term of his first presidency.

Being one of the first examples of the strategy of the new government to subordinate business to the political system, the Iukos-Khodorkovskii case marked the decisive break between liberal economists and the Putin government. Henceforth, the liberals criticised Putin's economic policy as a move towards "state capitalism" (Radygin 2004; Radygin and Entov 2005: 37; Abramov and Radygin 2007: 31).

In the early stages of Putin's first presidency, it had appeared that handing more power to the state was to serve the enforcement of the rule of law, as Vladimir Mau wrote. In the meantime, however, the government had started directly participating in economic activities (Mau 2006: 17). This direct state participation had already led to "nationalisation and quasi-nationalisation" (Nikolaev, Kalinin and Tolchikina 2005: 20), restricting the realm of market and competition and progressively blurring the lines of property rights (*razmyvanie*).[14]

Liberal authors agreed that in Putin's second term, a far-reaching redistribution of property was taking place, with state officials, especially bureaucrats, taking on the position of the former "oligarchs" (Men'shikov 2004: 31). According to liberal observers, this new fusion of state and economy (Popadiuk 2006: 148; Tsvetkov and Dzhumov 2007: 36) became clearest in the institution of "power-property" (*vlast-sobstvennost'*). The increasingly important role of the administration was most alarming, Vladimir Mau warned, as the administrative reforms had failed and Russian bureaucracy had become even less efficient (Mau 2006: 7).[15] As noted earlier by Iu. P. Voronov (2003: 14), a critical point had been reached, as staying on course would inevitably lead to a return to the planned economy.

According to Neshchadin, Kuznetsov and Kashin (2007: 9–10), the fact that the state was able to control vast parts of the economy meant that an economic counterpart of a "guided democracy" had emerged. From their point of view, the Russian economy had already been reverted to a mobilised economy. It only remained unclear as to whose interests it would serve in the long run. From a liberal point of view, the fact that the government was now pursuing its own interests, and was therefore less prone to conform to general rules, manifested itself in a less and less predictable economic policy (Iasin, Grigor'ev, Kuznetsov, Danilov and Kosygina 2006: 5; Golikova, Gonchar, Kuznetsov, Iakovlev and Iasin 2007: 15). Instead, a system of double standards had emerged in which the personal relationships between the entrepreneur and the representatives of the state determined which set of rules would be applied (Radygin and Entov 2005: 38). It was therefore no coincidence, Iasin et al. (2006: 9) concluded, that Russia's position had significantly deteriorated particularly in areas such as the independence of the legal system or the influence of personal relationships on decisions of state organs (as indicators such as those of *Transparency International* also showed).[16] In their eyes, the much discussed short-sightedness of Russian investors was not due to market failure but reflected a fully rational decline in trust towards the stability of property rights (Davydov 2007: 122; Rozmainskii and Skorobogatov 2006: 11; Alekseev and Kuznetsova 2004: 26). They saw the only path to continuous growth in a return to structural and institutional reforms that had been launched in 2000 but had almost come to a complete halt after 2003 (Kholodkov 2005: 42; Voronova 2003: 43; Gaidar 2004: 21; Mau 2004: 31). The liberals also started to more vehemently criticise the restrictions of civil liberties and called for a "democracy without adjective" (Iasin 2007: 15). This discussion culminated in the years 2007 to 2012, and I will continue this topic in the next chapter.

Economics or political economy?

The predominant judgment of market reforms modelled on Western examples having failed also led to an intensified debate on the applicability of Western economic theory to Russian economic reality. The journal *Rossiiski ekonomicheskii zhurnal* became the main organ for an "anti-economics" discourse, within which two currents can be distinguished: one arguing in favour of a "national economics", the other in favour of reviving Soviet-style political economy.

In 1996, Iurii Ol'sevich raised a demand for a new "national economic thought" (Ol'sevich 1996). This demand led to a discussion on a "Russian economic school", during the course of which nationalist and Slavophile ideas fused. In 2000, Leonid Abalkin organised a conference on "The Russian Economic School – Past and Present", in Moscow. In his plenary lecture, "The Russian Economic School: In the Search for Self-definition", Abalkin made very clear what was at stake in the debate:

> The question of a Russian school of economic thought . . . has come up relatively recently. It is in many ways connected with the reconsideration of Russian history, the awareness of her past and the concern about her future caused by today's crisis. It is also influenced by the attitude towards the attempts to obtrude upon her doubtful recipes of modernisation which have completely failed.
>
> (Abalkin 2000b: 7)

To put it briefly, the thesis that there had been something like a "Russian school" of economics is scientifically unsustainable (see e.g. Avtonomov 2003; Shirokorad 2003). Russian economic thinkers such as Sergei Iu. Witte, Vladimir I. Lenin, Nikolai K. Mikhailovskii, Pyotr B. Struve and Aleksandr I. Chuprov, who, according to Abalkin, all belonged to the "Russian school" (Abalkin 2000b: 31–32), were in fact adherents of different currents of thought, and their Russian nationality was the only thing they had in common (Shirokorad 2003). Moreover, the outstanding Russian liberal economist P. Struve (1870–1944) probably turned in his grave when Abalkin attributed to him the view of "the primacy of national, and, what is the same [*sic*], socially justified (politico-economic) interests over individual interests" (Abalkin 2000b, 21) – a view which Abalkin regarded as the main feature of this "school".

Unsurprisingly, the supporters of a national economics[17] often referred to Friedrich List (Martynov 2003b: 89; L'vov 2005: 8) and the German historical schools[18] (Val. Radaev2004: 32–33; Kul'kov 2004: 51–52) as examples of successful integration of national features into economic theory. As a result of the discussion, the ministry of education included "national economics" in the economics curriculum of Russian universities in 1999 (Zemliakov 2000: 75); but the definition was so vague that the authors of the first textbooks (Gradov 1997/2005; Vinogradov 2002; Savchenko 2005; Kudrov 2007) found themselves confronted with the task of defining precisely what this course was about. The following definition from the first textbook by Aleksandr P. Gradov (1997/2005: 43) illustrates how the image of a "national economy" was embedded in organismic patterns of thought that aimed at emphasising the unity of polity, economy, and national culture:

> The national economy – this is the economy of the country, its composition, structure, interdependence among its single elements . . . The country . . . acts as the organisational foundation: the economic activity of individuals, groups, the state, are all characterised by their integration and a certain degree of interdependence.

With the nationalist turn and the reappraisal of the planned economy in the early years of the new millennium, the discussion on the perceived strengths of Soviet-style political economy compared with economics, which had started in the mid-1990s, gained momentum. The first formal sign was an open letter to the Ministry of Education published in 2002 in the weekly journal *Ekonomika i zhizn* (Abalkin et al. [2002] 2003) signed by a group of prominent Russian economists (among them Abalkin and Aganbegian). The authors bemoaned the monopoly position of Western mainstream economics at Russian universities, argued that only political economy allowed to "systematically approaching the economy as a national, social economy and the problems related to the challenges of the information revolution and globalisation" and thus called for putting political economy back into the economics curricula.

In contrast to the debate of the 1990s, the supporters of Soviet-style political economy now explicitly referred to its founding father Nikolai A. Tsagolov*, chair of the faculty of political economy at Lomonosov University, Moscow, from 1957 to 1985. Tsagolov, certainly not a gifted scholar, but equipped with excellent organisational skills and the political instinct needed to make a career in the most ideological of Soviet sciences (Fomin 2006: 182), had first published the methodological programme of his economic theory of "developed socialism" in the official Party organ *Kommunist* in 1961 (Tsagolov 1961). His influential textbook *Kurs politicheskoi ekonomii* was first published in 1963.[19] In 2004, some of his former students published a collection of articles in praise of Tsagolov and his school (Dzarasov, Menshikov and Popov 2004).

The supporters of Soviet-style political economy based their rejection of Western economics both on methodological and on practical arguments. In terms of methodology, the criticism was mainly directed against the abstractness of Western mainstream economics (Zemliakov 2000: 76; Porokhovskii and Khubiev 2005: 32). Further, its Russian critics argued that its intrinsic coherence was based on the strict separation of the economy from all other social affairs. In contrast to this, and very much in line with the anthropocentric and holistic tradition of the Slavophile/populist current of Russian social philosophy, the authors of a special issue of the economics series of the "Messenger of Moscow University" dedicated to the tradition of Economics at the Lomonosov University argued that political economy in the spirit of Tsagolov had chosen "social" instead of "economic" man and the assumption of the "organic unity" [*tselostnost'*] of the economic system as its starting point (w/o author 2005: 10; similar Salikhov 2006: 11; Voeikov 2003: 103). Being based on materialism and utilitarianism, Western economics lacked a solid philosophical basis, according to some authors (Malakhinova 2003: 75; Kulikov 2004: 45). In particular, according to Iurii Osipov*, editor of the series on *Economic Theory at the Threshold of the 21st Century/Economic Theory in the 21st Century*, the "superficial" approach of Western economics could be contrasted with the "philosophical-essential" methodology of Soviet/Russian political economy (Osipov 1996: 8, 1998: 6). Another point that was – rather unsurprisingly – often criticised, was that economics lacked a "concept of the fundamental laws of development of contemporary economic systems and the system of economic relations" (Salikhov 2006: 10; Porokhovskii and Khubiev 2005: 16).

In political terms, it was now increasingly often argued that the outcome of the reforms had served as proof of the deficiency of the neoclassical paradigm (Buzgalin 2003: 114; Zhuravlova 2003: 84), which had been forced on Russia in the 1990s (Zemliakov 2000: 76; Kulikov 2004: 55). From their point of view, the broader and more complex methodology of political economy allowed for a deeper understanding of transition. It cannot be considered a coincidence, Kaisyn Khubiev* (2004: 43) claimed, that the first Russian textbook on the Russian transitional economy had been written by two representatives of the Tsagolov school.[20] The Chinese example demonstrated that it was possible to base transition on Marxist political economy, and the methodology of the Tsagolov school could have provided the foundation for a successful gradualist strategy (Khubiev 2003: 97).

The representatives of the school denied that Soviet political economy had been isolated from international science.[21] First of all, the foundation of the Tsagolov school of political economy coincided with the rise of the "new political economy" in the Western world (Kul'kov 2004: 49), and the increasing interest in "political economy" (public choice) in the West provided clear evidence of the topicality of the Tsagolov school (Porokhovskii 2003: 65). This last point clearly shows how little these authors knew about Western theories, as a stronger contrast between two methodological approaches than that between Public Choice and the Political Economy of the Tasgolov school is hard to imagine.

Russian economic science on the retreat from international discourse

The period under review in this chapter marks the end of any attempts of the political economy camp to re-integrate into the international scientific community. From now on, this camp openly rejected Western economics and explicitly returned to the ideational paths that had their beginnings in the thaw period in the Soviet Union. As empirical research shows, Russian economics today is not much more integrated into global economics than it was at the end of the 1980s. One might find this judgement too pessimistic and feel that a significant part of the problem might still be due to the difficulties of the older generation of Russian economists to adapt to modern, Western economics. However, this seems not to be the case. In our content analysis of current Russian doctoral dissertations (roughly an equivalent of a German/Austrian *Habilitation*),[22] Alexander Libman and I (2014) found that in these works of younger to middle-aged Russian economists, Adam Smith is by far the most frequently quoted author (followed by John Maynard Keynes and Karl Marx). Moreover, among the thirty authors most often quoted in Russian *doktorskie dissertatsii* only two – Gary Becker and Josef Stiglitz – are among the authors most often quoted by international economists. It deserves mention here that Becker's and Stiglitz's works have been translated into Russian, which also makes them accessible to those (in our estimation the vast majority) Russian economists who do not have proper English reading skills. The same applies to the methods used by the authors of Russian second dissertations. Whereas – for good or evil – international economics is strongly dominated by econometric methods, no more than 15% of authors of *doktorskie dissertatsii* made use of quantitative empirical methods. To be very explicit about this, with the majority of younger to middle-aged Russian economists showing no sign of integration into the international community, it is obvious that today's Russian economics students – at least outside the few lighthouses of modern science (Moscow, St. Petersburg, Ekaterinburg) – are receiving an education which does not reflect the state of the art of modern economic science.

Notes

1 See Sutela (2012: 89–97) for a careful assessment.

2 To make things worse, Russia had even fallen behind emerging markets such as India, China and South Korea, countries that had until recently been subject to Soviet development aid (Grigor'ev 2003: 101; Iasin 2007: 7).

3 As Valerii V. Poliakov (2006: 88) observed, the "romantic-utopian" idea of a Russian third way between Westernisation and domestic traditions had by now lost much of its appeal.

4 In one of his last interviews, Egor Gaidar (2009) said that he regarded the introduction of the Stabilisation Fund as one of the most important achievements of his career.

5 O'Sullivan is the correct spelling of the author's name but it was missspelled "O'Sallivan" in the book.

6 References here are to the second edition from 2001.

7 Kirdina's main contribution was to formulate Bessonova's basic idea in a more catchy terminology and style. In 2007, Bessonova explicitly criticised Kirdina for plagiarism of her ideas.

8 In the first edition she spoke of "Eastern" and "Western" matrices, terms she then substituted with X and Y in order to underline the general character of her concept. Without providing any explanation for this, she argues that the terms "Eastern" and "Western" or "X" and "Y" also stand for "female" and "male" (Kirdina 2001: 63).

9 "Immutability is the fundamental characteristic of institutional matrixes, constituting in the last order the specificity and significance of the theory of institutional matrixes" (Kirdina 2001: 70). See also Kirdina (2004: 96), Bessonova, Kirdina and O'Sullivan (1996: 11) and Bessonova (2006: 6, 12).

10 The term *mankurt*, stemming from a Turkic myth, was popularised by Soviet writer Dzhingis Aitmatov (1928–2008) in his novel *I dol'she veka dlitsia den'* (*The Day Lasts More Than a Hundred Years*). A *mankurt* is a person who in order to adapt to foreign influences loses her or his cultural identity. In the context of growing nationalism, the term has recently appeared more and more often in the Russian print media.

11 Another typical example is: "*Gosplan* of the SU put forward, substantiated and accomplished the solution of current and strategic challenges of industrial development, and on the basis of these very solutions formulated intentions, priorities and proportions of the five-year and annual economic plans" (Gubanov 2007: 7).

12 According to Ivanchenko and Ivanchenko (2005: 4): "there had not been a breakdown of the socialist economy. What happened was a self-transformation of a system of governance that had been deformed for different reasons (internal and external) and a search for a model more adequate to modern conditions of economising and economic development". For Senchagov, there was no doubt that the breakdown of the USSR was the result of purposeful actions of the Western powers, and in his view this had to be considered the "main lesson" of the 1980s for today's Russia. For a third example: "The modernising function of the Russian idea called to life under Stalin seemed dangerous to the enemies of our country. Given the opportunity to control the actions of our 'reformers', they made an effort to shape the economy of our country in such a way, that this function was suppressed. By doing so, a 'crusade' in the name of renewing Russia was proclaimed" (Leskov 2004: 133).

13 When the article this chapter is based on was submitted to *Europe-Asia Studies*, I received a very interesting comment by one of the anonymous referees: "I believe his scepticism about market reform began very early in the 1990s, though evidently at some point after he had written Khanin (1992). I met him in Moscow in late 1993 and went with him to visit . . . Vasilii Seliunin. Seliunin should, incidentally, be credited as Khanin's co-author of 'Lukavaia tsifra'. Khanin was very worried that his views had evolved to the point where he might fall out with his former co-author: Seliunin remained a completely convinced free market liberal. (In the event, Khanin need not have worried; Seliunin was unperturbed by the divergence in their views.) I can't cite documents, I'm afraid, but it was clear to me then that Khanin already had major doubts about the character of policy under the 'young reformers'".

14 The blurred lines between polity and economy, the liberal economists argued, find their clearest expression in the institution of the "state holding" in which the state passes state property over to private hands but is able to exert significant influence on strategic management decisions (Nikolaev et al. 2005: 60–61).

15 For a similar argument, see Tsvetkov and Dzhumov (2007: 36).

16 In 2002, Russia had occupied the 71st position in the Transparency International country ratings, while in 2007 it had dropped to position 143rd.

17 Key contributions were Zemliakov (2000), Sorokin (2001), Dement'ev (2002), Kul'kov (2004).

18 The economists of the German historical schools had explicitly regarded themselves as *Nationaloekonomen*, that is, national economists.

19 Second and third editions came out in 1970 and 1973, respectively.

20 The author refers to Val. Radaev and Buzgalin (1995); see last chapter.

21 In contrast, Matveenko and Zhelesniak (2005: 44) argued that the Soviet Union had been something of a protected area for this kind of political economy, and Andrei Zaostrovtsev (2008: 175) shows that the Tsagolov school did not have the slightest impact even on Western Marxian economics.

22 The advantage of these works is that they provide a very detailed picture of the scientific work of younger Russian economists at average Russian universities.

7 A new transition debate: 2007–2012

2007 as a turning point

The year 2007 marks an important turning point regarding Russia's relationship to the West and its trajectory of economic development. At his speech at the 43rd Munich Security Conference on 9 February, Vladimir Putin had – harshly criticising the NATO – made it unmistakably clear that Russia was not willing to accept a "monopolar world order". In terms of economic policy, 2007 saw the establishment of so-called "development institutions" and thus another visible policy shift towards state-led development.

From then on, the issue of a medium to long term strategy for Russia's development was also at the centre of Russian academic debates on economic policy. In the background of this discussion was the fear that Russia could have permanently lost its position among the leading nations of the world.[1] By 2007, it was obvious that the economy was stagnant and that the growth of the preceding years had done little if nothing to promote qualitative improvements. Throughout the period under review here, in Russian economic science there was a widespread consensus that the last few years had been marked by "growth without development" (Grinberg 2008: 57; Prazdnov 2011: 15; Kudrov 2012: 29), that the Russian economy was in a state of "*zastoi*" (Kudrov 2009: 126; Orekhovskii 2009: 99; Molchanov and Molchanova 2010; Iasin, Akindinova, Iakobson and Iakovlev (2013: 25) so that new concepts or even a new "paradigm" (Gref 2009: 29; Nabiullina 2009: 75; Grinberg 2012: 32) were needed to foster a new perestroika (Prazdnov 2011: 15; Glaz'ev 2012: 4) or "transition" (Sorokin 2011a: 29; Nabiullina 2009: 83). Among Russian economists was a widespread critique that the government was lacking "a unified understanding about the sources of growth and the methods of its stimulation", as a result of which contradictory compositions of individually correct measures were accomplished again and again (Tsentr Razvitiia 2009: 86; similar see Auzan and Satarov 2012: 66; Kudrov 2009: 125). In the harsh words of Evsei Gurvich (2013: 29),

> the attempts to stimulate economic growth by means of palliative measures while maintaining high state expenditures represents probably the greatest risk for the Russian economy for the next years.

Although in the scientific community there was a consensus that something had to be done: regarding the right strategy to solve the obvious problems, the gap between the different camps proved to be as wide as in the early 1990s. From a constructivist perspective, the inconsistency of Russian economic policy can at least partly be seen as an expression of the ongoing clashes between conflicting patterns of thought in Russian economics. In the words of Ruslan Grinberg* et al. (2007: 3):

> Russia is at a crossroads again. She is ready for changes, and everybody is asking for changes, but everybody has a different idea of what these changes should look like.[2]

In my view, two points stand out as important characteristics of the period from 2007 to 2012. First, the modernisation/innovation debate clearly illustrates how deep the gap between the two thought collectives in Russian economic science still is. As we will see, the participants of the debate, usually without making their particular understanding explicit, filled the terms "innovation" and "modernisation" with rather heterogeneous, often opposed, content. The same was true for the evaluation of economic policy concepts; some praised the transition to state led development strategy as a long overdue "Southkoreanisation", while others condemned it as a dangerous "Venezuelanisation" (Neshchadin et al. 2007: 5). Second, there are striking parallels between this debate and the economic policy debates during the Brezhnev period. On the one hand, it is obvious to most scholars and analysts that fundamental change is needed to prevent a further decline of the Russian economy. On the other, the political and economic elite (and in today's Russia, the economically and politically powerful form one unified group; see e.g. Kudrov 2009: 41) is not interested in fundamental change which they regard mainly as a danger for their power positions and the rents generated. In this constellation, theories that emphasise the role of the state in promoting structural change come in handy to defend rents against the threat of creative destruction that would result from market-led structural change.[3]The government, not least by issuing an impressive number of strategy papers on medium to long term development,[4] therefore promotes an intense pseudo-modernisation discourse and tends to restrict the issue of innovation/modernisation to its technological dimension.

Modernisation/innovation was a heavily politicised topic, and it has to also be seen in the context of a certain tension between the "innovation" and "stability" camps among the Russian elites. The divide can loosely be associated with the names of Dmitrii Medved'ev and Vladimir Putin, but much speaks in favour of the interpretation that it mainly regarded the presidential advisors (or the "circles" around the presidents) rather than the presidents themselves. In view of the embeddedness of the debate in political struggles, in this chapter I also look at policy reports, newspaper articles and internet sources. The chapter also differs slightly from the previous ones in that instead of giving a broader overview of the evolution of economic ideas and debates it concentrates on the discussion of modernisation and innovation which dominated the discourse in Russia between 2007 and 2012 (i.e. during and immediately after the period when

Dmitrii Medved'ev was president). Accordingly, the Russian discussion about the economic and financial crisis of 2008 and 2009 will be dealt with only insofar as it was relevant for the modernisation/innovation debate.[5]

This chapter is organised into two parts, the first of which deals with the academic debate and concentrates on the conflicting patterns of thought on the basis of which different meanings were attributed to the terms "innovation" and "modernisation". It will also look into the debate about re-industrialisation, which paved the way to the strategy of import-substitution which, especially after the implementation of Western sanctions, has been widely applied since 2014. The second major point puts the debate into its political context. In this section, I will illustrate how the "party of power", *Edinaia Rossiia*, and the stabilisation camp around Vladimir Putin handled the challenge of the innovation campaign initiated by Dmitrii Medved'ev in 2009.

Conflicting concepts of innovation and modernisation

As already mentioned, a key problem with the debate was that different authors had very different understandings of "modernisation" and "innovation" without being explicit about their particular definitions of the terms. As Tatiana Zaslavskaia (2011: 14) observed, the heterogeneity of concepts and understandings partly emerged out of the habit of many authors to use the terms to describe those changes they found desirable. In my view it also reflected the fact that up to the present day in Russia the demarcation line between economics and the other social sciences is still less strictly drawn than in Western economics. A short overview of the way the terms "modernisation" and "innovation" are usually used in economics and in the social sciences will hopefully help to avoid confusion in the present chapter.[6]

Modernisation and innovation in economics and in sociology

Economists (see e.g. Aghion and Howitt 2009) mainly understand modernisation as catch-up development, that is, a process in which "backward" countries try to imitate the technologies and products of "advanced" countries. Innovation, in contrast, is understood by most economists as a spontaneous process of "creative destruction" as a result of which new technologies and products emerge. Promoting the emergence of innovations is the fitting development strategy for emerging markets that are already close to the "frontier" of technological progress. For countries going through catch-up development, it is crucial to find the right timing of the shift from a modernisation to an innovation strategy. This shift can be politically difficult to accomplish, as modernisation often takes place in vertical and rather centralised structures, which tend to pose obstacles to innovation in the Schumpeterian sense. Accordingly, for economists, modernisation is a rather narrow term, as it relates to an effectively economic and technological matter, whereas innovations are bound to a political and social context that does not only equip agents with human capital but also provides them with the freedom they need for various kinds of experimentation.

For social scientists, the term "modernisation" is associated with modernisation theory which (at least in its original form) equates development with "becoming equal to today's Western developed countries" and, more importantly in our context, emphasises the complex interplay between the different parts of society in this process. For those following this understanding of modernisation, it is an all-encompassing concept (and among Russian economists often critically) associated with a Eurocentric normative bias on development processes. At the same time, those Russian economists who stand in the tradition of Marxist political economy rather than of the Western economics tradition, in general tend to have a low opinion (and, some would argue, a lack of understanding) of spontaneous processes. Therefore, to them, innovation is not so much something that automatically emerges if certain institutional prerequisites are given, but more a technological matter that can be promoted by industrial policy. It follows suit that in this interpretation, modernisation is the broader concept (dealing with the social and political context of economic processes), whereas innovation is a narrow economic and technological term.

Note that from the background of these different understandings, both a liberal and a Marxist author could speak out in favour of innovation and against modernisation meaning opposing things. The liberal demands deepening political and social change and warns against reducing the matter of innovation to its technological side, whereas the Marxist speaks out precisely in favour of such a narrow understanding of innovation and warns against political and social "destabilisation" that would be caused by modernisation qua democratisation.

The "coalitions for modernisation" debate

The debate on modernisation and innovation started with the "Coalitions for Modernisation" program initiated by the association of liberal economists SIGMA.[7] The discussion took off in the January number 2008 of *Voprosy ekonomiki*.[8] The idea of "modernisation coalitions" had been developed by Leonid Grigor'ev* and SIGMA (Grigor'ev et al. 2007). The basic idea was that in view of the previous unsuccessful reform efforts, new ways had to be found to gain public support for social and economic change. More important than the concept itself is how Grigor'ev and Tambovtsev (2008: 59) substantiated the motivation behind it:

> The general objectives of Russian modernisation in 2008 do not in principle differ from the objectives of transition in 1991; a democratic development of society; convergence of the wealth of citizens to European standards; a re-organisation of government in order to increase the efficiency of its institutions both for the successful solution of internal tasks and the accomplishment of competitiveness in the system of international relations.

A common feature of the contributions to the "modernisation coalitions" discussion (and this also became "state of the art" in the "official" policy papers on medium term development, see below) was the distinction made between different development scenarios (Tambovtsev 2008; Shastitko, Afontsev and Plaksin 2008; Grigor'ev, Plaksin and Salikhov 2008). The scenarios "inertia", "rentier", "mobilisation" and "modernisation" boiled down to the (sometimes explicit, sometimes implicit) reproach that the government had practiced "inertia" and had thus missed the opportunity to use the oil and gas boom for promoting structural change. This went hand in hand with the demand to proceed with a policy of modernisation which, according to these authors, had to be based on structural change and private entrepreneurship. The "coalitions for modernisation" debate clearly illustrates that the different interpretations of "modernisation" were not too tightly related to ideological positions. These liberals definitely had a broad "sociological" understanding of modernisation in mind when they demanded structural change. However, even though the basic idea was that institutional change had not kept pace with the high growth rates of GDP, all in all a certain optimism that this problem could be solved by not too radical a correction of political strategy seemed to have prevailed.[9] Note that a "re-organisation of government" in order to increase its efficiency is something entirely different from calls for fundamental changes of the political system as they were to come up pretty soon.

Discussions within the liberal camp

Possibly hoping for a window of opportunity, directly after the presidential elections in April 2008, the liberal camp started including the "modernisation/innovation" topic in the political agenda. On 8 April the daily newspaper *Nezavisimaia gazeta* (Sergeev 2008) quoted the then minister of economic development (and current head of the Russian Central Bank) Elvira Nabiullina with a statement that

> the growth model of the last eight years has already exhausted itself, [moreover one faces the situation that, JZ] Russia does not increase its global competitiveness, the structure of exports is frozen, and the foci of growth bear local character.[10]

This opportunity was seized by liberal economists Ksenia Iudaeva and Evgenii Iasin (2008) in the May edition of *Voprosy ekonomiki*. A system based on the "vertical of power", they argued, was appropriate for catch-up development but not for "development at the technological frontier" which Russia had now reached.

The divide concerning the issue of whether Russia was still in a process of catching-up or already had to rely on its own innovations moved directly through the ideological camps. "Russia in the XXI Century: Image of a Desirable Future", a 66-page strategy paper published in 2010 by the Institute of Contemporary Development (*Institut sovremennogo razvitiia*; INSOR) was perhaps the clearest formulation of the position of those liberals who believed that Russia's transition to an innovative knowledge society should be accomplished as quickly as possible. The paper was authored by Igor Iurgens* (the Director of INSOR) and Evgenii Gontmakher*, two liberal economists who were politically close to Medved'ev.[11] The message of "Russia in the XXI Century" is rather straightforward:

> The problem lies in the conditions, in the environment. If these same people abroad do marvels in creative work and become heroes of innovation, then the problem lies in institutions and practices. In this century, the innovation manoeuvre for Russia has its rise not even in investment, business incubators or techno parks, but rather in removing the obstacles and discharging the ballast, primarily on the part of the government. . . . The task is to create an economy generating innovations and not to generate innovations to tortuously introduce them into the economy.
>
> (INSOR 2010: 17)

While this passage regarding the economic strategy of modernisation is key, the authors also argued that "full-fledged modernisation programs of the post-industrial age are not realisable in principle given the lack of freedom" (ibid.: 8) and accordingly demanded a fundamental reformation of the political system (see also Sorokin 2011b).

The harshest among the reactions to the INSOR paper was that delivered by liberal economist Vladislav Inozemtsev* (2010) and bore the short and blunt title "Anti-Iurgens". Inozemtsev castigated the idea of Russia's imminent transition to a post-industrial society[12] as "utopian". In an earlier publication he had already poured scorn onto those who dreamed about Russia becoming a technological leader in the foreseeable future:

> An economy producing ten airliners a year, unable to launch a radically new model of a passenger car, and virtually non-existent on the market for personal computers, mobile communication and office equipment, is unlikely to become an innovation leader.
>
> (Inozemtsev 2009: 9)

Accordingly, he had demanded a catch-up strategy of new industrialisation combined with a systematic integration into the global economy.[13] In his reaction to the INSOR report, however, he concentrated on the political dimension of the matter and insisted that

> there is nothing more valuable for strengthening authoritarianism in the context of the coming economic recovery than allowing for democratisation in the context of the present economic decline. Today, Russian liberals should not demand democracy, but rather modernisation.[14]

The position of the gosudarstvenniki

For many of the economists trained in and still faithful to Soviet political economy, an "innovative economy" was not only a stage of economic development but a stage in social evolution in a much broader sense. As used by the *gosudarstvenniki*, it has to be seen as a link in a chain that leads from "developed socialism", "socialism with a human face" and "the post-industrial society" to the "innovative stage".[15] The Marx-oriented authors harshly criticised the depiction of Russia as a "backward" country facing the task of catching-up (e.g. Senchagov 2008: 121). To them, the Soviet planned economy had represented a higher developmental stage than capitalism. This perspective was amplified by a nationalist perspective in which the idea of catching-up was "not acceptable" for a country that "is able and should fight for an equal place in the highest league of world powers" (Maslennikov 2012a: 10). Instead of catching-up, Sergey Glaz'ev* (2012: 5–6), who has been the informal "spokesman" of the *gosudarstvenniki* since the early 1990s (see on Glaz'ev: Aslund 2013), argued that everything possible had to be done to directly acquire the technologies of the "fifth technological formation" which was just about to emerge. In short, these authors delivered yet another version of the idea of leap-frogging which occupied Russian thinkers from the times of Petr Chaadaev, Alexander Herzen and Nikolai Chernyshevskii.

However, there was now a significant shift in this discourse. The very same authors who for years had never tired of calling for Russia's transition into a post-industrial society now demanded a resolute state-led re-industrialisation of the country. This neo-Marxist discourse mainly took place on the pages of *Ekonomist*, the previous official organ of *Gosplan*. The content of this neo-Soviet debate effectively boiled down to the slogan "neo-industrialisation plus vertical integration" (Gubanov 2009) in order to achieve a new "integration of production, science and education" (Bodrunov 2015). At this point it is important to note that the idea of protectionism was visibly prevalent in this discussion, which can thus be seen as an important stepping stone towards import substitution.

The strengthening of economic nationalism also found an institutional reflection in the founding of an "Institute of new industrial development in the name of S. Iu. Witte" in St. Petersburg in 2011. The institute, allegedly founded on the private initiative of economists and economic practitioners, is headed by Sergei D. Bodrunov, a former politician. It received official state acknowledgement in 2011 and is now part of the system of the Russian Academy of Sciences. The institute publishes the journal *Russian Economic Renaissance* which has, apart from *Ekonomist*, become the main organ for what one may call Russian industrial nationalism.

In my view, two things are remarkable about the *gosudarstvennikis'* position on modernisation and innovation. First, it is striking to see the degree of overlap between the ideas of this camp and that of the then "progressive" economists of the Brezhnev period. In a collection of articles on *The Innovative Development of Russia,* edited by the "Russian Presidential Academy of National Economy and Public Administration" (the Rector of which is no less a figure than Vladimir Mau) Genadii Prazdnov (2011: 9) wrote:

> Innovative development is a part of the state's economic policy providing the enhancement of productive efficiency based on its intensification on all sides and by all means. Intensification is thereby a way to secure faster growth of the final product as compared to the costs of obtaining this product.

Not only is this definition of "innovative development" at odds with everything one could possibly read in a modern economics textbook, the connection with "intensification", one of the central topics of the economic debates under Brezhnev, is puzzling indeed. Second, it is notable how radically the *gosudarstvenniki* reduced the problem to its technological side and denied the very possibility of the spontaneous emergence of innovations. For example, A. A. Maslennikov (2012a: 7) explicitly criticised the equation of innovative development "with so-called modernisation" (having in mind a sociological understanding of modernisation) and made it plainly clear that to him "innovation" was an exclusively technological matter (Maslennikov 2012b: 349):

> What is at issue, first and foremost, is the creation of favourable conditions for capital formation and for the investment of this capital into the most high-tech and core industries, for doing research and training engineering and technical staff as well as highly-qualified workers.[16]

A. V. Kiva went a step further than that by calling for a "mobilising" strategy of modernisation and in this context positively referring to the large modernisation projects (a la "virgin soil", "intensification" and so on). As she argued:

> In other words, this [a liberal concept of, JZ] modernisation is such that excludes the mobilisation of society for the country's jump into the new economy – of the sort that happened in Japan, South Korea and is currently happening in China.
>
> (Kiva 2011: 42)

However, the most explicit denial of innovation as a spontaneous process was formulated by N. I. Ivanova, the editor of another collection of articles on innovation, published by the Institute of the World Economy and International Relations of the Russian Academy of Sciences.[17] In the introduction of the volume, she writes that the study is on "diversification, modernisation, innovatisation (*innovatizatsiia*)" (Ivanova 2010: 7) and later on defines the "innovatisation of the economy" as the "enhancement of innovative activity" (ibid.: 13). There is, in my view, no clearer a term than "innovatisation" to illustrate how deep the gap between certain strata of the Russian economics discourse and their Western counterparts is after twenty-five years of post-Soviet reforms.

The political dimension of the debate

In February 2008, in his speech at the Krasnoiarsk Economic Forum, the then presidential candidate Dmitrii Medved'ev had put forth his idea of the "Four I's" (institutions, infrastructure, innovation and investment) (Kosobokova 2008). One and a half years later, in an article "Forward, Russia!" (*Rossiia vperyod*!), which was published on 9 September 2009 in the Russian internet newspaper *gazeta.ru*, focusing on "five priorities of technological development", Medved'ev (2009a) made it clear that to him innovation was mainly a matter of technology. However, he also stated that "of course, an innovative economy does not emerge immediately. It is a part of culture, based on humanistic values".[18]

Conservative modernisation versus innovation

This latter aspect of the innovation agenda posed a problem not only for Vladimir Putin's camp, which saw it as a threat to stability, but also for the "party of power", *Edinaia Rossiia*, which portrayed itself as a conservative political force. In November 2009, that is, directly after Medved'ev had published his "Forward, Russia" article, at its 11th party congress, *Edinaia Rossiia* proclaimed its strategy of "conservative modernisation" (Ivanov 2009). In light of the fact that in 1998 the well-known demographer and economist Anatolii Vishnevskii* (1998) had published a much-recognised book *Sickle and Ruble. Conservative Modernization in the USSR*, this was a rather strange rhetorical choice. For Vishnevskii had shown in historical detail why a strategy of "technological and material progress based on traditional social institutions" (as Boris N. Mironov [2000: 333] defined Soviet modernisation) in the long run was doomed to fail. In April 2010, Vishnevskii (2010) reacted to *Edinaia Rossiia* in a speech on "The Traps of Conservative Modernisation" he gave at the Higher School of Economics on the occasion of his 75th birthday.

In my view, there is a certain analogy between the concept of "conservative modernisation" and that of "developed socialism" of the early 1970s, with which the politburo reacted to the increasingly far-reaching demands of reform-minded economists. As has been argued in chapter three, this concept was an attempt to channel the reform debate by reducing reforms to their technological side and by depicting them as improvements within the existing political and social order. As this amounted to technological modernisation within the given institutional framework, the concept of "developed socialism" had been inseparably connected with Soviet "conservative modernisation". However, there are important differences here, too. For one, the slogan "developed socialism" appeared after at least five years of intense discussion on economic reforms, whereas "conservative modernisation" was pulled out of the hat at a rather early stage in the debate. Also, as *Edinaia Rossiia* operated in a different political system than the Soviet Communist Party, it simply did not have the power and resources to suppress an unsolicited discussion.

Under the impression of the worldwide financial and economic crisis, the innovation debate turned into a true transition debate. In its course, the liberal participants of the debate more and more openly addressed the question of whether it was the political system that formed the main obstacle to the urgently needed economic changes. In a newspaper article that was published in *Vedomosti* in March 2010, Igor Bunin, head of the Centre for Political Technology, reported how the discussion at the Krasnoiarsk Economic Forum (at which in 2008 Medved'ev had held his "four I's" speech) had evolved over the previous years. Whereas in 2008 and 2009 it had still been restricted to the technological aspects of innovation, by 2010 this discussion had fully turned into a political one, causing, as Bunin observed, a "fear of perestroika" among the political elites (Bunin 2010).

The former editor of *Obshchestvo i ekonomika,* one of the major Russian economics journals, Konstantin Mikul'skii (2009), put forth a furious critique of the Putin system: The fusion of political power and economic privileges, he argued, had let to a situation in which "status rents" had become the decisive form of economic income. As the current social order was based on "administrative-violent redistribution of the social product" rather than on "national-economic accumulation", a "democratic perestroika" was the prerequisite to economic modernisation as well. In a similar vein, A. Martynov (2009) argued that the established system of state capitalism bore a contradiction between the short-term interests of the predominantly rent-seeking entrepreneurs and the goals of development as officially declared. As a result of this inner contradiction, he argued, the current model was unlikely to establish itself lastingly and could thus be characterised as "transitory".

It was in this context of the question of how the political system related to the developmental prospects of the country that parallels to the Brezhnev period and the phenomenon of *zastoi* were more and more frequently drawn. As Piotr Orekhovskii (2009: 93–94) pointed out, a "transition from extensive to intensive production" (Brezhnev era) and "overcoming resource dependence and becoming an innovative economy" were basically one and the same problem. He argued that the transition was likely to fail now as it had then, because "any innovation is a redistribution of power and, as such, entails not only economic, but also social and political consequences" which had been as intolerable for the Soviet elites under Brezhnev as they were for the "system Putin".

One of the most detailed critiques of the Putin system was provided by a group of authors from the Institute of Sociology of the Russian Academy of Sciences led by Iurii A. Krasin (2011). Summarising the work of three years of round table discussions, the authors sharply rebuffed the idea of "conservative modernisation" as well as all attempts to restrict innovation to its technological side and made it plainly clear that they regarded a thorough democratisation of the political system as the all-important prerequisite for a transition to an "innovative type of development". In contrast to the term "innovative development", Krasin (2011: 59) and his co-authors argued, the term "modernisation" was "extremely indefinite", which made it a well suited rhetorical means to "hug to death" the discussion about the political foundations of innovative development.

Innovation and modernisation in presidential speeches

In fact, as Krasin et al. noted, after the outbreak of the crisis, in the official documents a semantic shift from "innovation" to the broader and fuzzier term "modernisation" (ibid.: 80–81) could be observed. A similar remark was made by Mikhail A. Bendikov and Igor E. Frolov (2011: 44), who observed a threefold shift of policy priorities from "growth" via "innovation" to "modernisation". "And back to growth" should be added here; surprisingly for many, in 2011 then Prime Minister Vladimir Putin suddenly returned to the quantitative approach to development when repeating his demand to double GDP within ten years which he had originally made in 2003. As the deep-running reforms of the 1990s had resulted in shrinking GDP, Putin was obviously trying to exploit fears among the population that a new wave of reforms might in the short to medium term lead again to a loss of stability.

In order to verify Krasin et al.'s claim about the semantic shift in official documents, here I conduct a simple empirical exercise. As I argued, in Russian politics there was a certain political tension between "innovation" and "stability" camps, where the key terms reflecting these agendas were "innovation", "modernisation", "stability" and "growth". On this list, "innovation" unequivocally stands for the "innovation" camp and "stability" and "growth" for the stability agenda. The term "modernisation" is less clear. First, as has been argued earlier in this chapter, in the academic debate the term was attributed a range of different meanings. Second, as has been illustrated in the last paragraph, in the political debate it was sometimes used to channel the innovation debate in order to free it from its potentially "subversive" aspects. Using an extremely simple, but as I believe quite instructive empirical strategy, I have counted the number of times these four terms are mentioned in Medved'ev's and Putin's annual presidential addresses to the Federal Assembly (table 7.1).[19]

It is plain to see how the concepts of innovation and modernisation enter the political discourse in 2009. We also see clearly that the political tension between the innovation and the stability camps should not too tightly be connected to the names of Medved'ev and Putin, for as early as 2010 a shift from the potentially "subversive" term "innovation" to the much more ambiguous concept of "modernisation" took place. At the same time, there was certainly a rather sharp change after Putin was re-elected in 2012, with Putin not mentioning innovation at all and with "growth" being mentioned fourteen (!) times as compared to three times in 2011 and only once in 2010.[20]

Table 7.1 Innovation, modernisation, growth and stability in the presidential addresses to the Federal Assembly, 2008–2013.

Document	*Innovation*	*Modernisation*	*Growth*	*Stability*
Medved'ev (2008)	6	4	7	2
Medved'ev (2009b)	16	22	4	8
Medved'ev (2010)	6	26	1	2
Medved'ev (2011)	3	14	3	6
Putin (2012b)	0	3	14	3
Putin (2013)	3	1	1	5

A "fear of perestroika"?

There is no doubt that the beginning of the "Arab Spring" in early 2011 and the mass demonstrations in Moscow and St. Petersburg in the second half of the year decisively amplified the "fear of perestroika" which Igor Bunin had already observed in early 2010. In January 2012, almost exactly four years after Medved'ev had proclaimed his "Four I's" strategy in *Vedomosti*, Vladimir Putin (still in his role as Prime Minister and presidential candidate) published an article "About our Economic Tasks" which almost reads as an official announcement of neo-*zastoi*. Note how clearly the aspect of change is subordinated to stability and how it is reduced to technology and economic policy (I am quoting from the introductory part of the article):

> We are living in a period of radical change in the global economy. Technology is being modernised [*obnovlialis'*, that is, renewed, not modernised, in original – JZ] faster than ever before . . . The struggle for global leadership has become more acute than ever before . . . In these circumstances we must ensure sustainable progressive development of our economy and try to shield our citizens from the hardships of crises as much as possible, while at the same time consistently and rapidly modernising [*obnovlenie*] all economic sectors, from the material and technical base to approaches to our economic policy.
> (Putin 2012a)[21]

The government's blatant retreat from reforms brought on a number of critical comments from the liberal camp. For example, Vladimir Mau titled his traditional report on economic policy of 2012, "Between *zastoi* and modernisation" and stated that the current macroeconomic situation as well as the economic discourse reminded him of "the situation in the USSR at the turn of the 1970s and '80s", explicitly pointing at the fine line between stability and *zastoi* (Mau 2013: 16–17). In similar fashion, in his summary of 2012, Viktor Starodubrovskii (2013) warned of a "possibly enduring *zastoi*" and closed his article with the furious assertion that it was more than palpable that the whole social and political system, with its "vertical of power" and the permanent violation of property rights were the root of the decline of the Russian economy.

On the whole I agree with the Russian liberals that today's Russia is in a neo-*zastoi* state. The numerous strategy papers and official declarations dealing with modernisation of the Russian economy mainly serve the aim of simulating reform activity. In fact, any deep-reaching structural change would endanger the volatile equilibrium between those who enjoy privileged access to rents and is thus intolerable to those in power. As Kriukov (2013) put it, in the current institutional environment innovation is still the grass trying to grow under asphalt paving. In this sense, things appear now to have come full circle since the Brezhnev period. However, this is a statement about the "real" economy, whereas my book deals predominantly with ideas. This leads us to the question I will deal with in the last chapter: Does the parallel between the Brezhnev years and the current situation hold for the ideational dimension too?

Notes

1 As Russian sociologist N.E. Tikhonova (2008: 5) put it: "In a rapidly changing and globalising world, which in the last decades has been entering a new stage of its development, the question looms large of the role Russia can possibly play on an international level. The answer to this question depends crucially upon successful completion of modernisation processes – both of the Russian economy and of Russian society at large".

2 In similar terms, Nikolai Petrakov (2010: 3) declared that "today the Russian political leadership for the third time attempts to establish capitalism in our contry", and Valentin M. Kudrov* (2011: 29) emphasised that this time a failure of renewal would have particularly severe consequences, as the population was tired of reforms.

3 This at least is the clearly dominant liberal mainstream position in today's Western economics. However, there are Western economists (especially in industrial economics) who emphasise the role of industrial policy for stimulating technological change which is intended in turn to promote innovation, see, for example, Mazzucato (2014).

4 Between 2006 and 2012 three official or semi-official strategy papers on medium to long run development were ordered by the government. The first of these reports, the *Kontseptsiia dolgosrochnogo razvtiia Rossiiskoi Federatsii na period do 2020 goda* (Conception of the Long-Term Development of the Russian Federation in the Period to 2020) [http://economy.gov.ru/minec/activity/sections/strategicPlanning/concept/] had been commissioned in July 2006 by President Putin, authored by the Ministry of Economic Development under the direction of Deputy Minister Andrei Klepach and adopted by the government on 17 November 2008, that is, at the very time when the worldwide financial and economic crisis transgressed to Russia. It looks quite obvious that a strategy paper published at the beginning of a deep crisis quickly needed to be adapted to the new reality. On 31 December 2010, under the title *Innovatsionnaia Rossiia – 2020: Strategiia razvtiia innovatsionnoi politiki* (Innovative Russia – 2020. Strategy of Innovative Development of the Russian Federation in the Period to 2020) [http://adm-edu.spb.ru/sites/default/files/innovacionnaya_rossiya_2020.pdf] a preliminary version of a new paper was published at the website of the Ministry of Economic Development. The final version, jointly prepared by the Ministry of Education and Science and the Higher School of Economics, was adopted only in December 2011. However, as the preliminary version was received rather infavorably, already in early 2011 Vladimir Mau (Russian Presidential Academy of National Economy and Public Administration) and Iaroslav Kuzminov (Higher School of Economics) were assigned to compile a new strategy report. *Strategiia 2020 – novaia model' rosta – novaia sotsial'naia politika* (Strategy 2020 – A New Growth Model – a New Social Policy) [http://2020strategy.ru/data/2012/03/14/1214585998/1itog.pdf] covers more than 500 pages and was handed in to the government in December 2011.

5 The "Round Table: The economic crisis in the world and in Russia: Lessons and ways to overcome" that was published in *Zhurnal novoi ekonomicheskoi assotsiatsii* (Kruglyi stol' 2009) provides a good introductory overview about the different theoretical and ideological positions.

6 For a good overview of the discussion from a political economy perspective see Sutela (2012: 82–89).

7 SIGMA stands for *Setevaia Institutionalistskaia Gruppa Modernizatsionnogo Analiza* (Network Institutionalist Group of Modernisation Analysis). For more information about the association, see their website www.sigma-econ.ru/; last accessed 24 June 2017.

8 In 2007, the same group had already published an extensive report (67 pages) on Coalitions for the Future. A Strategy for the Development of Russia in the Years 2008–2016. However, the special issue of *Voprosy ekonomiki* marked the starting point of the academic debate. At the same time, Andrei Iakovlev (2007) published a paper in which

he identified "agents of modernization" in the form of entrepreneurs, and (especially) medium-sized businesses, but also regional elites, and members of various business associations.

9 This was later acknowledged by Grigor'ev (2013: 34).

10 An assessment that soon was to become a kind of generally accepted wisdom (e.g. Kuchukov 2009: 3; Aganbegian 2011: 50).

11 Russia in the 21st century provided what was indeed the foundation for a further report, *Gaining the Future: Strategy-2012* (published in 2012), by the same authors which served as a kind of pre-election program for Medved'ev (Taratuta 2011).

12 This was certainly the ideal postulated by Iurgens and Gontmakher, who, however, explicitly acknowledged that at the same time a certain re-industrialisation was needed.

13 In a similar vein, Viktor Polterovich (2008: 11), one of the "heavyweights" of Russian economics, called Russia a "backward" country point-blank and said that in the decades to come the country would have to concentrate on catching-up. Iuri Kniazev (2012: 3) was no less outspoken when he mocked those of his colleagues who sought to "overtake the whole world, without catching up with anyone".

14 This warning certainly reflected the fear that for a second time in recent Russian history in the minds of the Russian population democratisation might become associated with economic turmoil, but Inozemtsev also explicitly referred to the general experience that "mature democratic regimes more often emerge from liberal autocracies than from non-liberal democracies" (ibid.).

15 The "innovative economy" was sometimes associated with precisely the characteristics Marxists had attributed to the Communist future: "The economy of profit will historically give way to the human economy of spare time. Rather than accumulating value, the society begins to accumulate aggregate spare time as a time of the creative labor, expended for making science an immediate productive force" (Gubanov 2009: 5).

16 Or, in the words of Abel Aganbegian (2010: 54): "in the coming years we have to be engaged in modernisation: to develop high-level processing of raw materials – petrochemistry, processing of wood etc. The development of machine manufacturing is drawing other industries with it: metal industry, electronics, etc.; we need to invest into large-scale housing and social construction. At the same time, we need to actively develop innovative industries: only when their share reaches 15–20% of the GDP can we talk of the transition to the innovative type of development".

17 Ivanova is currently a deputy director of this Institute.

18 In his address to the Federal Assembly dating from the 12th of November 2009, Medved'ev (2009b) still spoke of a "all-round modernisation" but at the same time clearly focused on the technological modernisation of the economy.

19 I am very grateful to Andrei Iakovlev for his suggestion to compare the presidential addresses. These addresses are roughly the same length, and I have thus abstained from relating the frequency of mentions to the numbers of pages of the individual addresses.

20 After the Crimea affair, the agenda of the presidential addresses changed dramatically. In 2014, from the four words, only "growth" was mentioned five times. In 2015, modernisation emerged only once and merely as "technological modernisation", while "growth" also got only one mention.

21 I cite the official translation: http://archive.premier.gov.ru/eng/events/news/17888/.

8 Conclusion

From *zastoi* to *zastoi*?

As stated in the introduction, the present book seeks to contribute both to a better understanding of Russia's current political and economic order and to the theoretical debate on ideas and institutions. In line with this double intention, in this brief chapter I summarize my main findings regarding these two aspects and as a third step ask what implications my study might have for other empirical cases.

In the centre of the recent debate between historical and constructivist institutionalists lies the structure/agency problem. As I argued in the second chapter, in their eagerness to demonstrate the causal influence of ideas on institutions, constructivist institutionalists tend to focus on empirical cases in which the problem of deep ideational backgrounds may be neglected. This is problematic, because it leads to a bias towards "success stories" (that is, cases in which it can be shown how new ideas did indeed lead to lasting institutional change) and restricts the generalisability of empirical findings. As a second problem, I identified the (often implicit) image of the relative homogeneity of prevailing ideas that form the basis of an institutional equilibrium. Closely related to this is the notion of institutional change as a short term disturbance of this equilibrium which sooner or later will be replaced with a new equilibrium of ideas and institutions.

In this context, the case of post-Soviet Russia provides an empirical counterfactual which is also relevant for the recent attempts of historical institutionalists to contextualise critical junctures. The story told in this book is mostly a story of a clash between imported neo-liberal policy ideas and deep ideational background ideas held by a significant portion of the country's intellectual elite. This clash did not lead to a complete rejection of imported ideas (which would have been a possible equilibrium) but rather to a deep ideational divide within economic science and the emergence of a conflict between the adherents of mutually incompatible thought styles. Very much in line with the predictions of constructivist institutionalism, the ideational disequilibrium translated into inconsistent economic policy and, as a result, into institutional instability. The example of the Russian Stabilisation Fund clearly illustrates how this translation of ideational into institutional instability worked. The fact that two thought collectives of roughly equal strength each provide a focal point for a shared interpretation of social reality (or certain aspects thereof) bears the danger of quick shifts from one equilibrium to another or to compromises which try to accommodate both interpretations and lead to hybrid (and usually contradictory) institutional arrangements.

Regarding the other major intention of this book, I should like to take up the question I asked in the last chapter, namely whether the story told in this book is a story of a development "from *zastoi* to *zastoi*". According to this interpretation, the attempt to shift the country from one equilibrium to another has failed, and since around 2004 we have seen a restoration of a social order which resembles that of the Soviet Union of the 1970s and early 1980s: The political and the economic systems are again so firmly interwoven that creative economic destruction becomes threatening to political stability and thus has to be politically prevented. Now as with then, this story continues; the political oppression of economic dynamics goes hand in hand with an intense official rhetoric of innovation and modernisation.

As I see it, my book partly supports this interpretation but also and perhaps more importantly, advises that caution be taken not to overemphasise the parallels between the Brezhnev period and today. From the perspective of my analysis, the question of whether behind the current social order in Russia stands a more or less stable dominant shared interpretation of social reality represents the litmus test for the neo-*zastoi* thesis. Over the last number of years, in the struggle between the two thought collectives there certainly has been a shift of weight in favour of the conservative camp. Nowhere does the parallel to the Brezhnev period become as obvious as in the modernisation/innovation debate which I have dealt with in the last chapter. However, this very debate also shows that the liberal camp has certainly been weakened but is still present in the economic and political discourse. The only way to achieve a further unification would be violent enforcement, that is, the further restriction of the freedom of speech. The emigration of Russian liberal economists Ekatarina Zhuravskaia, Sergei Guriev* and Konstanin Sonin indicates that during the last few years the pressure has significantly increased. In my view, however, the present degree of political oppression cannot be equated to that of the Brezhnev years.

The classification of today's Russia as neo-*zastoi* might also partly reflect the (Western) observers' search for a convenient, complexity-reducing label. Such labels tend to postulate equilibrium where, under the surface of stability, there is in fact substantial ideological heterogeneity and conflict.[1] The third and fourth chapter of this book in particular demonstrated the role of generational change for ideational change. From the perspective of this book, this question is a black box, but the message is again that things might be much less stable than they appear to be. Finally, it is obvious that the Russian economy is in dramatic decline. There are of course no simple mechanics between economic crises and paradigm shifts in economic thought, but at the same time economic ideas do not evolve independently of economic reality. Whether the economic decline will boost economic nationalism or lead to a return of more pro-market ideas is difficult to predict, but at least a comeback of more liberal ideas does not seem impossible.

One of the reasons why Western scientific observers tend to interpret processes of fundamental change in non-Western societies as a movement towards a new equilibrium may be the fact that they themselves live and were socialised in societies that are – both in terms of ideas and institutions – extremely stable compared to most other societies (Levitsky and Murillo 2009: 116). In my view, Russia is a prime example of a "backward" country that under Peter the Great started its catch-up development and from this time on has been struggling with the fundamental problem we still observe today. The import of Western ideas (which were thought to deliver the ideational foundation of the new social order) clashed with traditional patterns of thought, and there emerged an ideological divide among the intellectual elite which translated into institutional instability and hybridity of social institutions. I believe that this problem is likely to emerge wherever a "latecoming" nation imports (sometimes voluntarily, sometimes under pressure or even force) ideas and institutions from more "advanced" countries. At the same time, in each case the basic problem will take on specific forms that reflect specific cultural traits of the particular society, and these specific features can have an impact on how deep the clash between imported and domestic ideas runs. I argued that in the case of Russia two specific features of Russian Orthodoxy, anthropocentrism and holism, proved to be particularly incompatible with the Western European pattern of functional differentiation, thus amplifying the tensions between a Western and a non-Western camp and as a result making Russia's social evolution particularly volatile to external shocks. As I have shown, these patterns were indeed a common thread in the critique of the political economy camp of the capitalist order.

If constructivist institutionalism means to contribute to a better understanding of transformational processes in non-Western societies, it has to take the problem of deep ideational backgrounds more seriously than has been done until now. As these backgrounds are historically embedded, dealing with them makes it necessary to take the intellectual history of countries into account. I should like to stress that this methodological demand shall in no way be equated with a call for "re-sticking institutions" and "re-fixing preferences and norms" (to paraphrase Vivien Schmidt, see Chapter 2). Rather, in cases of large-scale institutional change in non-Western societies, it is a matter of necessity to take structural factors into account in order to develop an adequate understanding of agency. This, in my view, is not only a theoretical matter but one that is also of practical relevance. If my analysis is correct, a central problem of today's Russia is the divide among the intellectual elite. To achieve lasting institutional stability, it would be necessary to find some kind of compromise between the two shared interpretations of social reality. This is a classical challenge for political entrepreneurs acting as cultural innovators engaging in bricolage and bounded innovation in order to reconcile imported ideas with deep domestic ideational backgrounds (see Zweynert 2009).

Note

1 It was interesting to see that the Russian mass protests 2011–2013 came as a much bigger surprise to Western than to Russian observers.

Appendix
Biographical index

Abalkin, Leonid Ivanovich (1930–2011) Abalkin was an important representative of the Political Economy of Socialism and of the *shestidesiatniki* generation of Soviet/Russian economists, one of the idea providers of perestroika and in the second half of the 1980s, a close economic advisor to Mikhail Gorbachev. He was one of the main critics of liberal economic policy during the 1990s and 2000s as well as a spokesman for a state-centered strategy of economic development. In 1952, Abalkin graduated from the Plekhanov Institute of Economics, Moscow. 1962 *kandidat*, 1971 *doktor* of economic science. From 1976 to 1985 he served as professor and dean of the faculty of Political Economy at the Academy of the Social Sciences at the Central Committee of the Communist Party. Further, he worked as director of the Economics Institute of the Soviet/Russian Academy of Sciences from 1986 to 2005, deputy chairman of the Council of Ministers of the Soviet Union from 1989 to 1991, and member of the politburo of the CPSU from 1990–1991.

Aganbegian, Abel Gezevich (b. 1932) One of the key Soviet *shestidesiatniki* economists, Aganbegian belonged to the close economic advisors to Mikhail Gorbachev during the 1980s. In 1955, he graduated from the Moscow State Economic Institute. He was awarded the title of *doktor* of economic science in 1963. From 1964 to 1984 he was director of the Institute of Economics and the Organisation of Industrial Production of the Novosibirsk branch of the Soviet Academy of Sciences, and from 1989–2002 he was director of the Academy of Economics at the Government of the Russian Federation. In 1970 he initiated *EKO*, the most intellectually open Soviet economic journal, and he acted as editor-in-chief for many years thereafter.

Auzan, Aleksandr Aleksandrovich (b. 1954) One of the pioneers of New Institutional Economics in Russia. In 1979 Auzan graduated from the faculty of economics of Lomonosov University, Moscow. 1982 *kandidat*, 1991 *doktor* of economic science. Currently, professor of applied institutional economics and dean of the faculty of economics of Lomonosov University, Moscow.

Avtonomov, Vladimir Sergeevich (b. 1955) Studied economics at Lomonosov University, Moscow; *kandidat* of economics 1986, *doktor nauk* 1996; since 1997, professor at Higher School of Economics, Moscow, dean of the economics faculty from 2000–2011 and since 1997 has been a corresponding member of the Russian Academy of Science. Avtonomov works predominantly in the field of the history of economic thought.

Belousov, Andrei Removich (b. 1959) Economist and Politician. Belousov has been the chief economic advisor to Vladimir Putin since 2013. In 1981, he graduated from the faculty of economics of Lomonosov University, Moscow, and under the supervision of the reformist Soviet macroeconomists Aleksandr Anchishkin (1933–1987) and Iuri Iaremenko (1935–1996), he started to work at the Central Economic-Mathematical Institute of the Soviet Academy of Sciences. 1988 *kandidat*, 2006 *doktor* of economic science. In 1986, he began working at the newly established Institute of Economics and Forecasting of Scientific-Technological Progress (IEPNTP). In 2000, he founded the Centre of Macroeconomic Analysis and Short-term Forecasting (TSMAKP). In 2006 Belousov became Deputy Minister of Economic Development, followed by Minister of Economic Development in 2012.

Bessonova, Ol'ga Ernestovna (b. 1958) Economic sociologist and member of the Novosibirsk school of economic sociology, Bessonova graduated from the faculty of economic cybernetics of Novosibirsk State University in 1980. She has worked at the Institute of Economics and the Organisation of Industrial Production of the Novosibirsk branch of the Academy of Sciences since 1980. Bessonova completed her doctoral studies under supervision of → Tatiana Zaslavskaia, 1989 *kandidat*, 2007 *doktor* of economic science. From the late 1990s onward, together with → Svetlana Kirdina, she developed the theory of the Russian "distributive economy" which argues that due to Russia's cultural specifity "westernising" reforms are doomed to fail.

Bogomolov, Oleg Timofeevich (1927–2015) One of the key reform-minded Soviet economists of the *shestidesiatniki* generation. Bogomolov graduated from the Institute of Foreign Trade of the Ministry of Foreign Trade in 1949 and in the following years worked as a consultant to the Ministry of Foreign Trade and to the Secretariat of the Council of Mutual Economic Assistance (CMEA) in the Central Committee of the CPSU (1962–1969). From 1967–1977 he held the chair of economic geography of foreign socialist countries at Lomonosov University, Moscow. From 1969 to 1998 he served as director of the Institute of the Economy of the World Socialist System (renamed into Institute of International Economic and Political Studies in 1991), which in Soviet times under his leadership offered a niche for reform-oriented economists and for the study of Western economic ideas. He was deputy of the Congress of People's Deputies of the USSR between 1989 and 1991 and of the State Duma of the Russian Federation between 1993 and 1995.

Buzgalin, Aleksandr Vladimirovich (b. 1954) Buzgalin studied economics at Lomonosov University, Moscow; 1979 *kandidat*, 1989 *doktor* of economic science. He has been professor of political economy at Lomonosov University, Moscow, since 1991 and is one of the most pronounced left-wing public intellectuals among Russian economics professors. Among other things, he initiated the left-wing journal *Alternatives* and the movement "Scientists for Democracy and Socialism" and acted as one of the initiators and organizers of the first and second Russian Social Forum.

Gaidar, Egor Timurovich (1956–2009) Gaidar is widely regarded as the "father" of the Russian Shock therapy. In 1978 he graduated from the faculty of economics of Lomonosov University, Moscow. In 1980 joined the All-Soviet Research Institute for Systems Research (VNIISI) where, under the guidance of → Stanislav Shatalin, a group of economists worked on problems of economic reforms. Between 1980 and 1987 worked as a researcher at the Russian Academy of Sciences (first at the Institute of System Research and later at the Institute of Economics and Forecasting). From 1987 to 1990 Gaidar worked as head of the economic section of the journal *Kommunist* and was then promoted to the same post at the newspaper *Pravda*. On 6 November 1991, he was appointed deputy chairman of the government of the Russian Federation on economic policy and in the first half of 1992 initiated the Russian "Shock Therapy". He was dismissed from government on 15 December 1992. In the following years he organised the liberal parties "Russian Democratic Choice" and the "Association of Right Forces" and founded the research institute and thinktank "Institute of the Economy in Transition" (since 2010: Gaidar Institute).

Glaz'ev, Sergei Iur'evich (b. 1961) Economist and politician. Glaz'ev has shown to be the leading left-wing Russian economist and critic of liberal reforms of his generation. Since 2012, presidential adviser on regional economic integration. Glaz'ev studied at Lomonosov University, Moscow; 1986 *kandidat*, 1990 *doktor* of economic science, became a professor in 1999 and corresponding member of the Russian Academy of Sciences in 2000. He served as Minister of Foreign Economic Relations of the Russian Federation from 1992 to 1993 and was twice elected to the Duma (the first time for the Democratic Party of Russia, the second time for the Communist party). In 2003, he founded the party *Rodina* (Homeland) and ran for President in the 2004 elections.

Gontmakher, Evgenii Shlemovich (b. 1953) Born in L'vov (Ukraine), Gontmakher graduated from the faculty of geography of Lomonosov University, Moscow in 1975. From then until 1991 he was involved with the Central Economic Research Centre (TSENII) of *Gosplan*. In 1992, he became head of the administration of the Ministry of Labour, then acted as Deputy Minister of Social Affairs from 1993–1994, then as head of the presidential administration in 1994 and 95 and finally as head of the department for social development of the government of the Russian Federation from 1999 to 2003. From 2003 to 2006 he held the position of Vice-President of the Russian Union of Industrialists and Entrepreneurs. Since 2008 Gontmakher has been a member of the board of directors of the "Institute of Modern Development".

Grigor'ev, Leonid Markovich (b. 1947) Liberal economist, one of the contributors to the "500 days" programme. In 1968, he graduated from the economic faculty of Lomonosov University, Moscow; 1973 *kandidat* of economic science. Until the breakdown of the Soviet Union, Grigor'ev developed his career at the Institute of World Economy and International Relations. In the early 1990s, he was integrally involved in the implementation of market reforms, first in the Shatalin group as contributor to the "500 days" programme, then, in 1991 and 1992, as deputy Minister of Finance and Economic Affairs. Grigor'ev is currently professor of economics at the Higher School of Economics, Moscow, and a leading member of the economic expert group SIGMA.

Grinberg, Ruslan Semenovich (b. 1946) One of the most prolific Russian critics of neoliberal ideas. Grinberg studied at Lomonosov University Moscow; 1971 *kandidat*, 1995 *doktor* of economic science, and he has been a corresponding member of the Russian Academy of Sciences since 2006. From 2003 to 2015 he occupied the position of director of the Institute of Economic and Political Studies// Institute of Economics [renamed 2005] at the Russian Academy of Sciences. He has been president of the "New Economic Association" since 2014, and he teaches at Lomonosov University, Moscow.

Gubanov, Sergei Semenovich (b. 1955) Professor of economics at Lomonosov University, Moscow, and since 2010 managing editor of the left-wing Russian economics journal *Ekonomist* (formerly *Planovoe khoziaistvo* ["Planned Economy"]). He is one of the main proponents of a neo-industrialisation of Russia and of a partial return to a planned economy.

Guriev, Sergei Maratovich (b. 1971) Former rector of the *New School of Economics* (2004–2013), Moscow, leading Russian liberal economist of his generation. Born in Ordzhonikidze into a family of scientists. In 1993, he graduated from the Moscow Physico-Technological Institute; in 1994 *kandidat* of physico-mathematical sciences. After a research stay at the MIT, from 1998 onward worked at the New School of Economics, where he received the title of *doktor* of economic science in 2001. In 2013, he emigrated to Paris, after his office had been searched by police forces as a reaction to his involvement with a group of experts who had criticised the prosecution of Mikhail Khodorkovskii. He is now chief economist of the European Bank of Reconstruction and Development and teaches at the SciencesPo in Paris.

Iakovlev, Andrei Aleksandrovich (b. 1966) Institutional economist, one of the authors of Strategy 2020. Studied economics at Lomonosov University, Moscow; 1993 *kandidat* of economic science. Has been occupied at the Higher School of Economics, Moscow, since 1993. He holds the position of director of the Institute for the Analysis of Enterprises and Markets and of the International Centre for the Analysis of Institutions and Development. In 2016, he became full professor at the Faculty of Social Sciences of the Higher School of Economics.

Iasin, Evgenii Grigor'evich (b. 1934) One of the leading Russian liberal economists. Studied at the Odessa Institute of Civil Construction and afterwards at the faculty of economics of Lomonosov University, Moscow. 1968 *kandidat*, 1976 *doktor* of economic science, since 1979 professor. From 1973 to 1989 he headed a Laboratory at the Central Institute of Economics and Mathematics of the Academy of Sciences. In the late 1980s, he belonged to the first academic economists who called for radical market reforms. He was minister of economic affairs from 1994 to 1997 and has been Academic Supervisor of the University – Higher School of Economics. Since 2000 he has also acted as president of the foundation 'Liberal Mission'.

Inozemtsev, Vladislav Leonidovich (b. 1968) Economist, sociologist and liberal politician. Born in Gor'kii (Belorus). In 1989 he graduated from the faculty of economics of Lomonosov University, Moscow, then in 1991–1992 worked as economic expert for the parliamentary group of "Svobodnaia Rossiia" (Free Russia) in the Higher Council of the Russian Federation. In 1994, he received the title *kandidat*, in 1999 that of *doktor* of economic sciences. In 1996, he founded the thinktank "Centre for the Study of Post-Industrial Society". He was chief editor of the journal *Svobodnaia mysl* ("Free Thought") between 2003 and 2012 and has been teaching economics at the Higher School of Economics, Moscow, since 2014.

Iurgens, Igor Iur'evich (b. 1952) Economist, president of the Institute of Modern Development (INSOR). In 1974, he graduated from the faculty of economics of Lomonosov University; 1999 *kandidat* of economic sciences. From 1974 to 1980, and from 1985 to 1991, he worked for the Central Union of Trade Unions of the Soviet Union (and from 1991 to 1997 for the successor organisation) and from 1980 to 1985 for the UNESCO in Paris. After his post as President of the Russian Union of insurance companies and the Russian employers' association, he became president of the "Institute of Contemporary Development" (INSOR) in 2008. Since 2007 he has also been working as a professor at the Higher School of Economics, Moscow.

Khanin, Grigorii Isaakovich (b. 1937) Khanin is an economist and statistician who in the late Soviet Union was a harsh critic of the planned economy and is today a proponent of a return to a Stalin-type planned economy. In 1959 Khanin graduated from the Leningrad Institute of Finance and Economics; 1968 *kandidat*, 1973 *doktor* of economic science. Between 1965 and 1972 he worked as lecturer at Novosibirsk State University before being dismissed for "oppositional views". In the early 1970s, he began working on alternative macroeconomic models of the Soviet economy. Together with the well-known journalist → Vasilii Seliunin, in 1987, under the title "Lukavaia Tsifra" (Arcane Number) he published a sensational article which painted a gloomy picture of the condition of the Soviet Economy. After the Russian crisis of 1998, Khanin published a number of papers in which he praised Iosif Stalin and recommended a return to a planned economy. Khanin is editor of the Russian economic journal *Eko* and professor at Novosibirsk Technical State University.

Khubiev, Kaisyn Azretovich (b. 1948) Economist, representative of the so-called Tsagolov School of Political Economy. In 1972, he graduated from Rostov State University. From 1974 to 1977 he pursued his PhD studies (*aspirantura*) under the supervision of → Nikolai Tsagolov. In 1978, he received the title of *kandidat* and in 1991 that of *doktor* of economic sciences. Khubiev has been professor at Lomonosov University, Moscow, since 1978.

Kirdina, Svetlana Georgievna (b. 1955) Economic sociologist, member of the Novosibirsk school of sociology. Kirdina graduated from the faculty of economics of Novosibirsk University in 1997. From 1977 to 1982 she worked as an economist at the Sibirsk Research Institute of Agricultural Economics and between 1983 and 1985 pursued her PhD studies (*aspirantura*) in economic sociology under supervision of → Tatiana Zaslavskaia. In 1986, she received the title of *kandidat* and in 2002 that of a *doktor* of economic sciences. Until 1999 she had worked at the Institute of Economics and the Organisation of Industrial Production of the Novosibirsk branch of the Academy of Sciences, before she moved to the Institute of Economics of the Academy of Sciences since 2002. From the late 1990s, together with Olga Bessonova, she developed the theory of the Russian "distributive economy", which she later popularised as a theory of "X" and "Y" patterns of social evolution.

Kleiner, Georgii Borisovich (b. 1946) Institutional economist who follows the lines of original institutionalism and belongs to the more prominent group of Russian critics of neo-liberal and monetarist ideas. In 1969, he graduated from the Faculty of Mechanics and Mathematics of Lomonosov University, Moscow. 1972 *kandidat* of physico-mathematical sciences, 1989 *doktor* of economic sciences. From 1969 to 1991 he worked at the Institute of Electronic Control Machines of the Ministry of Instrumentation, Automation and Control Systems of the USSR, then in 1991 joined the Central Institute of Mathematical Economics of the Russian Academy of Sciences. Since 2003 he has been a corresponding member of the Russian Academy of Sciences.

Kudrin, Aleksei Leonidovich (b. 1960) From 2000 to 2011 Kudrin was the Minister of Finance of the Russian Federation. In 1983, he graduated from the faculty of economics of Leningrad State University and in 1988 was awarded the title of *kandidat nauk* by the Economics Institute of the Soviet Academy of Sciences. In the early 1990s, he started work in the administration of St. Petersburg's liberal Mayor Anatoly Sobchak and in 1996 took on work in the Presidential Administration of Boris El'tsin. Kudrin was appointed Finance Minister in 2000, a post he held until 2011, and Deputy Prime Minister from 2000 to 2004 and 2007 to 2011.

Kudrov, Valentin Mikhailovich (b. 1932) Economist and Americanist. In 1954 graduated from the faculty of economics of Lomonosov University, Moscow; 1961 *kandidat*, 1969 *doktor* of economic sciences, 1975 professor of political economy. He worked for the central council of the Soviet trade unions, at the research institute of *Gosplan* and later at the Institute of the World Economy and International Relations. From 1990 onward he occupied the position of head of the Centre for Comparative Economic Studies at the Institute of Europe at the Russian academy of sciences. He teaches in the department of international economics at the Higher School of Economics, Moscow.

Latsis, Otto Rudol'fovich (1934–2005) One of the key figures in the Soviet economic reform debates of the 1960s. In 1956, Latsis graduated from the Faculty of Journalism of Lomonosov University, Moscow, in 1956 and from 1964 to 1971 was "economic observer" of the newspaper *Izvestiia*. 1970 *kandidat*, 1980 *doktor* of economic science. From 1975 to 1986 he worked at the Institute of the Economy of the World Socialist System of the Soviet Academy of Sciences. Afterwards (1987–1991) he became deputy chief editor of *Kommunist*. In 1991, he returned to his post as political correspondent to *Izvestiia* and later worked for *Russkii kurier* and *Moskovskie novosti*. Latsis joined the CPSU in 1959 and between 1990 and 91 was a member of its Central Committee.

Lisichkin, Gennadii Stepanovich (b. 1929) Economist, sociologist and journalist, one of the key figures of the reform debates of the 1960s. He graduated from the Moscow State Institute of International Relations, worked as research fellow of the Institute of Sociological Research (ICI) of the Soviet Academy of Sciences from 1968 to 1975 and from then on at the Institute of the Economics of International Political Systems (IEMCC).

L'vov, Dmitrii Semenovich (1930–2007) One of the most visible Marxist opponents of market reforms affiliated to the Russian Academy of Sciences. In 1954 L'vov graduated from the machine-building Faculty of the Ordzhonikdze Institute of Engineering and Economics, in 1961 was awarded the title of *kandidat* and in 1969 that of *doktor* of economic science. In 1987, he became corresponding member of the Soviet Academy of Sciences, in 1994 a full member of the Russian Academy of Sciences. From 1996 to 2002, he served as academic secretary of its economics department.

Mau, Vladimir Aleksandrovich (b. 1959) Besides → Egor Gaidar one of the key figures behind the economic reforms of the early 1990s, up to the present one the politically most influential Russian liberal economists. In 1981, he graduated from the Plekhanov Institute of Economics; 1986 *kandidat*, 1994 *doktor* of economic science. From 1981 to 1991 he worked as research fellow at the economics institute of the Soviet Academy of Sciences. In 1992 became economic advisor to Egor Gaidar, from 1993 to 97 was the vice director of the Institute of the Economy in the Transition Period and from 1997 to 2002 was head of the working group on economic reforms at the government of the Russian Federation. Mau has been director of the Academy of Economics at the Government of the Russian Federation since 2002.

Medved'ev, Vadim Andreevich (b. 1929) Important representative of the *shestidesiatniki* generation of Soviet economics and during perestroika one of the close advisors to Mikhail Gorbachev. In 1951, Medved'ev graduated from the faculty of economics of Leningrad State University where he later became lecturer and professor. During the 1970s and -80s he served in different positions (related to propaganda, education and science) at the Central Committee of the CPSU and from 1986 to 1990 became its secretary. From 1988 to 1990 he was a member of the politburo.

Naishul, Vitali Arkad'evich (b. 1949) After having graduated from the faculty of mechanical mathematics of Lomonosov University, Moscow, in 1971, Naishul started to work at the economic research institute at *Gosplan* and then in the Central Economic-Mathematical Institute (TSEMI) of the Soviet Academy of Sciences. Since 1992 he has been the director of the Institute of the National Model of the Economy (*Institut national'noi model'i ekonomiki*). In 1985 (under a pseudonym) he published the book "Drugaia zhizn" (Another Life) in which he compared the standard of life in the USA and the Soviet Union and suggested a kind of voucher privatisation for the USSR.

Oleinik, Anton (b. 1972) Sociologist and economist, studied economics at Lomonosov University, Moscow and Sociology at the Collège Universitaire Français in Moscow and l'École des Hautes Études en Sciences Sociales, Paris (E.H.E.S.S.); *kandidat* of economic science 1996, PhD in Sociology at E.H.E.S.S. in 2000. Since 2004 he has worked as a professor of sociology at Memorial University, Newfoundland, Canada.

Ol'sevich, Iurii Iakovlev (b. 1929) Economist and proponent of neo-Slavophile economic ideas. In 1951, Ol'sevich graduated from the faculty of economics of Lomonosov University, Moscow, and in 1973 he received the title of *doktor* of economic science. He is Professor of economics at Lomonosov University, Moscow and senior researcher of the Centre for historico-economic research at the Institute of Economics of the Russian Academy of Sciences.

Osipov, Iurii Mikhailovich (b. 1941) Economist and Philosopher. Studied economics at Lomonosov University, Moscow; 1973 *kandidat*, 1987 *doktor* of economic science. From 1970 to 2000 he taught political economy at Lomonosov University, where he founded the Laboratory of Economic Philosophy in 2000. He is editor of the journal *Filosofiia khoziaistvsa* (Economic Philosophy).

Petrakov, Nikolai Iakovlevich (1937–2014) Important representative of Soviet mathematical economics and of the *shestidesiatniki* generation of Soviet political economists. In 1959, he graduated from the faculty of economics of Lomonosov University, Moscow; 1963 *kandidat*, 1972 *doktor* of economic science. He was involved with different economic research institutes, particularly at the Central Economic-Mathematical Institute. One of the close economic advisors to Mikhail Gorbachev in the late 1980s.

Pevzner, Iakov Aleksandrovich (1914–2003) Economist, political scientist, Japanologist. After having graduated from the Faculty of Eastern Studies of Lomonosov University, Moscow, Pevzner joined the Institute of World Economy and World Politics (IMKHMP). In 1941, he received the title of *kandidat* and in 1961 that of a *doktor* of economic science. In 1956, he began working at the newly established Institute of World Economy and International Relations, where he was head of the department of Japanology. In the late 1980s, he belonged to the first academic economists who criticised perestroika and demanded radical market reforms.

[Popkova-]Piiashcheva, Larisa Ivanovna (1947–2003) One of the earliest and most radical proponents of market reforms. After having graduated from the Plekhanov Institute of economics in 1969, up until 1990 Piiasheva was occupied in the economics department of the Institute of the International Workers Movement of the Soviet Academy of Sciences. In 1987 under the title "Where are the *Pirogi* Meatier?" in the journal *Novyi mir*, she published a letter to the editors in which, for the first time in the public press, a demand for radical market reforms was raised. In the early 1990s, she temporarily held a high-ranking position at the mayor's office of Moscow and from 1993 until her death worked as head of the department of economics and law at Moscow Open University.

Polterovich, Viktor Moisevich (b. 1937) Leading Russian economist in the field of general equilibrium theory. In 1962, he graduated from an engineering programme of the Moscow Oil and Gas Institute and in 1966 from the Mathematics Faculty of Lomonosov University, Moscow. In 1966, he joined the Central Economics and Mathematics Institute of the Soviet Academy of Science (since 1991: Russian Academy of Sciences), where he is currently head of the Laboratory of Mathematical Economics. 1971 *kandidat* of mathematics, 1991 *doktor* of economic science. From 1994 to 2004 Polterovich was professor of Economics at Lomonosov University, Moscow and since 2004 at the New School of Economics, Moscow. In 2000, he became corresponding member of the Russian Academy of Sciences and in 2003 a full member.

Popov, Gavriil Kharitonovich (b. 1936) In the late 1980s and early 1990s, Popov was one of the key proponents of radical economic reforms. In 1959, he graduated from the faculty of economics of Lomonosov University, Moscow, where he also pursued a *kandidat* of economic science and in 1963 became lecturer and later professor. From 1988 to 1991, he was the chief editor of the most central Soviet/Russian economics journal *Voprosy ekonomiki*. He was the mayor of Moscow from 1991 to 1992.

Radaev, Vadim Valer'evich (b. 1961) One of the leading Russian economic sociologists. Son of → Valerii Viktorovich Radaev. In 1983, he graduated from the faculty of economics of Lomonosov University Moscov; 1986 *kandidat*, 1997 *doktor* of economics. He has worked as a professor of sociology at the Higher School of Economics, Moscow, since 2003.

Radaev, Valerii Viktorovich (b. 1932) Father of → Vadim Valer'evich Radaev. Studied economics at Lomonosov University, Moscow. 1972 *doktor* of economic science and has been professor of political economy at Lomonosov University since 1974.

Seliunin, Vasilii Illarionovich (1927–1994) Economist and journalist, key figure of the public debate about economic reforms in the perestroika period. In 1954, he graduated from the journalism faculty of Lomonosov University, Moscow. In the 1960s, he received an economics education at *Gosplan*. In the late 1980s, he was among the first authors to argue that perestroika had failed and that radical market reforms were needed. Together with → Grigorii Khanin, in 1987, under the title "Lukavaia Tsifra" (Arcane Number), he published a sensational article which painted a gloomy picture of the condition of the Soviet Economy. At a time when *glasnost'* and perestroika were still framed as the completion of the ideas of Lenin, Seliunin also was one of the first authors who heavily criticized Lenin and drew attention to his involvement in terror. In 1993, he was elected to the State Duma.

Shastitko, Andrei Evgen'evich (b. 1965) One of the pioneers of new institutional economics in Russia. In 1989, he graduated from the faculty of economics of Lomonosov University, Moscow; 1991 *kandidat*, 1999 *doktor* of economic science. Since 2000 he has been working as a professor of economics at Lomonosov University, Moscow. In 1998, he published one of the first Russian textbooks of neo-institutional economic theory and is a member of the liberal group of economists SIGMA.

Shatalin, Stanislav Sergeevich (1934–1997) Important representative of the cybernetic current of Soviet economics and co-author of the 500 days programme of economic transition. In 1958, Shatalin graduated from the faculty of economics of Lomonosov University, Moscow. 1965 *kandidat*, 1970 *doktor* of economic science. From 1976–1986 he worked at the All-Soviet Research Institute of Systems Research and from 1986 to 1989 at the Institute of Economic and Scientific Forecasting of Scientific Progress of the Soviet Academy of Sciences. For many years he held the chair of economic cybernetics at Lomonosov University. In December of 1989 he was appointed member of the State Commission of Economic Reform and in 1990 became head of the working group which authored the "500 days" programme. From 1990–1991 he was a member of the central committee of the CPSU.

Shmelev, Nikolai Petrovich (1936–2014) In the late 1980s, one of the earliest proponents of market reforms, later a severe critic of → Egor Gaidar and the radical reforms of the 1990s. Shmelev studied economics at Lomonosov University, Moscow; 1961 *kandidat*, 1969 *doktor* of economic science, and he became a corresponding member of the Academy of Sciences in 1969 and a full member in 2000. From 1983 to 1992 he worked at the Institute of the USA and Canada of the Soviet/Russian Academy of Sciences and has since then worked at its Institute of Europa of which he became director in 2000 and remained as such until his death. In 1987, in *Novyi mir*, Shmelev published an article "Advances and Debts," in which he ruthlessly criticised the state of the socialist economies and called for far-reaching reforms. The article received much attention both in the Soviet Union and abroad and is considered to have significantly influenced Gorbachev's economic reforms.

Tsagolov, Nikolai Aleksandrovich (1904–1985) Key figure of the Soviet Political Economy of Socialism and founder of the "Tsagolov School" of Soviet political economy. In 1924 Tsagolov graduated from the Moscow Institute of Agricultural Economics. 1929 *kandidat*, 1949 *doktor* of economic science. In

1932, he became scientific secretary of the Institute of economic research of *Gosplan*. From 1937 to 1958 he was a research fellow at the Institute of Economics of the Soviet Academy of Sciences and from 1957 to 1985 the chair of Political Economy at Lomonosov University, Moscow.

Vishnevskii, Anatolii Grigor'evich (b. 1935) Economist and demographer. In 1958 Vishnevskii graduated from the faculty of economics of Kharkov University with a specialisation in statistics. In 1967, he was awarded the title *kandidat nauk* by the Economics Institute of the Soviet Academy of Sciences. In 1971, he began work in the demographic department of the Statistical Research Institute of the Soviet Academy of Sciences. Vishnevskii is regarded as one of the leading Russian demographers. In 1998, he published a book *Serp i Rubl. Konservativnaia modernizatsiia SSSR* (*The Sickle and the Ruble. The Conservative Modernisation of the USSR*) in which he provided a fundamental critique of the Soviet project of modernisation.

Volkonskii, Viktor Aleksandrovich (b. 1932) Studied mathematics at Lomonosov University, Moscow; 1960 *kandidat* of physical-mathematical sciences, 1967 *doktor* of economic science. From 1960 to 1963 he worked under V.S. Nemchinov at the Laboratory of Mathematical Economics and from 1963 to 1989 acted as director of the Central Economic Mathematical Institute (TSEMI) of the Russian Academy of Science. Since 1989 he has occupied a position at the Institute of Economic Forecasting (INP) of the Russian Academy of Sciences.

Zaslavskaia, Tat'iana Ivanovna (1927–2013) Economic sociologist and key representative of the *shestidesiatniki* generation of Russian social scientists. In 1950, Zaslavskaia graduated from the faculty of economics of Lomonosov University, Moscow. In 1963, on invitation of Abel Aganbegian, she joined the Institute of Economics and the Organisation of Industrial Production of the Novosibirsk branch of the Soviet Academy of Sciences. From 1967 onward, she headed the department of social problems which became a country-wide centre of economic sociology. In 1983, Zaslavskaia published the highly controversial "Novosibirsk Manifesto", in which she demanded far-reaching economic reforms. In 1987 she returned to Moscow, where she became director of the newly established All-Soviet Centre of Opinion Research (VTSIOM).

References

Abalkin, L.I. (1973) *Khoziaistvennyi mekhanizm razvitogo sotsialisticheskogo obshchestva*, Moscow: Mysl'.

Abalkin, L.I. (1981) "The USSR: Economic Development and Improvement of the Economic Mechanism," in Fedoseev, P.N. (ed) *Developed Socialism: Economy, Policy, Ideology*, Moscow: Academy of Sciences: 66–87.

Abalkin, L.I. (1987) "Ekonomicheskie protivorechiia sotsializma (k itogam diskussii)," *Voprosy ekonomiki*, 5: 3–13.

Abalkin, L.I. ([1989] 1990) "Rynok v ekonomicheskoi sisteme sotsializma," *Voprosy ekonomiki*, 7: 3–12 [English translation: Abalkin, L.I. "The Market in a Socialist Economy," *Problems of Economics*, 10: 6–19].

Abalkin, L.I. (1993) "Ekonomicheskaia teoriia na puti k novoi paradigme," *Voprosy ekonomiki*, 1: 4–17.

Abalkin, L.I. (1994) "O natsional'no-gosudarstvennykh interesakh Rossii," *Voprosy ekonomiki*, 2: 4–16.

Abalkin, L.I. (1997) *Otlozhennye peremeny ili poteriannyi god*, Moscow: Institut ekonomiki RAN.

Abalkin, L.I. (2000a) "Evoliutsionnaia ekonomika v sisteme pereosmysleniia bazovykh osnov obshchestvovedeniia," in Abalkin, L.I. (ed) *Evoliutsionnaia ekonomika i "meinstrim"*, Moscow: Nauka: 7–14.

Abalkin, L.I. (2000b) *Rossiiskaia shkola ekonomicheskoi mysli: poisk samoopredeleniia*, Moscow: IE RAN.

Abalkin, L.I. et al. (1989) "Sotsialisticheskaia sobstvennost: problemy perestroiki (po materialam doklada instituta RAN)," *Voprosy ekonomiki*, 4: 82–92.

Abalkin, L.I., Petrakov, N.Ia. and Shatalin, S.S. (1994a) "Sotsial'no-ekonomicheskaia situatsiia v Rossii: Itogi, problemy, puti stabilizatsii," *Voprosy ekonomiki*, 2: 126–160.

Abalkin, L.I., Petrakov, N.Ia. and Shatalin, S.S. (1994b) "Esli v strane krepchaet beda, znachit reformy idut ne tuda," *Rabochaia Tribuna*, 4 February 1994: 4–5 (part 1); 5 February 1994: 3 (part 2); 8 February 1994: 3 (part 3).

Abalkin, L.I. et al. ([2002] 2003) "Otkrytoe pis'mo gruppy uchenykh-ekonomistov ministru obrazovaniiu RF," *Rossiiskii ekonomicheskii zhurnal*, 4: 80 [first published in *Ekonomika i zhizn'*, 48, 2002].

Abramov, A. and Radygin, A. (2007) "Finantsovyi rynok Rossii v usloviiakh gosudarstvennogo kapitalizma," *Voprosy ekonomiki*, 6: 28–44.

Afanasenko, I.D. (2001) *Ekonomika i dukhovnaia programma Rossii*, St Petersburg: Trete Tysiacheletie.

Afontsev, S.A. (2002) "National'naia ekonomicheskaia bezopasnost': na puti k teoreticheskomu konsensusu," *Mirovaia ekonomika i mezhdunarodnye otnosheniia*, 10: 10–39.

Aganbegian, A.G. (2001) "Vremia ne stol'ko podvodit' itogi, skol'ko rabotat' na budushchee," *Obshchestvo i ekonomika*, 9: 9–27.

Aganbegian, A.G. (2010) "Uroki krizisa: Rossii nuzhna modernizatsiia i innovatsionnaia ekonomika," *EKO*, 1: 34–60.

Aganbegian, A.G. (2011) "O meste ekonomiki Rossii v mire," *Voprosy ekonomiki*, 5: 43–55.

Aghion, P. and Howitt, P. (2009) *The Economics of Growth*, Cambridge, MA: MIT Press.

Akinin, A.A., Shevelev, A.A. and Pochikovskaia, E.A. (2004) "Praviashaia elita i perspektivy modernizatsii v Rossii," in Osipov, Iu.M., Chekmarev, V.V. and Zotova, E.S. (eds) *Ekonomicheskaia teoriia v xxi veke 2 (9), vol. 2*, Moscow: Ekonomist: 892–902.

Aleksandrov, Iu.G. (1999) *Perekhodnaia ekonomika: rossiiskaia versiia*, Moscow: IV RAN.

Alekseev, A.B. and Kuznetsova, N.N. (2004) "Dlia udvoeniia VVP osnovanii net," *EKO*, 4: 2–26.

Alekseev, S.I. (1991) "Rynok kak predmet revogo," *Literaturnaia gazeta*, 3 July, 26 (5352).

Alekseev, S.I. (2005) "2005g.: Mezhdu stagnatsii i depressiei," *EKO*, 4: 51–55.

Alston, L.J., Melo, M.A., Mueller, B. and Pereira, C. (2016) *A Conceptual Framework for Understanding Critical Transitions*, NBER Working Paper No. 22144.

Anan'in, O.I. (1988) "Politicheskaia ekonomiia sotsializma: stereotipy i tochki zreniia," *Voprosy ekonomiki*, 5: 69–80.

Anan'in, O.I. (1992) "Ekonomicheskaia teoriia: krizis paradigmy i sud'ba nauchnogo soobshchestva," *Voprosy ekonomiki*, 10: 81–99.

Arkhipov, A.I. (1994) "Ekonomicheskaia bezopasnost': otsenki, problemy, sposoby obespecheniia," *Voprosy ekonomiki*, 12: 36–44.

Arkhipov, A.I. (1999) "Osobennosti i puti utverzhdeniia novogo ekonomicheskogo myshleniia," *Ekonomist*, 12: 70–75.

Armstrong, J.A. (1978) *Ideology, Politics, and Government in the Soviet Union: An Introduction*, 4th edn, New York: Praeger.

Arthur, B.W (1988) "Self-reinforcing Mechanisms in Economics," in Andersen, P.W. et al. (eds) *The Economy as an Evolving Complex System*, Redwood City: Addison-Wesley: 9–31.

Aslund, A. (2013) "Sergey Glazyev and the Revival of Soviet Economics," *Post-Soviet Affairs*, 29, 5: 375–386.

Auktsionek, S.P. (1995) *Teoriia perekhoda k rynku*, Moscow: Argus.

Auktsionek, S.P. (1996) "Teoriia perekhodnoi ekonomiki i ee mesto v riadu ekonomicheskikh nauk," *Mirovaia ekonomika i mezhdunarodnye otnosheniia*, 10: 11–19.

Auzan, A. (1989) "Politicheskaia ekonomiia sotsializma: Perestroika stavit problemy," *Kommunist*, 1 (1335), January: 5–14.

Auzan, A. and Satarov, G. (2012) "Prioritety institutional'nykh preobrazovanii v usloviiakh ekonomicheskoi modernizatsii," *Voprosy ekonomiki*, 6: 65–74.

Avtonomov, V.S. (1996) "Politicheskaia ekonomiia perekhodnogo perioda," *Mirovaia ekonomika i mezhdunarodnye otnosheniia*, 9: 5–15.

Avtonomov, V.S. (2003) "Istoriia ekonomicheskoi mysli i ekonomicheskogo analiza: mesto Rossii," in Abalkin, L.I. (ed) *Ocherki istorii rossiiskoi ekonomicheskoi mysli*, Moscow: Nauka: 116–122.

Avtonomov, V.S., Anan'in, O., Kuz'minov, Ia., Lipsits, I., Liubimov, L., Nureev, R. and Radaev, V. (2001) "Ekonomicheskaia nauka, obrazovanie i praktika v Rossii v 90-e gody," *Voprosy ekonomiki*, 1: 84–95.

Baburin, S.N. (2004) "Globalizatsiia i bor'ba Rossii za svoe national'noe razvitie," in Osipov, Iu.M., Chekmarev, V.V. and Zotova, E.S. (eds) *Ekonomicheskaia teoriia v xxi veke 2 (9), 2 vol. 2*, Moscow: Ekonomist: 177–186.

Bachurin, A.V. (1993) "Gosudarstvennoe regulirovanie neobkhodimo," *Ekonomist*, 10: 3–10.

Balatskii, E. (2007) "Nechetkie instituty, kul'tura naseleniia i institutional'naia entropiia," *Obshchestvo i ekonomika*, 5–6: 37–53.

Barnett, V. (1992) "Conceptions of the Market Among Russian Economists: A Survey," *Soviet Studies*, 44, 6: 1087–1098.

Basina, T.D. and Shereveva, M.Iu. (1993) "Istoki i osobennosti razvitiia khoziaistvennykh traditsii v Rossii," *Vestnik Moskovskogo universiteta*, 4: 29–38.

Béland, D. and Cox, R.H. (eds) (2011a) *Ideas and Politics in Social Science Research*, Oxford: Oxford University Press.

Béland, D. and Cox, R.H. (2011b) "Introduction. Ideas and Politics," in Béland, D. and Cox, R.H. (eds) (2011a): 9–20.

Bell, S. (2011) "Do We Really Need a New 'Constructivist Institutionalism' to Explain Institutional Change?" *British Journal of Political Science*, 44, 4: 883–906.

Bell, S. (2012) "Where Are the Institutions? The Limits of Vivien Schmidt's Constructivism," *British Journal of Political Science*: 42, 3: 714–719.

Belousov, A. (2005) "Dolgosrochnye tendentsii rossiiskoi ekonomiki. Stsenarii ekonomicheskogo razvitiia Rossii do 2020 goda," *Obshchestvo i ekonomika*, 12: 114–229.

Bendikov, M.A. and Frolov, I.E. (2011) "Vysokotekkhnologichnyi sektor promyshlennosti Rossii v aspektakh sistemnogo i global'nogo finantsovo-ekonomicheskogo krizisov," *Ekonomika i matematicheskie metody*, 47, 2: 43–53.

Berdiaev, N.A. ([1937] 1990) *Istoki i smysl' russkogo kommunizma*, Moscow: Nauka.

Bessonova, O.E. (1997) *Instituty razdatochnoi ekonomiki Rossii: retrospektivnyi analiz*, Novosibirsk: IEIOPP SO RAN.

Bessonova, O.E. (1998) "Teoriia razdatochnoi ekonomiki: novyi vzgliad na khoziaistvennoe razvitie Rossii," *Obshchestvo i ekonomika*, 8/9: 219–240.

Bessonova, O.E. (1999) *Razdatok: Institutional'naia teoriia khoziaistvennogo razvitiia Rossii*, Novosibirsk: IEIOPP SO RAN.

Bessonova, O.E. (2006) *Razdatochnaia ekonomika Rossii*, Moscow: Rosspen.

Bessonova, O.E. (2007) "Fenomen teorii institutional'nykh matrits: Restavratsiia ustarevshei paradigmy," *Ekonomicheska nauka sovremennoi Rossii*, 2: 23–33.

Bessonova, O.E., Kirdina, S. and O'Sullivan, R. (1996) *Rynochnyi eksperiment v razdatochnoi ekonomike Rossii. Demonstratsionnye proekty v zhilishchnom khoziastve*, Novosibirsk: IEIOPP SO RAN.

Block, F. (2001) "Introduction," in Polanyi, K. (ed) *The Great Transformation: The Political and Economic Origins of Our Time*, Boston: Beacon Press: xvii–xli.

Blyth, M. (1997) "Any More Bright Ideas? The Ideational Turn of Comparative Political Economy," *Comparative Politics*, 29, 2: 229–250.

Blyth, M. (2002) *Great Transformations: Economic Ideas and Institutional Change in the Twentieth Century*, Cambridge: Cambridge University Press.

Blyth, M. (2006) "Great Punctuations: Predictions, Randomness, and the Evolution of Comparative Political Science," *American Political Science Review*, 100, 4: 493–498.

Blyth, M., Helgadottir, O. and Kring, W. (2016) "Ideas and Historical Institutionalism," in Fioretos, O., Falleti, T.G. and Sheingate, A. (eds) *The Oxford Handbook of Historical Institutionalism*, Oxford: Oxford University Press: 142–162.

Bockman, J. and Eyal, G. (2002) "Eastern Europe as a Laboratory for Economic Knowledge: The Transnational Roots of Neoliberalism," *American Journal of Sociology*, 108, 2: 310–352.

Bodrunov, S. (2015) "Integratsiia proizvodstva, nauki i obrazovaniia kak osnova reindustrializatsiia RF," *Mirovaia ekonomika i mezhdunarodyne otnosheniia*, 10: 94–104.

Bogomolov, O.T. ([1989] 1990) "Meniaiushchisia oblik sotsializma," *Kommunist*, 11 [English translation: "The Changing Nature of Socialism," *Problems of Economics*, 32, 11: 15–29].

Bondarenko, I.A. (1995) "Institutional'naia ekonomicheskaia teoriia: nekotorye osnovnye voprosy," *Mirovaia ekonomika i mezhdunarodnye otnosheniia*, 11: 31–35.

Borozdin, I.V. (1987) "Zakon stoimosti i tsena v sotsialisticheskoi khoziaistve," *Voprosy ekonomiki*, 12: 62–70.

Brezhnev, L.I. (1967) *Fifty Years of Great Achievements of Socialism*, Moscow: Novosti Press.

Brue, S.L. and MacPhee, C.R. (1995) "From Marx to Markets: Reform of the University Curriculum in Russia," *Journal of Economic Education*, 2 (Spring): 182–194.

Buchanan, J. (1962) *The Calculus of Consent*, Ann Arbor, MI: University of Michigan Press.

Buchanan, J. (1975) *The Limits of Liberty*. Chicago, IL: The University of Chicago Press.

Bunin, I. (2010) "Diskussiia o modernizatsii: strakh perestroiki," *Vedomosti*, 3 March 2010, available online at: www.politcom.ru/9705.html, last accessed 30 April 2017.

Buss, A.E. (2003) *The Russian-Orthodox Tradition and Modernity*, Leiden: Brill.

Buzgalin, A.V. (1993) "Otechestvennaia ekonomicheskaia teoriia: ot krizisa k novoi paradigme?" *Voprosy ekonomiki*, 1: 42–52.

Buzgalin, A.V. (1995) *Perekhodnaia ekonomika. Zakonomernosti, modeli, perspektivy*, Moscow: Ekonomicheskaia demokratiia.

Buzgalin, A.V. (2003) "Evristicheskii potentsial politicheskoi ekonomii sotsializma v XXI veke," *Voprosy ekonomiki*, 3: 112–131.

Buzgalin, A.V. and Kolganov, A.I. (1998) "K kritike ekonomiks (teoreticheskoe obosnovanie neobkhodimosti korrektsii gospodstvuiushchei modeli uchebnogo kursa po ekonomicheskoi teorii)," *Voprosy ekonomiki*, 6: 87–107.

Bzhilianskii, Y. (1973) "K voprosu ob ekonomicheskoi zakanomernosti," *Voprosy ekonomiki*, 10: 62–72.

Bzhilianskii, Iu. (1975) "Ekonomicheskie zakonomernosti razvitogo sotsializma," *Voprosy ekonomiki*, 11: 56–66.

Cable, V. (1995) "What Is International Economic Security?" *International Affairs*, 71, 2: 305–324.

Campbell, J.L. (1998) "Institutional Analysis and the Role of Ideas in Political Economy," *Theory and Society*, 27, 3: 377–409.

Campbell, J.L. (2002) "Ideas, Politics, and Public Policy," *Annual Review of Sociology*, 28: 21–38.

Campbell, R.W. (1974) *Soviet-Type Economies: Performance and Evolution*, 3rd edn, Boston: Houghton Mifflin.

Campbell, R.W. (2012) *A Biographical Dictionary of Russian and Soviet Economists*, London: Routledge.

Capoccia, G. and Kelemen, R.D. (2007) "The Study of Critical Junctures: Theory, Narrative, and Counterfactuals in Historical Institutionalism," *World Politics*, 59, 3: 341–369.

Capoccia, G. and Ziblatt, D. (2010) "The Historical Turn in Democratization Studies: A New Research Agenda for Europe and Beyond," *Comparative Political Studies*, 43, 8/9: 931–968.

Cherkasov, P. (2004) *IMEiMO: Portret na fone epokhi*, Moscow: Ves' mir.

Cherkovets, O. (2003) "Vozmozhnosti i perspektivy ekonomicheskogo sblizheniia Rossii i Belorusii (tochka zreniia ekonomista)," *Rossiiskii ekonomicheskii zhurnal*, 7: 43–58.

Cherkovets, V. (1973) "Problemy razvitogo sotsializma v politicheskoi ekonomii," *Voprosy ekonomiki*, 12: 3–15.

Coase, R. (1988) *The Firm, the Market and the Law*, Chicago: University of Chicago Press.

CPSU (1985) *Proekt novoi redaktsii programmy Kommunisticheskoi Partii Sovetskogo Soiuza*, Moscow: CPSU.

Dabrowska, E. and Zweynert, J. (2015) "Economic Ideas and Institutional Change. The Case of the Russian Stabilisation Fund," *New Political Economy*, 20, 4: 518–544.

Davydov, A.Iu. (2007) "Budushchee rossiiskoi ekonomiki v svete zarubezhnogo opyta," *EKO*, 12: 119–137.

Dawisha, K. and Ganev, V. (2005) "The Role of Ideas in Post-Communist Politics: A Reevaluation," *East European Politics and Societies*, 19, 3: 339–342.

Dement'ev, V. (2002) "Teoriia national'noi ekonomiki i mezoekonomicheskaia teoriia," *Rossiiskii ekonomicheskii zhurnal*, 4: 71–82.

Denton, G.R. (1971) *A New Economic Mechanism: Economic Reform in Hungary*, London: PEP.

Deriabin, A.A. (1987) "Sovershenstvovanie sistemy tsen," *Planovoe khoziaistvo*, 1: 81–87.

Diskin, I.E. (1997) "Sotsial'naia sostavliaiushchaia razvitie perekhodnoi ekonomiki," *Obshchestvo i ekonomika*, 1–2: 147–174.

Dolan, E.G. and Lindsey, D.E. (1974) *Basic Macroeconomics*, Hinsdale, IL: Dryden Press.

Dugin, A.G. (2003) "Ekonomicheskie aspekty neoevraiistva (liberal-evraistvo)," in Osipov, Iu.M., Baburin, S.N., Belolipetskii, V.G. and Zotova, E.S. (eds) *Ekonomicheskaia teoriia na poroge XXI veka, t. 7: Global'naia ekonomika*, Moskva: Iurist: 194–204.

Duncan, P. (2000) *Russian Messianism. Third Rome, Revolution, Communism and After*, London: Routledge.

Dvorkin, I.N. (1970) "The Scientific-Technical Revolution and Bourgeois Economic Theories of Socialism," *Problems of Economics*, 12, 9: 59–76.

Dynkin, A. (2003) "Does Russia Have a Chance in the Global Economy," *Problems of Economic Transition*, 46, 12: 49–80.

Dzarasov, S., Menshikov, S. and Popov, G. (eds) (2004) *Sud'ba politicheskoi ekonomii i ee sovetskogo klassika*, Moscow: Alpina Biznes buks.

Eddie, S.M. (1996) "Hungarian Economic Reform, 1968–1989: The Illusions and Delusions of the New Economic Mechanism," in Berend, I.T. et al. (eds) *A Gazdaságtörténet Kihívásai. Anulmányok Berend T. Iván 65. Zszületésnapjára*, Budapest: Godi: 383–394.

Efremov, V.A. (1987) "Tseny v sisteme planovogo upravleniia proizvodstvom," *Voprosy ekonomiki*, 6: 52–60.

Ekspert (2006) "Start natsional'nykh investproektov," *Ekspert*, 24, 26 June: 21–22.

Emel'ianov, A.M. ([1988] 1989) "Ekonomicheskii mekhanizm i sotsialisticheskii rynok sredtsv proizvodstva," *Voprosy ekonomiki*, 7: 92–98 [English translation: Emel'ianov, A.M. "The Economic Mechanism and the Socialist Market for the Means of Production," *Problems of Economics*, 10: 95–107].

Engels, F. (1967) "Brief an Joseph Bloch," in *MEW*, vol. 37, Berlin: Dietz: 462–65.

Eremin, A. (1992) "Kakoi put' vyvodit iz krizisa?" *Ekonomist*, 9: 37–47.

Evans, A.B. (1977) "Developed Socialism in Soviet Ideology," *Soviet Studies*, 29, 3: 409–428.

Falleti, T.G. and Lynch, J.F. (2009) "Context and Causal Mechanisms in Political Analysis," *Comparative Political Studies*, 42, 9: 1143–1166.

Farrell, H. and Finnemore, M. (2016) "Global Institutions without a Global State," in Fioretos, O., Falleti, T.G. and Sheingate, A. (eds) *The Oxford Handbook of Historical Institutionalism*, Oxford: Oxford University Press: 572–589.

Fedorenko, N.P. (2003) "O tseliakh i strategii sotsial'no-ekonomicheskogo razvitiia Rossii," *Ekonomika i matematicheskie metody*, 39, 2: 3–13.

Fedoseev, P.N. (1974) "Postroenie razvitogo sotsialisticheskogo obshchestva v SSSR: Torzhesvto idei Leninizma'," *Kommunist*, 2: 20–32.

Fetisov, G. (2007) "Al'ternativy 'syr'evoi' modeli razvitiia Rossiiskoi ekonomiki," *Rossiiskii ekonomicheskii zhurnal*, 9–10: 3–15.

Fisher, S., Dornbusch, R. and Schmalensee, R. (1988) *Economics*, 2nd edn, New York: McGraw-Hill.

Fleck, L. ([1935] 1979) *Genesis and Development of a Scientific Fact*, Chicago: University of Chicago Press.

Fomin, D.A. (2006) "Politicheskaia ekonomiia: panegirik vmesto epitafii? Razmyshleniia nad knigoi 'Sud'ba politicheskoi ekonomii i ee sovetskogo klassika'," *EKO*, 7: 166–190.

Fourcade, M., Ollion, E. and Algan, Y. (2015) "The Superiority of Economists," *Journal of Economic Perspectives*, 29, 1: 89–114.

Gaidar, E.T. (1994) *Novyj kurs? Vozrozhdenie gosudarstvennogo regulirovaniia obogashchaet bogatykh i razoriaet bednykh*, Moscow: Nachala-Press.

Gaidar, E.T. (2003) *State and Evolution: Russia's Search for a Free Market*, Seattle, WA: University of Washington Press.

Gaidar, E.T. (2004) "Recovery Growth and Key Features of the Current Economic Situation," *Problems of Economic Transition*, 46, 10: 6–23.

Gaidar, E.T. (2007) *Collapse of an Empire. Lessons for Modern Russia*, Washington, DC: Brookings Institution Press.

Gaidar, E.T. (2009) *Interview for the Russian Television (First Channel) on 02 March 2009*, available online at: http://pozneronline.ru/2009/03/5569/, last accessed 16 April 2017.

Gaidar, E.T. and Mau, V. (2004) "Marksizm. Mezhdu nauchnoi teorii i svetskoi religii (liberal'naia apologiia)," *Voprosy ekonomiki*, 5: 4–27; 6: 28–56.

Gatovskii, L.M. (1987) "Stoimost' i potrebitel'naia stoimost' v usloviiakh intensifikatsii," *Voprosy ekonomiki*, 6: 15–24.

Gel'man, V., Travin, D. and Marganiia, O. (2014) *Reexamining Economic and Political Reforms in Russia, 1985–2000: Generations, Ideas, and Changes*, Lanham, MD: Lexington Books.

Gel'vanovskii, M.I. (2003) "Globalizatsiia i national'naia konkurrentosposobnost'," in Osipov, Iu.M., Baburin, S.N., Belolipetskii, V.G. and Zotova, E.S. (eds) *Ekonomicheskaia teoriia na poroge XXI veka, t. 7: Global'naia ekonomika*, Moskva: Iurist: 214–226.

Gerner, K. and Hedlund, S. (1989) *Ideology and Rationality in the Soviet Model: A Legacy for Gorbachev*, London: Routledge.

Gerschenkron, A. (1978) "Samuelson in Russia: A Report," *Journal of Economic Literature*, 16, 2: 560–573.

Glaz'ev, S.Iu. (1996) *Za kriticheskoi chertoi. O kontseptsii makroekonomicheskoi politiki v svete obespecheniia ekonomicheskoi bezopasnosti strany*, Moscow: Rossiiskii ekonomicheskii zhurnal.

Glaz'ev, S.Iu. (2007) "Perspektivy razvitiia rossiiskoi ekonomiki v usloviiakh global'noi konkurrentsii," *Rossiiskii ekonomicheskii zhurnal*, 3: 4–25.

Glaz'ev, S.Iu. (2012) "Strategiia 2020 – antimodernizatsionnyi dokument," *Rossiiskii ekonomicheskii zhurnal*, 2: 3–9.

Glaz'ev, S.Iu. et al. (2011) "O strategii razvitiia ekonomiki Rossii," *Ekonomicheskaia nauka sovremennoi Rossii*, 54, 3: 7–31.

Glezerman, G.E. (1981) "Methodological Problems of the Theory of Developed Socialism," in Fedoseev, P.N. (ed) *Developed Socialism: Economy, Policy, Ideology*, Moscow: Academy of Sciences: 45–65.

Gnatovskaia, N. (1987) "Privatizatsiia – ekonomicheskaia politika," *Mirovaia ekonomika i mezhdunarodnye otnosheniia*, 12: 114–116.

Gofas, A. and Hay, C. (eds) (2010) *The Role of Ideas in Political Analysis: A Portrait of Contemporary Debates*, London: Routledge.

Goldschmidt, N., Grimmer-Solem, E. and Zweynert, J. (2016) "On the Purpose and Aims of the Journal of Contextual Economics," *Schmollers Jahrbuch*, 136, 1: 1–14.

Golikova, V., Gonchar, K., Kuznetsov, B., Iakovlev, A. and Iasin, E. (2007) "Rossiiskaia promyshlennost' na pereput'e: chto meshaet nashim firmam stat' konkurentosposobnymi?" *Voprosy ekonomiki*, 3: 4–35.

Gorbachev, M. (1987) "O zadachakh partii po korennoi perestroike upravleniia ekonomikoi," *Kommunist*, 10, July: 5–47.

Goricheva, L.G. (1993) "Ekonomicheskie problemy i natsional'noe samosoznanie," *Voprosy ekonomiki*, 8: 44–53.

Goricheva, L.G. (2002) "Kul'turno-istoricheskaia tsel'nost' national'no-gosudarstvennogo khoziaistva," *Mirovaia ekonomika i mezhdunarodnye otnosheniia*, 1: 81–89.

Gorlanov, G.V. (1988) "Ekonomicheskoe soderzhanie obshchenarodnoi sobstvennosti i mekhanizm ee realizatsii," *Voprosy ekonomiki*, 3: 34–41.

Gorodetskii, A. (1990) "Reforma i rynok," *Voprosy ekonomiki*, 12: 37–49.

Gradov, A.P. (1997/2005) *National'naia ekonomika (kurs lektsii)*, St Petersburg: Spetsial'naia literatura, 2nd edn; Moskow: Piter.

Gref, G. (2009) "Ekonomicheskii krizis i perspektivy rossiiskoi ekonomiki," *Ekonomicheskaia politika*, 6: 20–29.

Gregory, P.R. and Stuart, R.C. (1998) *Russian and Soviet Economic* Peformance *and Structure*, 6th edn, Boston: Addison-Wesley.

Grigor'ev, L. (2003) "Nereshennye problemy na fone ekonomicheskogo rosta," *Obshchestvo i ekonomika*, 9: 97–105.

Grigor'ev, L. (2013) "Stsenarii razvitiia i ekonomicheskie instituty," *Ekonomicheskaia politika*, 3: 33–60.

Grigor'ev, L. and Tambovtsev, V. (2008) "Modernizatsii cherez koalitsii," *Voprosy ekonomiki*, 1: 59–70.

Grigor'ev, L. et al. (2007) *Koalitsii dlia budushchego. Strategii razvitiia Rossii*, Moscow: RIO.

Grigor'ev, L., Plaksin, S. and Salikhov, M. (2008) "Postkrizisnaia struktura ekonomiki i formirovanie koalitsii dlia innovatsii," *Voprosy ekonomiki*, 4: 25–43.

Grimmer-Solem, E. and Romani, R. (1998) "The Historical School, 1870–1900: A Cross-National Reassessment," *History of European Ideas*, 24: 267–299.

Grinberg, R. (2005) "Neskol'ko myslei na temu 'Rossiiskaia reforma i zapad'," *Rossiiski ekonomicheskii zhurnal*, 3: 3–6.

Grinberg, R. (2008) "Rossiiskaia strukturnaia politika: Mezhdu neizbezhnost'iu i neizvestnostiu," *Voprosy ekonomiki*, 3: 56–63.

Grinberg, R. (2012) "O novoi bolshoi privatizatsii i prochikh nepopuliarnykh reform," *Rossiiskii ekonomicheskii zhurnal*, 3: 27–32.

Grinberg, R. et al. (2007) "Reformatsionnyi pragmatizm kak osnova modernizatsii," *Rossiiskii ekonomicheskii zhurnal*, 3: 3–14.

Grishin, A.M. and Stepanov, Iu.V. (1994) "Problemnyi analiz tendentsii v ekonomike Rossii perekhodnogo perioda," *Voprosy ekonomiki*, 4: 23–35.

Groshev, I. and Iur'ev, V. (2005) "Ekonomicheskie preobrazovaniia i mental'nost' Rossiian: Est li vzaimodeistvie?" *Obshchestvo i ekonomika*, 10–11: 192–221.

Gubanov, S. (2001) "Vertikal'naia integratsiia – magistral'nyi put' razvitiia," *Ekonomist*, 1: 35–49.

Gubanov, S. (2005a) "Inertsiia syr'evogo rosta," *Ekonomist*, 10: 3–15.

Gubanov, S. (2005b) "Sistemnye usloviia razvitiia," *Ekonomist*, 9: 16–29.

Gubanov, S. (2007) "Sistemnyi vybor Rossii (k itogam 2006 g.)," *Ekonomist*, 4: 3–36.

Gubanov, S. (2009) "K politike neoindustrializatsii Rossii," *Ekonomist*, 9: 3–20.

Gurvich, E. (2013) "Dolgosrochnye perspektivy rossiiskoi ekonomiki," *Ekonomicheskaia politika*, 3: 7–31.

Gutnik, V.P. (1995) "Rynochnye instituty i transformatsiia rossiiskoi ekonomiki," *Mirovaia ekonomika i mezhdunarodnye otnoshcheniia*, 7: 50–64.

Gutnik, V.P. (1996) "Renessans teorii ekonomicheskogo poriadka," *Mirovaia ekonomika i mezhdunarodnye otnosheniia*, 10: 5–10.

Haas, P.M. (1992) "Introduction: Epistemic Communities and International Policy Coordination," *International Organization*, 46, 1: 1–35.

Hall, P.A. (ed) (1989) *The Political Power of Economic Ideas: Keynesianism Across Nations*, Princeton, NJ: Princeton University Press.

Hall, P.A. (1993) "Policy Paradigms, Social Learning, and the State: The Case of Economic Policymaking in Britain," *Comparative Politics*, 25, 3: 275–296.

Hall, P.A. (1997) "The Role of Interests, Institutions, and Ideas in the Political Economy of the Industrialized Nations," in Lichbach, M.I. and Zuckerman, A.S. (eds) *Comparative Politics: Rationality, Culture, and Structure*, Cambridge: Cambridge University Press: 174–206.

Hanson, P. (2003) *The Rise and Fall of the Soviet Economy: An Economic History of the USSR from 1945*, London: Longman.

Hay, C. (2006a) "Constructivist Institutionalism," in Rhodes, R.A., Binder, S. and Rockman, B. (eds) *The Oxford Handbook of Political Institutions*, Oxford: Oxford University Press: 56–74.

Hay, C. (2006b) "Political Ontology," in Goodin, R.E. and Tilly, C. (eds) *The Oxford Handbook of Contextual Political Analysis*, Oxford: Oxford University Press: 78–96.

Hellman, S., Jones, E. and Kaufmann, D. (2003) "Seize the State, Seize the Day: State Capture and Influence in Transition Countries," *Journal of Comparative Economics*, 31, 4: 751–773.

Heynes, P.T. (1973) *The Economic Way of Thinking*, Chicago: Science Research Association.

HSE (2006) *Round Table on the Russian SF from 18 April 2006*, available online at: www.ria-arbitr.ru/news.htm?id=21853, last accessed 16 April 2017.

Iakovets, Iu.V. (1994) "Rossiia i mirovoi progress," *Voprosy ekonomiki*, 2: 75–84.

Iakovets, Iu.V. (1999) "Formirovanie postindustrial'noi nauchnoi paradigmy v Rossii," *Obshchestvo i ekonomika*, 3/4: 97–105.

Iakovlev, A. (2006) "The Evolution of Business – State Interaction in Russia: From State Capture to Business Capture?" *Europe-Asia Studies*, 58, 7: 1033–1056.

Iakovlev, A. (2007) *Agenty modernizatsii*, Moscow: HSE.

Ianowitch, M. (1991) *Controversies in Soviet Social Thought: Democratization, Social Justice, and the Erosion of Official Ideology*, Armonk, NY and London, UK: Sharpe.

Iaremenko, Iu. (1995) "Statement in Round-Table Discussion 'Istoricheski sud'by, uroki i perspektivy radikal'noi ekonomicheskoi reformy'," *Voprosy ekonomiki*, 4: 60–62.

Iasin, E.G. ([1989] 1990) "Sotsialisticheskii rynok ili iarmarka illiuzii?" *Kommunist*, 15, 134: 53–62 [English translation: Iasin, E. "A Socialist Market or a Fair of Illusions?" *Problems of Economics*, 1: 25–41].

Iasin, E.G. (1990) "Problemy perekhoda k reguliruemoi rynochnoi ekonomike," *Voprosy ekonomiki*, 1: 3–20.

Iasin, E.G. (2003) "Modernizatsiia ekonomiki i sistema tsennostei," *Voprosy ekonomiki*, 4: 4–36.
Iasin, E.G. (2006) "Gosudarstvo i ekonomika na etape modernizatsii," *Voprosy ekonomiki*, 4: 4–30.
Iasin, E.G. (2007) "Modernizatsiia i obshchestvo," *Voprosy ekonomiki*, 5: 4–29.
Iasin, E.G., Akindinova, N., Iakobson, L. and Iakovlev, A. (2013) "Sostoitsia li novaia model' ekonomicheskogo rosta Rossii?" *Voprosy ekonomiki*, 5: 4–39.
Iasin, E.G., Grigor'ev, L., Kuznetsov, O., Danilov, Iu. and Kosygina, A. (2006) "Investitsionnyi klimat v Rossii," *Obshchestvo i ekonomika*, 5: 3–56.
Iasinskaia, I.B. (2002) "Filosofskie osnovy national'noi ekonomicheskoi modeli," in Osipov, Iu.M. and Zotova, E.S. (eds) *Ekonomicheskaia teoria na poroge XXI veka, vol. 6, Filosofiia khoziaistva, teoreticheskaia ekonomiia*, Moscow: Iurist: 292–311.
Iavlinskii, G.A. (1993) "O novoi politike pravitel'stva," *Voprosy ekonomiki*, 2: 112–123.
Ickes, B.W. and Ryterman, R. (1993) "Roadblock to Economic Reform: Interenterprise Debt and the Transition to Markets," *Post-Soviet Affairs*, 9, 3: 231–252.
Ignatovskii, P. (1974) *Razvitoi sotsializm: Obshchestvenno-ekonomicheskaia dinamika*, Moscow: Politicheskaia literatura.
Ignatovskii, P. (2007) "Otechestvennyi opyt planirovaniia ubezhdaet . . . ," *Ekonomist*, 7: 12–23.
Illarionov, A.N. (1995) "Contribution to Round-Table Discussion 'Istoricheskie sud'by, uroki i perspektivy radikal'noi ekonomicheskoi reformy'," *Voprosy ekonomiki*, 4: 4–66.
Innovatsionnaia Rossiia – 2020 (2011) *Strategiia razvitiia innovatsionnoi politiki*, available online at: http://adm-edu.spb.ru/sites/default/files/innovacionnaya_rossiya_2020.pdf, last accessed 02 July 2017.
Inozemtsev, V.L. (1997) "Lichnoie protiv chastnogo? (razmyshleniia o putiakh transformatsii otnoshenii sobstvennosti)," *Obshestvo i ekonomika*, 9/10: 3–22.
Inozemtsev, V.L. (ed) (2009) *Prinuzhdenie k innovatsiiam. Sbornik statei i materialov*, Moscow: Tsentr issledovanii post-industrialnogo obshchestva, available online at: https://pronicks.ru/t16/index.html#/3/zoomed, last accessed 24 June 2017.
Inozemtsev, V.L. (2010) *Anti-Iurgens*, available online at: www.mk.ru/economics/article/2010/02/08/426404-antiiurgens.html, last accessed 16 April 2017.
INSOR (2010) *Rossiia XXI veka: Obraz zhelaemogo budushchego*, available online at: http://rosglobal.polpred.com/upload/pdf/Obraz_gel_zavtra.pdf, last accessed 16 April 2017.
INSOR (2012) *Obretenie budushchego*, available online at: www.insor-russia.ru/files/Finding_of_the_Future%20.FULL_.pdf, last accessed 16 April 2017.
Iokhin, V.Ia. (2006) "National'naia model' ustoichivogo razvitiia Rossii," in Osipov, Iu.M., Sizov, V.S. and Zotova, E.S. (eds) *Ekonomicheskaia teori v XXI veke, 4 (11), Instituty ekonomiki*, Moscow: Ekonomist: 355–366.
Iudaeva, K. and Iasin, E. (2008) "Strategiia 2050: Spravitsia Rossiia s vyzovami globalizatsii?" *Voprosy ekonomiki*, 5: 4–21.
Iurchak, A. (2005) *Everything Was Forever, Until It Was No More: The Last Soviet Generation*, Princeton, NJ: Princeton University Press.
Iur'ev, M.Z. (2003) "Novyi ekonomicheskii nationalizm," in Osipov, Iu.M., Baburin, S.N., Belolipetskii, V.G. and Zotova, E.S. (eds) *Ekonomicheskaia teoriia na poroge XXI veka, t. 7, global'naia ekonomika*, Moskva: Iurist: 202–214.
Ivanchenko, V. (2007) "K poisku modeli dinamichnogo razvitiia," *Ekonomist*, 12: 24–30.
Ivanchenko, V. and Ivanchenko, V. (2005) "K sistemnomu razvitiiu Rossii," *Ekonomist*, 11: 3–9.
Ivanov, V.V. (2006) "Inovatsionnaia politika pri perekhode k ekonomike znanii," *Ekonomicheskaia nauka sovremennoi Rossii*, 1: 47–58.

Ivanov, V.V. (2009) "Konservativnaia modernizatsiia," *Izvestiia*, 30 November 2009, available online at: http://izvestia.ru/news/355942, last accessed 16 April 2017.

Ivanova, N.I. (ed) (2010) *Modernizatsiia rossiiskoi ekonomiki: strukturnyi potential*, Moscow: IMEMO RAN, available online at: www.imemo.ru/files/File/ru/publ/2010/10010.pdf, last accessed 16 April 2017.

Jacobsen, J.K. (1995) "Much Ado About Ideas: The Cognitive Factor in Economic Policy," *World Politics*, 47, 2: 283–310.

Kalashnikov, M. (2003) *Vpered, v SSSR-2*, Moscow: Iauza.

Kapeliushnikov, R.I. (1987) "Reprivatizatsiia i teoriia obobshchestvleniia," *Mirovaia ekonomika i mezhdunarodnye otnosheniia*, 1: 71–73.

Kapeliushnikov, R.I. (1989) "Filosofiia rynka F. Khaeka," *Mirovaia ekonomika i mezhdunarodnye otnosheniia*, 12: 15–26.

Kapeliushnikov, R.I. (2001) "'Gde nachalo togo kontsa?' (k voprosy ob okonchanii perekhodnogo perioda v Rossii," *Voprosy ekonomiki*, 1: 138–156.

Kashin, V.N. (1996) "Ob odnoi tendentsii postindustrial'noi ekonomiki," *Ekonomika i matematicheskie metody*, 32, 1: 31–37.

Kelley, D.R. (1977) *The Politics of Developed Socialism: The Soviet Union as a Post-Industrial State*, New York: Greenwood Press.

Khanin, G.I. (1989) "Opredelenie dinamiki optovykh tsen v sovetskoi ekonomike za 1929–1985," *Ekonomika i matematicheskie metody*, 25, 3: 540–548.

Khanin, G.I. (1992) "Economic Growth in the USSR in the Eighties," *Problems of Economics*, 34, 12: 30–39.

Khanin, G.I. (2003a) "Kak lechit' rossiiskuiu ekonomiku? (otvet na stat'iu E.B. Kibalova 'Nuzhny li nam radikal'nye peremeny?'," *EKO*, 4: 76–90.

Khanin, G.I. (2003b) "Sovetskoe ekonomicheskoe chudo: mif ili real'nost'?" *Svobodnaia mysl'*, XXI: 7–12 (four parts).

Khanin, G.I. (2004) "Teoriia ryvka i opyt Rossii," *EKO*, 9–10: 80–97.

Khanin, G.I. (2005a) "Ekonomicheskie programmy i prognozy, ili manilovshchina i samoobman," *EKO*, 4: 3–19.

Khanin, G.I. (2005b) "'Ottepel' i 'perestroika' nachalis . . . pri Staline?" *EKO*, 9: 70–100.

Khanin, G.I. (2007) "Periody stanovleniia postsovetskoi ekonomiki," *EKO*, 5: 30–50.

Khanin, G.I. and Seliunin, V. (1987) "Lukavaia tsifra," *Novyi Mir*, 2: 181–204.

Khavina, S.A. (1977) "Kritika burzhuaznoi teorii industrial'nogo obshchestva," *Voprosy ekonomiki*, 2: 112–120.

Khavina, S.A. (1994) "Gosudarstvennoe regulirovanie v sovremennoi smeshannoi ekonomike," *Voprosy ekonomiki*, 11: 80–91.

Kholodkov, V.G. (2005) "Faktory rosta rossiiskoi ekonomiki v period stabilizatsii," *Vestnik Moskovskogo universiteta*, 6, 3: 22–42.

Khubiev, K.A. (1988) "Osnovnaia struktura ekonomicheskoi systemy sotsializma v usloviiakh ego vsestoronnego sovershenstvovaniia," *Vestnik Moskovskogo universiteta, seriia 6 (ekonomika)*, 3: 11–21.

Khubiev, K.A. (1993) "Sostoianie rossiiskoi ekonomiki i puti vykhoda iz krizisa," *Vestnik Moskovskogo universiteta, seriia 6 (ekonomika)*, 4: 64–69.

Khubiev, K.A. (2003) "Aktual'nyi potentsial 'shkoly tsagolova'," in Porokhovskii, A.A. (ed) *Ekonomicheskaia teoriia v sovremennoi Rossii. Global'nye tendentsii i national'nye traditsii*, Moscow: TEIS: 96–103.

Khubiev, K.A. (2004) "Razvitie kafedry politicheskoi ekonomii pod rukovodstvom N.A. Tsagolova (1957–1985)," *Vestnik Moskovskogo universiteta*, 3: 34–47.

King, A.E. (1979) "The Macroeconomic Impact of the Czechoslovak New Economic Mechanism," *Economics of Planning*, 15, 2/3: 99–125.

Kirdina, S.G. (2000) *Institutional'nye matritsy i razvitie Rossii*, Moscow: TEIS.

Kirdina, S.G. (2001) *Institutional'nye matritsy i razvitie Rossii*, 2nd edn, Novosibirsk: IEIOPP SO RAN.

Kirdina, S.G. (2004) "Institutional'naia struktura sovremennoi Rossii: Evolutsionnaia modernizatsiia," *Voprosy ekonomiki*, 10: 89–98.

Kireeva, N.V. (2003) "Sovremennaia Rossiia: Konflikt tsennostei pod natiskom ekonomicheskoi globalizatsii," in Osipov, Iu.M., Baburin, S.N., Belolipetskii, V.G. and Zotova, E.S. (eds) *Ekonomicheskaia teoriia na poroge XXI veka, t. 7, global'naia ekonomika*, Moskva: Iurist: 695–709.

Kiva, A.V. (2011) "Mnogolikost' rossiiskoi modernizatsii," *Obshchestvennye nauki i sovremennost*, 1: 42–51.

Kleiner, G.B. (2000) "Institutional'nye faktory dolgovremennogo ekonomicheskogo rosta," *Ekonomicheskaia nauka sovremennoi Rossii*, 1: 5–20.

Kleiner, G.B. and Petrosian, D. (2005) "Vzaimodeistvie gosudarstva i obshchestva pri formirovanii ekonomicheskoi politiki," *Obshchestvo i ekonomika*, 4: 48–69.

Klotsvog, F. and Chernova, L. (2004) "O strategii upravliaemogo razvitiia," *Ekonomist*, 9: 56–63.

Kniazev, Iu.K. (2003) "Obshchemirovye tendentsii ekonomichskogo razvitii i rossiiskaia samobytnost'," *Obshchestvo i ekonomika*, 1: 5–30.

Kniazev, Iu.K. (2012) "Puti razvitiia Rossii: lozhnye orientiry i real'nost," *Obshchestvo i ekonomika*, 6: 3–16.

Kokurin, D.I. and Shalenkova, O.K. (2003) "Ekonomicheskii potentsial i stsenarii razvitiia Rossii," in Osipov, Iu.M., Baburin, S.N., Belolipetskii, V.G. and Zotova, E.S. (eds) *Ekonomicheskaia teoriia na poroge XXI veka, t. 7, global'naia ekonomika*, Moskva: Iurist: 966–976.

Kolganov, A.I. (1995) "Zakonomernosti perekhodnoi ekonomiki: ekonomicheskie tendentsii i modeli," *Voprosy ekonomiki*, 2: 50–60.

Kollontai, A.V. (1987) "Reprivatizatsiia – zveno v obshchem pereraspredelenii ekonomicheskikh funktsii," *Mirovaia ekonomika i mezhdunarodnye otnosheniia*, 4: 79–82.

Komin, A.N. (1987) "Perestroika tsennevogo khoziaistva," *Voprosy ekonomiki*, 3: 107–114.

Kondrashev, D.D. (1988) "Voprosy sovershenstvovaniia tsenoobrazovaniia," *Voprosy ekonomiki*, 1: 93–96.

Kontseptsiia dolgosrochnogo razvitiia Rossiiskoi Federatsii na period do 2020 goda, available online at: http://economy.gov.ru/minec/activity/sections/strategicPlanning/concept/, last accessed 2 July 2017.

Kosal, L.Ia. (2000) "Rossiiskii put' k kapitalizmu: mezhdu kitaem i vostochnoi evropoi," *Mirovaia ekonomika i mezhdunarodnye otnosheniia*, 10: 14–20.

Kosobokova, T. (2008) "Chetyre 'I' Medved'eva," *RBK*, 15 February 2008.

Kozlov, G.A. (1973) "Ob osnovnom ekonomicheskom zakone v usloviiakh razvitogo sotsializma," *Voprosy ekonomiki*, 5: 3–16.

Kozlov, G.A. (1977) *Razvitoi sotsializm: Voprosy ekonomicheskoi teorii*, Moscow: Mysl.

Krasin, Iu.A. (ed) (2011) *Innovatsionnaia modernizatsiia Rossii. Politologicheskie ocherki*, Moscow: Institut sotsiologii RAN.

Kriukov, V.A. (2013) "Trava pod asfal'tom," *EKO*, 10: 2–4.

Kruglyi stol' (2009) "Kruglyi stol': Ekonomicheski krizis v mire i v Rossii: Uroki, puti preodeleniia," *Ekonomicheskii zhurnal novoi ekonomicheskii assotsiatsii*, 1–2: 224–264.

Kubik, J. (2003) "Cultural Legacies of State Socialism: History Making and Cultural-Political Entrepreneurship in Postcommunist Poland and Russia," in Ekiert, G. and Hanson, S.E. (eds) *Capitalism and Democracy in Central and Eastern Europe: Assessing the Legacy of Communist Rule*, Cambridge: Cambridge University Press: 317–351.

Kuchukov, R. (2009) "Rol' gosudarstva v formirovanii innovatsionnoi politiki," *Ekonomist*, 6: 3–13.

Kudrin, A. (2007) "Stabilisation Funds: International and Russian Experience," *Problems of Economic Transition*, 50, 1: 6–26.

Kudrov, V.M. (2005) "Ekonomika 'trekh Evrop' (sopostavitel'nyi analiz)," *Obshchestvo i ekonomika*, 2: 3–43.

Kudrov, V.M. (2007) *National'naia ekonomika*, Moscow: Delo.

Kudrov, V.M. (2009) "Rossiiskaia ekonomika: Permanentnost' nereshennykh problem," *Obshchestvo i ekonomika*, 2: 118–139.

Kudrov, V.M. (2011) "Ekonomika Rossii i Evropy v mire: proshloe, nastoiashchee i budushchee," *Obshchestvennye nauki i sovremennost'*, 5: 21–33.

Kudrov, V.M. (2012) "K otsenke rossiiskoi sotsial'no-ekonomicheskoi sistemy," *Obshchestvo i ekonomika*, 9: 25–34.

Kuhn, T.S. (1962) *The Structure of Scientific Revolutions* (references are to the 1973 edition), Chicago: University of Chicago Press.

Kul'kov, V.M. (1993) "Rossiiskaia sotsial'naia traditsiia," *Vestnik Moskovskogo universiteta, seriia 6 (ekonomika)*, 3: 13–22.

Kul'kov, V.M. (2004) "National'nyi kontekst ekonomicheskoi teorii: proshloe i nastoiashchee," *Vestnik Moskovskogo universiteta seriia 6*, 3: 60–71.

Kulikov, V.V. (1986) "Protivorechiia ekonomicheskoi sistemy sotsializma kak istochnik ee razvitiia," *Voprosy ekonomiki*, 1: 117–128.

Kulikov, V.V. (1989) "Obshchestvennaia sobstvennost' i demokratizatsiia ekonomicheskoi zhizni," *Voprosy ekonomiki*: 5: 47–60.

Kulikov, V.V. (2004) "'Tsagolovskaia shkola' i ee nyneshnee zvuchanie," *Rossiiskii ekonomicheskii zhurnal*, 4: 60–71.

Kurishchak, A. (1995) "Contribution to Round-Table Discussion 'Istoricheskie sud'by, uroki i perspektivy radikal'noi ekonomicheskoi reformy'," *Voprosy ekonomiki*, 4: 4–66.

Kushlin, V.I. (1997) "Rossiia i ekonomicheskii poriadok XXI veka," *Ekonomist*, 12: 3–12.

Kuz'minov, I.I. (1975) "Politicheskaia ekonomiia – nauchnaia osnova rukovodstva khoziaistvom," in Kuz'minov, I.I. and Rochagov, S.V. (eds) *Politicheskaia ekonomiia sotsializma – nauchnaia osnova rukovodstva narodnym khoziaistvom*, Moscow: Mysl: 3–28.

Kuz'minov, Ia.I. (1992) "Sovetskaia ekonomicheskaia kul'tura: nasledie i puti modernizatsii'," *Voprosy ekonomiki*, 3: 44–57.

Kuz'minov, Ia.I. (1999) *Uchebno-metodicheskoe posobie k kursu lektsii institutional'noi ekonomiki*, Moscow: Vysshaia shkola ekonomiki.

Kuz'minov, Ia.I. and Iudkevich, M. (2000) *Institutsional'naia ekonomika*. Moscow: Vysshaia shkola ekonomiki.

Kuznetsov, O.L. (2005) "Problemy postroeniia obshchestva znanii v sovremennoi Rossii: mify, rify, perspektivy," *EKO*, 8: 40–46.

Kuznetsov, V.I. (1986) "Gosudarstvennoe regulirovanie i chastnoe predprinimatel'stvo v kapitalisticheskikh stranakh: Evoliutsiia vzaimootnosheniia," *MEiMO*, 10: 85–87.

Kuznetsov, V.I. (1994) "K teorii perekhodnoi ekonomiki," *Mirovaia ekonomika i mezhdunarodnye otnosheniia*, 12: 5–14.

Kuznetsova, T.E. (2000) *Ekonomist rossiiskoi shkoly*, Moscow: Nauka.

Lakatos, I. (1965) "Falsification and the Methodology of Scientific Research Programmes," in Lakatos, I. and Musgrave, A. (eds) *Criticism and the Growth of Knowledge: Proceedings of the International Colloquium in the Philosophy of Science* (references are to the 1974 edition), London: Cambridge University Press: 132–177.

Latysheva, G. and Sergeev, A. (1978) "Vysshaia tsel' obshchestvennogo proizvodstva pri sotsializme," *Voprosy ekonomiki*, 12: 94–105.

Ledeneva, A.V. (1998) *Russia's Economy of Favours. Blat, Networking and Informal Exchange*, Cambridge: Cambridge University Press.

Leont'ev, M., Privalov, A., Sokolov, M. and Fadeev, V. (2003) *Memorandum serafimovskogo kluba: Ot politika strakha k politike rosta*, avalilabe online at: https://regnum.ru/news/polit/80279.html, last accessed 16 April 2017.

Leskov, L.V. (2004) "Postmodern russkoi idei," in Osipov, Iu.M., Baburin, S.N., Belolipetskii, V.G. and Zotova, E.S. (eds) *Ekonomicheskaia teoriia na poroge XXI veka, t. 7, global'naia ekonomika*, Moskva: Iurist: 73–91.

Levikov, A. (1988) "Kak preodelet' izobilie defitsita: Tsena i rynok," *Literaturnaia Gazeta*, 50, 14 December 1988: 10.

Levita, R. (1996) "O sotsial'no-psikhologicheskoi komponente institutsional'nykh izmenenii v ekonomike," *Ekonomika i matematicheskie metody*, 32, 4: 91–106.

Levitsky, S. and Murillo, V. (2009) "Variation in Institutional Strength," *Annual Review of Political Science*, 12: 115–133.

Liberman, E.G. ([1956] 1971) "Means to Raise the Profitability of the Socialistic Enterprise," reprinted in Liberman, E.G. (ed) *Economic Methods and the Effectiveness of Production*, White Plains, NY: International Arts and Science Press.

Libman, A. and Zweynert, J. (2014) "Ceremonial Science: The state of Russian Economics Seen Through the Lens of the Work of 'Doctor of Science' Candidates," *Economic Sytems*, 38, 3: 360–378.

Lieberman, R.C. (2002) "Ideas, Institutions, and Political Order: Explaining Institutional Change," *American Political Science Review*, 96, 4: 697–712.

Lisichkin, G.S. (1966) *Plan i rynok*, Moscow: Ekonomika.

Louzek, M. (2011) "The Battle of Methods in Economics: The Classical Methodenstreit, Menger vs. Schmoller," *American Journal of Economics and Sociology*, 70, 2: 439–463.

L'vov, D.S. (1994) "Real'nyi kurs ekonomicheskikh preobrazovanii," *Ekonomika i matematicheskie metody*, 30, 1: 5–18.

L'vov, D.S. (1997) "Teoreticheskoe iadro sotsial'no-ekonomicheskogo razvitiia strany," *Ekonomist*, 1: 7–16.

L'vov, D.S. (2005) "Missiia Rosii," *EKO*, 2: 3–8.

Mahoney, J. and Thelen, K. (2010) "A Theory of Gradual Institutional Change," in Mahoney, J. and Thelen, K. (eds) *Explaining Institutional Change. Ambiguity, Agency, and Power*, Cambridge: Cambridge University Press: 1–37.

Maiminas, E.Z. (1992) "Otechestvennaia ekonomicheskaia nauka na pereput'e," *Ekonomika i matematicheskie metody*, 28, 4: 520–533.

Maiminas, E.Z. (1996) "Rossiiskii sotsial'no-ekonomicheskii genotip," *Voprosy ekonomiki*, 9: 131–141.

Makarevich, L. (2003) "Gosudarstva Rossii dolzhno nauchitsia upravliat' rynochnymi reformami," *Obshchestvo i ekonomika*, 9: 5–76.

Makasheva, N.A (1989) "F. fon Khaiek: Mirovozrencheskii kontekst ekonomicheskoi teorii," *Voprosy ekonomiki*, 4: 146–156.

Malakhinova, R.P. (2003) "K voprosu ob osnove vydeleniia ekonomicheskikh system," in Porokhovskii, A.A. (ed) *Ekonomicheskaia teoriia v sovremennoi Rossii. Global'nye tendentsii i national'nye traditsii*, Moscow: TEIS: 72–86.

Martynov, A. (2003a) "Postsotsialisticheskaia transformatsiia: Kak otsenit' ee rezul'taty?" *Obshchestvo i ekonomika*, 12: 5–35.

Martynov, A. (2003b) "Postindustrial'naia modernizatsiia i budushchee postsotsializma," *Obshchestvo i ekonomika*, 9: 77–96.

Martynov, A. (2009) "I vnov' ogosudarstvlenie rossiiskogo obshchestva?" *Obshchestvo i ekonomika*, 1: 5–20.

Maslennikov, A.A. (2012a) "Vvedenie," in Fedorov, V.P. (ed) *Institut Evropy Rossiiskoi Akademii Nauk: Innovatsionnoe razvitie ekonomiki. Mezhdunarodnyi opyt i problemy Rossii*, Moscow and St. Petersburg: Nestor-Istoriia: 7–14.

Maslennikov, A.A. (2012b) "Zakliuchenie," in Fedorov, V.P. (ed) *Institut Evropy Rossiiskoi Akademii Nauk: Innovatsionnoe razvitie ekonomiki. Mezhdunarodnyi opyt i problemy Rossii*, Moscow and St. Petersburg: Nestor-Istoriia: 347–352.

Materialy (1971) *Materialy xxiv. s'ezda kpss*, Moscow: Gospolitizdat.

Matveenko, V.D. and Zhelezniak, T.I. (2005) "Politicheskaia ekonomiia i 'ekonomiks': edinstvo ili antagonizm?" *Ekonomicheskaia nauka sovremennoi Rossii*, 1: 39–46.

Mau, V.A. (1995) "Perestroika: teoreticheskie i politicheskie problemy ekonomicheskikh reform," *Voprosy ekonomiki*, 67, 2: 6–29.

Mau, V.A. (1999) "Rossiia ekonomicheskie reformy glazami zapadnykh kritikov," *Voprosy ekonomiki*, 11: 4–23.

Mau, V.A. (2000) "Polit-ekonomicheskie problemy provedeniia rynochnykh reform v postkommunisticheskoi Rossii," *Obshchestvo i ekonomika*, 7: 3–38.

Mau, V.A. (2001) "Ekonomicheskaia politika Rossii: v nachale novoi fazy," *Voprosy ekonomiki*, 3: 4–22.

Mau, V.A. (2004) "Itogi 2003 goda i itogi cheterekhletiia: politika protiv ekonomiki," *Voprosy ekonomiki*, 3: 4–23.

Mau, V.A. (2006) "Ekonomicheskaia politika 2006 goda: na puti k investitionnomu rostu," *Voprosy ekonomiki*, 2: 4–25.

Mau, V.A. (2013) "Mezhdu modernizatsiei i zastoem: Ekonomicheskaia politika 2012 goda," *Voprosy ekonomiki*, 2: 4–23.

Mazzucato, M. (2014) *The Entrepreneurial State: Debunking Public vs. Private Sector Myths, Revised*, London: Anthem Press.

McConnell, C.R. and Brue, S.L. (1990) *Economics: Principles, Problems, and Policies*, 11th edn, New York: McGraw-Hill.

Medved'ev, D. (2008) *Poslanie Federal'nomu Sobraniiu Rossiiskoi Federatsii*, 5 November, available online at: www.kremlin.ru/events/president/transcripts/messages/1968, last accessed 16 April 2017.

Medved'ev, D. (2009a) "Rossiia, vpered!," *gazeta.ru*, 10 September 2009, available online at: www.gazeta.ru/comments/2009/09/10_a_3258568.shtml, last accessed 16 April 2016.

Medved'ev, D. (2009b) *Poslanie Federal'nomu Sobraniiu Rossiiskoi Federatsii*, 12 November, available online at: www.kremlin.ru/events/president/transcripts/messages/5979, last accessed 16 April 2017.

Medved'ev, D. (2010) *Poslanie Federal'nomu Sobraniiu Rossiiskoi Federatsii*, 30 November, available online at: www.kremlin.ru/events/president/transcripts/messages/9637, last accessed 16 April 2017.

Medved'ev, D. (2011) *Poslanie Federal'nomu Sobraniiu Rossiiskoi Federatsii*, 22 December 2011, available online at: www.kremlin.ru/events/president/transcripts/messages/14088, last accessed 16 April 2017.

Medved'ev, V.A. (1980) *Razvitoi sotsializm: Voprosy formirovaniia obshchestvennogo soznaniia*, Moscow: Politizdat.

Medved'ev, V.A. (ed) (1988) *Politicheskaia ekonomiia. Uchebnik dlia vysshikh uchebnykh zavedenii*, Moscow: Politizdat.

Medved'ev, V.A. (1993) "Nekotorye razmyshleniia o novoi paradigme ekonomicheskoi teorii," *Voprosy ekonomiki*, 1: 22–29.

Medved'ev, V.A. (1995) "Contribution to Round-Table Discussion 'Istoricheskie sud'by, uroki i perspektivy radikal'noi ekonomicheskoi reformy'," *Voprosy ekonomiki*, 4: 4–66.

Medved'ev, V.A. (2004) "Globalizatsiia ekonomiki: tendentsii i protivorechiia," *Mirovaia ekonomikai i mezhdnarodnye otnosheniia*, 2: 3–10.

Ménard, C. (1990) *L'économie des organisations*, Paris: Éd. La Découverte.

Men'shikov, S. (2004) "Nash kapitalizm: Mezhdu oligarkhicheskim i biurokraticheskim," *Svobodnaia mysl'*, 10: 25–32.

Miasoedov, B. and Lobova, A. ([1989] 1990) "On the Culture of Politico-Economic Publication (An Editor's Note)," originally: *Voprosy ekonomiki*, 10: 75–83, here: *Problems of Economic Transition*, 32, 10: 75–83.

Mikhailovskii, N.K. ([1869] 1906) "Chto takoe progress?" in *Polnoe sobranie sochinenii*, 4th edn, vol. 1, St. Petersburg: Znanie: 18–166 (translation of the verbal quotation is according to Walicki ([1969] 1975: 53).

Mikul'skii, K. (2009) "Rossiskaia ekonomika: Imperativ sotsial'noi modernizatsii," *Obshchestvo i ekonomika*, 11–12: 39–43.

Mileikovskii, A. (1975) "Is Galbraith Crossing the Rubicon," *Problems of Economics*, 18, 2: 78–98.

Mironov, B.N. (2000) *The Social History of Imperial Russia, 1700–1917*, 2 vols, Boulder, CO: Westview Press.

Mirowski, P. and Plehwe, D. (eds) (2009) *The Road From Mont Pèlerin: The Making of the Neoliberal Thought Collective*, Cambridge, MA: Harvard University Press.

Mochernyi, S.V. (1987) "K voprosu ob istoricheskoi perspektive gosudarstvenno-monopolisticheskogo kapitalizma," *Mirovaia ekonomika i mirovye otnosheniia*, 7: 94–98.

Moiseev, N.N. (1998) "Mozhno li govorit' o Rossii v budushchem vremeni? Rossiia v kontekste 'sud'by tsivilizatsii'," *Ekonomicheskaia nauka sovremennoi Rossii*, 2: 68–79.

Molchanov, M. and Molchanova, V. (2010) "Modernizatsionnye reformy: Vzaimovsiaz ekonomicheskogo i sotsial'no-politicheskogo razvitiia," *Obshchestvo i ekonomika*, 7: 5–21.

Movsesian, A.G. (1998) "Institutsional'nyi podkhod k strategii sotsial'no-ekonomicheskogo razvitiia," *Ekonomist*, 4: 24–29.

Mukherji, R. (2013) "Ideas, Interests, and the Tipping Point: Economic Change in India," *Review of International Political Economy*, 20, 2: 363–389.

Murav'ev, A.I. (ed) (1995) *Ocherki teorii perekhodnoi ekonomiki*, St Petersburg: Sankt-Peterburgskii universitet ekonomiki i finansov.

Nabiullina, E. (2009) "Ekonomicheskaia politika v usloviiakh krizisa – analis i perspektivy," *Ekonomicheskaia politika*, 3: 73–85.

Nekipelov, A.D. (2002) "O nekotorykh kontseptual'nykh voprosakh ekonomicheskikh preobrazovanii v Rossii," *Mirovaia ekonomika i mezhdunarodnye otnosheniia*, 2: 20–31.

Neshchadin, A., Kuznetsov, O. and Kashin, V. (2007) "Rossiiskaia ekonomika: Tendentsii ogosudarstvleniia," *Obshchestvo i ekonomika*, 8: 3–27.

Neshitoi, A.S. (2007) "Rost bez razvitiia (k itogam sotsial'no-ekonomicheskogo polozheniia Rossii v 2006)," *EKO*, 4: 2–12.

Nesterenko, A.N. (2000) "Perekhodnyi period zakonchil'sia: chto dal'she?" *Voprosy ekonomiki*, 6: 4–17.

Netreba, P. (2006) "Alexei Kudrin prizval pravitel'stvo otkazat'sia ot boltovni," *Kommersant*, 16 June 2006.

Nikolaev, I., Kalinin, A. and Tolchikina, O. (2005) "Rynochnaia transformatsiia ekonomiki: Itogi proidenogo etapa," *Obshchestvo i ekonomika*, 9: 48–81.

North, D.C. (1990) *Institutions, Institutional Change and Economic Performance*, Cambridge: Cambridge University Press.

Nosova, S.S. (2004) "Ekonomika Rossii v nachale XXI veka: kak zhit' dal'she?" in Osipov, Iu.M., Inshakov, O.V. and Zotova, E.S. (eds) *Ekonomicheskaia teoriia v XXI veke, 1 (8), Ekonomika postmoderna*, Moscow: Iurist: 709–715.

Novosel'skii, V. (2005) "Obshchestvennoe soznanie i ekonomicheskaia politika," *Ekonomist*, 1: 46–51.

Nureev, R. and Latov, Iu. (2001) "Plody prosveshcheniia (novaia rossiiskaia ekonomicheskaia nauka na poroge III tysiachiletiia)," *Voprosy ekonomiki*, 1: 96–116.

Oleinik, A.L. (1997) "Izderzhki i perspektivy reform v Rossii: institutsional'nyi podkhod," *Mirovaia ekonomika i mezhdunarodnye otnosheniia*, 12: 25–36.

Oleinik, A.L. (1998) "Izderzhki i perspektivy reform v Rossii: institutsional'nyi podkhod," *Mirovaia ekonomika i mezhdunarodnye otnosheniia*, 1: 18–28.

Oleinik, A.L. (2000) *Institutional'naia ekonomika*, Moscow: INFRA-M/Voprosy ekonomiki.

Oleinik, A.L. (2006) "The More Things Change, the More They Stay the Same: Institutional Reforms Seen Through the Lens of Reforms in Russia," *Journal of Economic Issues*, 40, 4: 919–940.

Oleinikov, A.A. (2006) "Traditionalizm v kachestve institutional'noi osnovoi modeli national'nogo khoziaistva Rossii," in Osipov, Iu.M., Sizov, V.S. and Zotova, E.S. (eds) *Ekonomicheskaia teoriia v XXI veke, 4 (11), Instituty ekonomiki*, Moscow: Ekonomist: 152–161.

Ol'sevich, Iu.Ia. (1992) "Khoziaistvennaia sistema i etnos," *Voprosy ekonomiki*, 8: 7–16.

Ol'sevich, Iu.Ia. (1996) "O natsional'nom ekonomicheskom myshlenii," *Voprosy ekonomiki*, 9: 117–130.

Ol'sevich, Iu.Ia. (1999) "Institutsionalizm: novaia panatseia dlia Rossii?" *Voprosy ekonomiki*, 6: 27–42.

Olson, M. (1965) *The Logic of Collective Action*, Cambridge, MA: Harvard University Press.

Olson, M. (1982) *The Rise and Decline of Nations*, New Haven: Yale University Press.

Orekhovskii, P. (2009) "Vlast' i innovatsii (pochemu v Rossii ne poluchaetsia postroit' innovatsionnuiu ekonomiku)," *Obshchestvo i ekonomika*, 8–9: 93–116.

Osadchaia, I.M. (1986) "Sdvigi v kontseptsii i praktike gosudarstvennogo regulirovaniia ekonomiki," *Mirovaia ekonomika i mezhdunarodnye otnosheniia*, 12: 99–101.

Osipov, Iu.M. (1996) "Po puti novogo tvorcheskogo poiska," in Osipov, Iu.M. and Puliarev, V.T. (eds) *Ekonomicheskaia teoriia na poroge XXI veka*, St Petersburg: Petropolis: 5–21.

Osipov, Iu.M. (1998) "K poisku novoi paradigmy," in Osipov, Iu.M., Puliarev, V.T., Riazanov, V.T. and Zotova, E.S. (eds) *Ekonomicheskaia teoriia na poroge XXI veka*, vol. 2, Moscow: Iurist: 5–16.

Ostrovitianov, K.V. (1954) *Politicheskaia ekonomiia. Uchebnik*, Moscow: Izdatel'stvo Politicheskoi Literatury.

Ovsienko, Iu. (2005) "Institutional'nye bar'ery rossiiskoi modernizatsii," *Ekonomika i matematicheskie metody*, 41, 2: 44–55.

Ovsienko, Iu. and Petrakov, N. (2004) "Rossiiskaia transformatsiia i ee rezul'taty," *Voprosy ekonomiki*, 5: 59–72.

Pakhomov, Iu.M. (2000) "Ob ekonomicheskom, sotsial'nom i tsivilizatsionnom aspektakh rynochnykh reform," *Obshchestvo i ekonomika*, 8: 3–18.

Pakhomov, Iu.M. and Vrublevskii, V.K. (1987) "Formirovanie i razreshenie ekonomicheskikh protivorechii sotsializma," *Voprosy ekonomiki*, 3: 86–95.

Pan'kov, V.S. (1987) "Deregulirovanie i evoliutsiia khoziaistvennogo mekhanizma GMK," *Mirovaia ekonomika i mezhdunarodnye otnoshenia*, 4: 72–76.

Panova, G.S. (ed) (2008) *Stabilizatsionnyi fond Rossiiskoi Federatsii: Genezis razvitiia*, Moscow: Finansy i Statistika.

Petrakov, N.I. ([1987] 1987) "Planovaia tsena v sisteme upravleniia narodnym khoziaistvom," *Voprosy ekonomiki*, 1: 44–55 [English translation: "The Plan Price in the National Economy's System of Management," *Problems of Economics*, 30, 3: 38–53].

Petrakov, N.I. (2010) "K voprosu o modernizatsii ekonomiki," *Ekonomist*, 12: 3–6.

Petrosian, D. (2007) "Psikhologicheskie metody modernizatsii institutional'noi sistemy ekonomiki Rossii," *Obshchestvo i ekonomika*, 7: 80–98.

Petrov, V.K. (1995) "Sostoitsia li shestaia Rossiia?" *Obshchestvo i ekonomika*, 5: 3–12.

Pevzner, Ia. (1987) "Gosudarstvennaia sobstvennost' kak chast' sistemy ekonomicheskogo regulirovaniia," *Mirovaia ekonomika i mezhdunarodnye otnosheniia*, 3: 56–60.

Pevzner, Ia. (1988) "Novoe myshlenie i neobkhodimost' novykh podkhodov v politicheskoi·ekonomii," *Mirovaia ekonomika i mezhdunarodnye otnosheniia*, 6: 5–22.

Pierson, P. (2000) "The Limits of Design: Explaining Institutional Origins and Change," *Governance*, 13, 4: 475–499.

Pindyck, R.S. and Rubinfeld, D.L. (1989) *Microeconomics*, New York: Macmillan.

Pinsker, B.S. (1990) "Illiuziia miagkoi posadki," *Literaturnaia Gazeta*, 38, 18 September 1990: 11.

Pinsker, B.S. and Popkova-Piiasheva, L.I. (1989) "Sobstvennost' i svoboda," *Novyi mir*, 11: 184–198.

Platonov, D.N. (1993) "Pravoslavie v ego khoziaistvennykh vozmozhnostiakh (zametki istorika-ekonomista)," *Voprosy ekonomiki*, 8: 82–87.

Platonov, O.A. (1993) *Russkii put' v ekonomike*, Moscow: AKIRN.

Plotitsyna, L.A. (2003) "Nekotorye osobennosti transformationnykh protsessov v Rossii v usloviiakh globalizatsii," in Osipov, Iu.M., Baburin, S.N., Belolipetskii, V.G. and Zotova, E.S. (eds) *Ekonomicheskaia teoriia na poroge XXI veka, t. 7, global'naia ekonomika*, Moskva: Iurist: 471–480.

Plyshevskii, B. (2004) "O promyshlennoi politike," *Ekonomist*, 9: 3–16.

Polanyi, K. ([1944] 2001) *The Great Transformation: The Political and Economic Origins of Our Time*, Boston: Beacon Press.

Poliakov, V. (2006) "Syrevaia orientatsiia rossiiskogo eksporta," *Mirovaia ekonomika i mezhdunarodnye otnosheniia*, 1: 88–95.

Polterovich, V.M. (2001a) "Transplantatsiia ekonomicheskikh institutov," *Ekonomicheskaia nauka sovremennoi Rossii*, 3: 24–50.

Polterovich, V.M. (2001b) "Institutional Traps," in Klein, L.R. and Pomer, M. (eds) *The New Russia: Transition Gone Awry*, Stanford: Stanford University Press: 93–116.

Polterovich, V.M. (2008) "Strategii modernizatsii, instituty i koalitsii," *Voprosy ekonomiki*, 4: 4–24.

Popadiuk, N. (2006) "Chastnia li chastnaia sobstvennost' v Rossii? (veroiatnye stsenarii razvitiia biznessa)," *Voprosy ekonomiki*, 1: 144–155.

Popkova-Piiasheva, L.I. ([1987] 1988) "Gde pyshnee pirogi?" *Novyi Mir*, 5: 239–241 [English translation: Popkova-Piiasheva, L.I. "Where Are the Pirogi Meatier?" *Problems of Economics*, 2: 44–48].

Popkova-Piiasheva, L.I. (1990) "Kak my budem zhit' v usloviiakh rnyka? Prognoz optimista," *Literaturnaia gazeta*, 22, 30 May 1990: 10.

Popkova-Piiasheva, L.I. and Pinsker, B.S. (1988) *Ekonomicheskii neokonservatizm: teoriia i mezhdunarodnaia praktika*, Moscow: Mezhdunarodnye otnosheniia [Shortened English translation: "Neo-conservative Economics: Theory and International Practice," *International Journal of Political Economy*, 19, 2: 13–97].

Popov, G. (1988) "Diskussiia o problemakh biurokratizma," *Voprosy ekonomiki*, 12: 3–6.

Popov, G. ([1989] 1990) "Vosstanie protiv Keinsianstva: Milton Fridmen," *Voprosy ekonomiki*, 12: 139–140 [English translation: Popov, G. "The Rebellion Against Keynesianism: Milton Friedman," *Problems of Economics*, 5: 99–103].

Popova, E. (2007) "K obshchegosudarstvennoi programme planogo-indikativnogo razvitiia," *Ekonomist*, 3: 3–10.

Porokhovskii, A.A. (2002) "Rossiiskaia rynochnaia model': put' realizatsii," *Voprosy ekonomiki*, 10: 35–46.

Porokhovskii, A.A. (2003) "Contribution to Round Table 'O statuse politicheskoi ekonomii v vuzovskom prepodovanii ekonomicheskikh distsiplin'," *Rossiiskii ekonomicheskii zhurna*l, 5–6: 63–66.

Porokhovskii, A.A. and Khubiev, K.A. (2005) "Formirovanie rossiiskoi modeli sotsial'noi rynochnoi ekonomiki," *Vestnik Moskovskogo universiteta*, 6, 4: 3–21.

Prazdnov, G.S. (2011) "Strategiia innovatsionnogo razvitiia ekonomiki Rossii," in Prochenko, O.D. (ed) *Innovatsionnoe razvitie Rossii*, Moscow: 8–21.

Pribram, K. (1983) *A History of Economic Reasoning*, Baltimore and London: John Hopkins University Press.

Prokhozhev, A.A. and Kornilov, M. (2003) "O probleme kriteriev i otsenok ekonomicheskoi bezopasnosti," *Obshchestvo i ekonomika*, 4/5: 225–239.

Ptushenko, A. (2004) "K voprosu o kriteriiakh effektivnosti ekonomiki," *Obshchestvo i ekonomika*, 10: 157–167.

Putin, V. (2012a) "Nam nuzhna novaia ekonomika", *Vedomosti*, 30 January 2012, available online at: www.vedomosti.ru/politics/articles/2012/01/30/o_nashih_ekonomicheskih_zadachah, last accessed 16 April 2017.

Putin, V. (2012b) *Poslanie Federal'nomu Sobraniiu Rossiiskoi Federatsii*, 12 December, available online at: www.kremlin.ru/events/president/transcripts/messages/17118, last accessed 16 April 2017.

Putin, V. (2013) *Poslanie Federal'nomu Sobraniiu Rossiiskoi Federatsii*, 12 December, available online at: www.kremlin.ru/events/president/transcripts/messages/19825, last accessed 16 April 2017.

Radaev, Vad. V. (1995) "Khoziaistvennaia sistema Rossii skvoz' prizmu ideologicheskikh sistem," *Voprosy ekonomiki*, 2: 30–39.

Radaev, Vad. V. and Auzan, A.A. ([1989] 1990) "Sotsializm: Vozmozhnye varianty," *Voprosy ekonomiki*, 9: 109–119 [English translation: Radaev, V.V. and Auzan, A.A. "Socialism: Possible Variants," *Problems of Economics*, 1: 59–77].

Radaev, Vad. V., Auzan, A.A., Gerasimenko, V.V., Krasnikova, E.V., Shastitko, A.E. and Shekht, N.I. (1994) "Perekhodnaia ekonomika v Rossii: metodologiia analiza," *Vestnik Moskovskogo universiteta*, 3: 3–12.

Radaev, Val. V. (1992a) "O kriteriiakh obshchestvennogo razvitiia," *Ekonomist*, 4: 71–80.

Radaev, Val. V. (1992b) "Obnovlenie ekonomicheskoi teorii: puti i problemy," *Voprosy ekonomiki*, 10: 113–120.

Radaev, Val. V. (2003) "Traditsii rossiiskoi ekonomicheskoi mysli i ekonomicheskaia teoriia," in Porokhovskii, A.A. (ed) *Ekonomicheskaia teoriia v sovremennoi Rossii. Global'nye tendentsii i national'nye traditsii*, Moscow: TEIS: 14–22.
Radaev, Val. V. (2004) "Vazhnye usloviia razvitiia ekonomicheskoi teorii," *Vestnik Moskovskogo universiteta*, 6, 3: 9–33.
Radaev, Val. V. and Buzgalin, A.V. (eds) (1995) *Ekonomika perekhodnogo perioda*, Moscow: Izdatel'stvo Moskovskogo universiteta.
Radygin, A. (2004) "Rossiia v 2000–2004 godakh: na puti k gosudarstvennomu kapitalizmu?" *Voprosy ekonomiki*, 4: 42–65.
Radygin, A. and Entov, R. (2005) "Institutional'nye komponenty ekonomicheskogo rosta," *Voprosy ekonomiki*, 11: 14–38.
Rakitskii, B.V. ([1987] 1988) "Problemy perestroiki politicheskoi ekonomiki sotsializma," *Voprosy ekonomiki*, 12 [English translation: Rakitskii, B.V. "Problems of Restructuring the Political Economy of Socialism," *Problems of Economics*, 31, 4: 24–41].
Robinson, N. (1995) *Ideology and the Collapse of the Soviet System: A Critical History of Soviet Ideological Discourse*, Aldershot: Edward Elgar.
Rodrik, D. (2014) "When Ideas Trump Interests: Preferences, Worldviews, and Policy Innovations," *Journal of Economic Perspectives*, 28, 1: 189–208.
Rostowski, J. (1994) *Interenterprise Arrears in Post-Communist Economies*, Washington, DC: IMF, Research Department.
Rozmainskii, I.V. and Skorobogatov, A.S. (2006) "Investitionnaia blizorukost' kak institutionl'nyi ogranichitel' ekonomicheskogo rosta v postsovetskoi Rossii," *Ekonomicheskaia nauka sovremennoi Rossii*, 4: 7–21.
Rubanov, V. (2004) "Ideia tekhnologicheskoi modernizatsii i budushchee Rossii," *Svobodnaia mysl'*, 7: 20–32.
Rutland, P. (2013) "Neoliberalism and the Russian Tradition," *Review of International Political Economy*, 20, 2: 332–362.
Ryvkin, A.A. (1989) "Ekonomicheskaia teoriia i real'nost'," *Voprosy ekonomiki*, 1: 130–141.
Safarov, S.I. (1983) *Razvitoi sotsializm. Vozdeistvie nadstroechnykh faktorov na ekonomiku*, Moscow: Ekonomika.
Salikhov, B. (2006) "Adekvatna li politicheskaia ekonomiia sovremennym obshchestvennym realiiam?" *Obshchestvo i ekonomika*, 3: 10–22.
Samsonov, K.P. (1994) "Elementy kontseptsii ekonomicheskoi bezopasnosti," *Voprosy ekonomiki*, 12: 14–24.
Samuelson, P. (1948) *Economics*, New York: McGraw-Hill Books.
Sandle, M. (2002) "Brezhnev and Developed Socialism: The Ideology of Zastoi?" in Bacon, E. and Sandle, M. (eds) *Brezhnev Reconsidered*, Basingstoke: Palgrave Macmillan: 165–187.
Savchenko, L.V. (ed) (2005) *National'naia ekonomika: uchebnik*, Moscow: Ekonomist.
Schmidt, V.A. (2008) "Discursive Institutionalism: The Explanatory Power of Ideas and Discourse," *Annual Review of Political Science*, 11 (June): 303–326.
Schmidt, V.A. (2012) "A Curious Constructivism: A Response to Professor Bell," *British Journal of Political Science*, 42, 3: 705–713.
Schull, J. (1992) "What Is Ideology? Theoretical Problems and Lessons From Soviet-type Societies," *Political Studies*, XL: 728–741.
Schumpeter, J.A. ([1954] 1967) *History of Economic Analysis*, 6th printing, London: George Allen and Unwin.
Seleznev, A. (1994) "Traditsii v ekonomicheskoi politike i sovremennost'," *Ekonomist*, 4: 49–58.

Seliunin, V. (1989) "Chernye dyry ekonomiki," *Novyi mir*, 10: 153–178.

Seliunin, V. (1990) "Poslednii shans," *Literaturnaia gazeta*, 18, 2 May 1990: 2.

Senchagov, V.K. (ed) (1998) *Ekonomicheskaia bezopasnost': proizvodstvo, finansy, banki*, Moscow: Finstatinform.

Senchagov, V.K. (2007) "Ekonomicheskaia bezopasnost' Rossii," *EKO*, 5: 2–20.

Senchagov, V.K. (2008) "Strategiia razvitiia Rossii: orientiry i ogranicheniia," *Voprosy ekonomiki*, 8: 119–130.

Sergeev, A. (1974) "O sisteme ekonomicheskikh zakonov v usloviiakh razvitogo sotsializma," *Voprosy ekonomiki*, 1: 55–65.

Sergeev, M. (2008) "Minfin stavit krest na svetlom budushchem," *Nezavisimaia gazeta*, 9 April 2008.

Sergeeva, O.A. (2003) "Ob ekonomicheskoi teorii, praktike, mentalitete, tsennostiakh i prochem," in Osipov, Iu.M., Baburin, S.N., Belolipetskii, V.G. and Zotova, E.S. (eds) *Ekonomicheskaia teoriia na poroge XXI veka, t. 7, global'naia ekonomika*, Moskva: Iurist: 558–573.

Shapiro, A.L. (1987) "Demontazha GMK ne bylo i net," *Mirovaia ekonomika i mezhdunarodnye otnosheniia*, 6: 82–88.

Shastitko, A.E. (1995) "Neoklassicheskaia ekonomicheskaia teoriia: kriticheskii analiz predposylok," *Mirovaia ekonomika i mezhdunarodnye otnosheniia*, 3: 18–31.

Shastitko, A.E. (1997) "Neoinstitutionalizm," *Vestnik Moskovskogo universiteta*, 12: 3–22.

Shastitko, A.E. (1998) *Neoinstitutional'naia ekonomicheskaia teoriia*, Moscow: TEIS.

Shastitko, A.E. (1999) "Fridrikh Khaiek i neoinstitutsionalizm," *Voprosy ekonomiki*, 6: 43–53.

Shastitko, A.E., Afontsev, S. and Plaksin, S. (2008) "Strukturnye al'ternativy sotsial'no-ekonomicheskogo razvitiia Rossii," *Voprosy ekonomiki*, 1: 71–85.

Shavaev, A.G. (ed) (2001) *Ekonomicheskaia bezopasnost'. Entsiklopediia*, Moscow: Iuridicheskoe prosveshchenie.

Sheinis, V.L. (1988) "Kapitalizm, sotsializm i ekonomicheskii mekhanizm sovremennogo proizvodstva," *Mirovaia ekonomika i mezhdunarodnye otnosheniia*, 9: 5–23.

Shemiatenkov, V.G. (2003) "Al'ternativnye sistemy kapitalizma (ob odnoi tendentsii v zapadnoi ekonomicheskoi mysli)," *Mirovaia ekonomika i mezhdunarodnye otnosheniia*, 3: 3–11.

Shirokorad, L.D. (2003) "Sushestvuet li rossiiskaia shkola ekonomicheskoi mysli?" in Abalkin, L.I. (ed) *Ocherki istorii rossiiskoi ekonomicheskoi mysli*, Moscow: Nauka: 51–61.

Shkolnikova, N.N. (2004) "Rossiia na puti k novoi tsivilizatsii," in Osipov, Iu.M., Chekmarev, V.V. and Zotova, E.S. (eds) *Ekonomicheskaia teoriia v xxi veke 2 (9)*, 2 vols., vol. 2, Moscow: Ekonomist: 652–660.

Shmelev, N.P. ([1987] 1988) "Avansy i dolgi," *Novyi mir*, 6: 142–158 [English translation: Shmelev, N.P. "Advances and Debts," *Problems of Economics*, 10: 7–43].

Shmelev, N.P. ([1989] 2006) "Libo sila, libo rubl'," in Shmelev, N. (ed) *V poiskakh zdravogo smysla. Dvatsat' let rossiskikh ekonomicheskikh reform*, Moscow: Ves' mir: 61–92.

Shmelev, N.P. (1990) "Ob ekstrennykh merakh po predotvrashcheniiu razvala sovetskoi ekonomiki," *Voprosy ekonomiki*, 1: 19–25 [English translation: Shmelev, N.P. (1990) "On Urgent Measures to Prevent the Collapse of the Soviet Economy," *Problems of Economics*, 6: 29–39].

Shmelev, N.P. (1996) "Ekonomika i obshchestvo," *Voprosy ekonomiki*, 1: 17–32.

Shmelev, N.P. (1999) "O konsensuse v rossiiskoi ekonomicheskoi i sotsial'noi politike," *Voprosy ekonomiki*, 8: 49–63.

Shvyrkov, Iu.M. (1996) "Gosudarstvennoe regulirovanie ekonomiki," *Ekonomist*, 8: 35–48.
Sidorovich, A.V. (2001) "Formirovanie natsional'noi modeli ekonomiki v perekhodnykh obshchestvakh," *Obshchestvo i ekonomika*, 11/12: 28–41.
SIGMA (2007) *Koalitsii dlia budushchego, RIO tsentr*, Moscow, available online at: http://sigma-econ.ru/.files/2172/SIGMA-100%20final%20rus%281%29.pdf, last accessed 16 April 2017.
Simoniia, N. (2003) "Nekotorye problemy transformatsionogo perioda," *Obshchestvo i ekonomika*, 6: 106–124.
Slater, D. and Simmons, E. (2010) "Informative Regress: Critical Antecedents in Comparative Politics," *Comparative Political Studies*, 43, 7: 886–917.
Smirnov, V. (2006) "O vneshnekonomicheskoi strategii Rossii," *Obshchestvo i ekonomika*, 11–12: 125–136.
Soifer, H.D. (2012) "The Causal Logic of Critical Junctures," *Comparative Political Studies*, 45, 12: 1572–1597.
Sokolov, V.V. (1996) "Natsional'nye ekonomicheskie interesy: vyrabotka konsensusa," *Mirovaia ekonomika i mezhdunarodnye otnosheniia*, 3: 5–18.
Sokolov, V.V. (1997) "Sovremennyi mir i natsional'naia ekonomicheskaia politika," *Mirovaia ekonomika i mezhdunarodnye otnosheniia*, 10: 5–20.
Sorgin, V. (1993) "Novaia ideologiia dlia Rossii: drama iz sovremennoi istorii," *Mirovaia ekonomika i mezhdunarodnye otnoshenia*, 10: 5–16.
Sorokin, D.E. (2001) "Politicheskaia ekonomiia dlia Rossii," *Rossiiskii ekonomicheskii zhurnal*, 2: 78–84.
Sorokin, D.E. (2004) "Traektoriia sotsial'no-ekonomicheskogo razvitiia Rossii: 1999–2007," *EKO*, 7: 48–68.
Sorokin, D.E. (2011a) "Russia's Development Strategy," *Problems of Economic Transition*, 53, 9: 29–44.
Sorokin, D.E. (2011b) "Mekhanizmy tormozheniia innovatsionnogo rosta," *EKO*, 2: 72–83.
Starodubrovskii, V. (2013) "Dinamika zastoia: Rossiiskaia ekonomika v 2012 godu," *Ekonomicheskaia politika*, 2: 141–207.
Stepanov, Iu.V. (1993) "Regulirovanie ekonomiki v perekhodnyi period," *Ekonomist*: 10–20.
Stepin, V. (1995) "Kul'tura i stanovlenie tsivilizovannogo rynka v Rossii," *Voprosy ekonomiki*, 7: 74–81.
Strategy 2020 (2013) *Strategiia – 2020: Novaia model' rosta – novaia sotsial'naia politika*, 2 Vols., Moscow: Delo, available online at: http://im.kommersant.ru/content/pics/doc/doc1753934.pdf, last accessed 16 April 2017.
Struve, P.B. (1894) *Kriticheskie zametki k voprosu ob ekonomicheskom razvitii Rossii*, St Petersburg: Tipografiia Skorokhodova.
Studentsov, V.B. (1986) "Burzhuaznaia natsionalizatsiia i privatizatsiia v mekhanizme gosudarstvenno-monopolisticheskogo kapitalizma," *Mirovaia ekonomika i mezhdunarodnye otnosheniia*, 10: 87–96.
Studentsov, V.B. (1989) "Sdvigi v gosudarstvennom regulirovanii i ekonomicheskaia rol' gosudarstva," *Mirovaia ekonomika i mezhdunarodnye otnosheniia*, 1: 5–22.
Subetto, A.I. (2003) "Dilemma globalizatsii: kapitalisticheskaia gibel' chelovechestva ili proryv k noosfernomu, dukhovnomu sotsializmu," in Osipov, Iu.M., Baburin, S.N., Belolipetskii, V.G. and Zotova, E.S. (eds) *Ekonomicheskaia teoriia na poroge XXI veka, t. 7, global'naia ekonomika*, Moskva: Iurist: 125–135.
Superfin, L.G. (1993) "Znanie obshchetsivilizatsionnogo sdviga i problemy vyrabotki novoi paradigmy v sotsial'no-ekonomicheskoi mysli zapada," *Voprosy ekonomiki*, 1: 53–65.

Sutela, P. (1991) *Economic Thought and Economic Reform in the Soviet Union*, Cambridge: Cambridge University Press.

Sutela, P. (2008) "Soviet Economics After Stalin: Between Orthodoxy and Reform," in Barnett, V. and Zweynert, J. (eds) *Economics in Russia: Studies in Intellectual History*, Burlington, VT: Ashgate: 157–172.

Sutela, P. (2012) *The Political Economy of Putin's Russia*, London: Routledge.

Sutela, P. and Mau, V. (1998) "Economics Under Socialism: The Russian Case," in Wagener, H.-J. (ed) *Economic Thought in Communist and Post-Communist Europe*, London and New York: Routledge: 33–79.

Swidler, A. (1986) "Culture in Action: Symbols and Strategies," *American Sociological Review*, 51, 2: 273–286.

Tambovtsev, V.L. (1994) "Ob'ekt ekonomicheskoi bezopasnosti Rossii," *Voprosy ekonomiki*, 12: 45–53.

Tambovtsev, V.L. (2008) "Koalitsii dlia budushchego. Strategii razvitiia Rossii," *Voprosy ekonomiki*, 3: 124–133.

Taratuta, Iu. (2011) "Dmitriiu Medved'evu napisali novuiu programmu," *Vedomosti*, 16 March 2011, available online at: www.vedomosti.ru/politics/articles/2011/03/16/2012_protiv_2020, last accessed 16 April 2017.

Terry, S.M. (1984) "Theories of Socialist Development in Soviet-East European Relations," in Terry, S.M. (ed) *Soviet Policy in Eastern Europe*, New Haven and London: Yale University Press: 221–252.

Tikhonova, N.I. (2008) "Sotsiokul'turnaia modernizatsiia v Rossii (Opyt empiricheskogo analiza)," *Obshchestvennye nauki i sovremennost'*, 2: 5–23.

Tropin, Iu. (1987) "Deistvennost' mekhanizma tsen," *Voprosy ekonomiki*, 9: 113–119.

Tsagolov, N.A. (1961) "Voprosy razrabotki nauchnogo kursa politicheskoi ekonomiki," *Kommunist*, 10.

Tsagolov, N.A. (ed) (1963) *Kurs politicheskoi ekonomii*, Moscow: Ekonomizdat.

Tsentr Razvitiia (2009) "Institut 'Tsentr Razvitiia GU – VSHE': Rossiiskaia ekonomika na fone mirovogo krizisa: Tekushchie tendentsii i perspektivy razvitiia," *Voprosy ekonomiki*, 9: 71–92.

Tsvetkov, V.A. (2006) "Rossiiskaia ekonomika v 2005 godu: Polnaia neopredelonnost' pri blagopriiatnoi koniunkture," *EKO*, 5: 3–24.

Tsvetkov, V.A. and Dzhumov, A. (2007) "Gosudarstvennaia sobstvennost' i effektivnost' ekonomiki," *Ekonomist*, 4: 27–36.

Uliukaev, A.G. (1996) "Perekhod (o politiko-ekonomicheskikh problemakh sistemnoi transformatsii v Rossii)," *Voprosy ekonomiki*, 10: 4–22.

Vardul, N. (2000) "Strana Sovetov," *Kommersant*, 11 October 2000.

Vasil'chuk, Iu.A. (1997) "Postindustrial'naia ekonomika i razvitie cheloveka," *Mirovaia ekonomika i mezhdunarodnye otnosheniia*, 9: 74–86.

Veber, A.B. (1989) "Vot takie pirogi," *Mirovaia ekonomika i mezhdunarodnye otnosheniia*, 8: 122–124.

Vinogradov, V.V. (2002) *Ekonomika Rosii: Uchebnoe posobie*, Moscow: Iurist.

Vishnevskii, A.G. (1998) *Serp i rubl'. Konservativnaia modernizatsiia SSSR*, Moscow: OGI.

Vishnevskii, A.G. (2010) "Lovushki konservativnoi modernizatsii," Speech, given at 27 April at the Higher School of Economics, Moscow, available online at: http://polit.ru/article/2010/05/20/traps/, last accessed 16 April 2017.

Vissarionov, A. and Fedorova, I. (2003) "Gosudarstvennyi sektor: Granitsy, kontrol', upravlenie," *Ekonomist*, 6: 3–12.

Voeikov, M. (2003) "Evraziiskaia teoriia khosiaistvovaniia' kak sostavnaia chast' rossiiskoi ekonomicheskoi shkoly," *Voprosy ekonomiki*, 11: 95–119.

Volkonskii, V.A. (1998) "O dvukh ekonomicheskikh paradigmakh i preodolenii rossiiskogo krizisa," *Ekonomicheskaia nauka sovremennoi Rossii*, 4: 7–16.

Volkonskii, V.A. (1999) "Institutsionnal'nyi podkhod k problemam krizisa rossiiskoi ekonomiki," *Ekonomika i matematicheskie metody*, 35, 1: 11–27.

Volkonskii, V.A. (2000) "Dukhovnaia drama sovremennoi Rossii," *Ekonomicheskaia nauka sovremennoi Rossii*, 3–4: 119–134.

Volkonskii, V. (1990) "The 'Cultured Huckster' Among Us. On the Restructuring of Economic Priorities," *Kommunist*, 1: 58–64 [English translation: Volkonskii, V. *Problems of Economics*, 8: 42–53].

Voronov, Iu.P. (2003) "Est' li v Rossii sobstvenniki?" *EKO*, 2: 3–14.

Voronova, T. (2003) "Konkurrentnye pozitsii Rossii na mirovom rynke investitsii," *Ekonomist*, 9: 38–43.

Wagener, H.-J. (ed) (1998a) *Economic Thought in Communist and Post-Communist Europe*, London: Routledge.

Wagener, H.-J. (1998b) "Between Conformity and Reform: Economics Under State Socialism and Its Transition," in Wagener, H.-J. (ed) *Economic Thought in Communist and Post-Communist Europe*, London: Routledge: 1–32.

Walicki, A. ([1969] 1989) *The Controversy Over Capitalism: Studies in the Social Philosophy of the Russian Populists*, Notre Dame, IN: University of Notre Dame Press.

Walicki, A. ([1975] 1989) *The Slavophile Controversy: History of a Conservative Utopia in Nineteenth-Century Russian Thought*, Oxford: Clarendon Press.

Williamson, J. (1990) "What Washington Means by Policy Reform," in Williamson, J. (ed) *Latin American Adjustment, How Much Has Happened?* Washington, DC: Institute for International Economics: 5–20.

Williamson, O. (1985) *The Economic Institutions of Capitalism*, New York: Free Press.

w/o Author (2005) "Nauka na ekonomicheskom fakul'tete: Proshloe, nastoiashchee i budushchee," *Vestnik Moskovskogo universiteta, seriia 6*, 1: 3–26.

Zagashvili, V.S. (1997) *Ekonomicheskaia bezopasnost' Rossii*, Moscow: Iurist.

Zagladin, N. (2005) "Global'noe informatsionnoe obshchestvo i Rossiia," *Mirovaia ekonomika i mezhdunarodnye otnosheniia*, 7: 15–31.

Zaitseva, L.I. (1994) "Umom Rossiiu ne poniat'," *Voprosy ekonomiki*, 2: 95–107.

Zalygina, E.A. and Mel'nichuk, Iu.K. (2003) "Rossiia i ugotovannaia ei rol' v protsesse globalizatsii," in Osipov, Iu.M., Baburin, S.N., Belolipetskii, V.G. and Zotova, E.S. (eds) *Ekonomicheskaia teoriia na poroge XXI veka, t. 7, global'naia ekonomika*, Moskva: Iurist: 498–504.

Zaostrovtsev, A. (2008) "From Marxist Economics to Post-Soviet Nationalism," in Barnett, V. and Zweynert, J. (eds) *Economics in Russia: Studies in Intellectual History*, Burlington, VA: Ashgate: 173–185.

Zaslavskaia, T. ([1986] 1987) "Chelovecheskii faktor razvitiia ekonomiki i sotsial'naia spravedlivost'," *Kommunist*, 13: 61–73 [English translation: Zaslavskaia, T. "Social Justice and the Human Factor in Economic Development," *Problems of Economics*, 30, 1: 5–26].

Zaslavskaia, T. (2011) "O sotsial'nykh aktiorakh modernizatsii Rossii," *Obshchestvennye nauki i sovremennost'*, 3: 13–25.

Zemliakov, D. (2000) "Distsiplina 'national'naia ekonomika': metodologo-teoreticheskie i metodicheskie osnovy," *Rossiskii ekonomicheskii zhurnal*, 9: 75–83.

Zen'kovsky, V.V. ([1948] 2003) *A History of Russian Philosophy*, London and New York: Routledge.
Zhuravlova, G.P. (2003) "Statement in Round-Table Discussion 'O statuse politicheskoi ekonomii v vuzovskom prepodovanii ekonomicheskih distsiplin'," *Rossiiskii ekonomicheskii zhurnal*, 4: 84–86.
Zilberman, D.B. (1977) "Orthodox Ethics and the Matter of Communism," *Studies in Soviet Thought*, 17, 4: 341–419.
Zolotareva, A.B., Drobyshevskii, S.M., Sinel'nikov, S.G. and Kadochnikov, P.A. ([2001] 2002) "The Prospects for Creating a Stabilisation Fund in The Russian Federation," *Problems of Economic Transition*, 45, 2: 5–85; Russian original (2001), available online at: https://iep.ru/ru/publikatcii/publication/380.html, last accessed 30 April 2017.
Zotov, V.V., Presniakov, V.F. and Rozental', V.O. (1998) "Analiz sistemykh funktsii ekonomiki: institutsional'nyi aspekt," *Ekonomika i matematicheskie metody*, 34, 2: 5–16.
Zotov, V.V., Presniakov, V.J. and Rozental', V.O. (2001) "Institutsional'nye problemy realizatsii sistemnykh funktsii ekonomiki," *Ekonomicheskaia nauka sovremennoi Rossii*, 3: 51–69.
Zweynert, J. ([2002] 2007) *Eine Geschichte des ökonomischen Denkens in Rußland. 1805–1905*, Marburg: Metropolis [Russian translation: *Istoriia ekonomicheskoi mysli v Rossii. 1805–1905*, Moscow: GU VSHE].
Zweynert, J. (2004) "Patristic Legacies in Russian Economic Thought and Their Significance for the Transformation of Russia's Economy and Society," in Barens, I., Caspari, V. and Schefold, B. (eds) *Political Events and Economic Ideas*, Cheltenham: Elgar: 263–274.
Zweynert, J. (2006) "Economic Ideas and Institutional Change: Evidence From Soviet Economic Debates 1987–1991," *Europe-Asia Studies*, 58, 2: 169–192.
Zweynert, J. (2007) "Conflicting Patterns of Thought in the Russian Debate on Transition: 1992–2002," *Europe-Asia Studies*, 59, 1: 47–69.
Zweynert, J. (2009) "Interests versus Culture in the Theory of Institutional Change?" *Journal of Institutional Economics*, 5, 3: 339–360.
Zweynert, J. (2010) "Conflicting Patterns of Thought in the Russian Debate on Transition: 2003–2007," *Europe-Asia Studies*, 62, 4: 547–569.
Zweynert, J. (2014) "'Developed Socialism' and Soviet Economic Thought in the 1970s and Early '80s," *Russian History*, 41, 3: 354–372.
Zweynert, J. and Boldyrev, I. (2017) "Conflicting Patterns of Thought in the Russian Debate on Innovation and Modernization: 2008–2013,"*Europe-Asia Studies*, 69, 6: 921–939.

Index

For Product Safety Concerns and Information please contact our EU representative GPSR@taylorandfrancis.com Taylor & Francis Verlag GmbH, Kaufingerstraße 24, 80331 München, Germany